SUICIDE AND THE SCHOOLS

SUICIDE AND THE SCHOOLS

A Handbook For
Prevention, Intervention, and Rehabilitation

By

S.W. JOHNSON

University of Alaska-Anchorage

and

L.J. MAILE

Anchorage Suicide Prevention and Crisis Center

CHARLES C THOMAS • PUBLISHER
Springfield • Illinois • U.S.A.

Published and Distributed Throughout the World by
CHARLES C THOMAS • PUBLISHER
2600 South First Street
Springfield, Illinois 62794-9265

© *1987 by* CHARLES C THOMAS • PUBLISHER

ISBN 0-398-05302-2

Library of Congress Catalog Card Number: 86-23085

With THOMAS BOOKS *careful attention is given to all details of manufacturing
and design. It is the Publisher's desire to present books that are satisfactory as to their
physical qualities and artistic possibilities and appropriate for their particular use.*
THOMAS BOOKS *will be true to those laws of quality that assure a good name
and good will.*

Printed in the United States of America
Q-R-3

Library of Congress Cataloging in Publication Data

Johnson, Stanley W., 1928-
    Suicide and the schools.

    Bibliography: p.
    Includes
    1. Youth--United States--Suicidal behavior.
2. Suicide--United States--Prevention.
3. Personnel service in education--United States.
4. Crisis intervention (Psychiatry)--United States.
I. Maile, L. J. II. Title. [DNLM: 1. Adolescent
Behavior. 2. Crisis Intervention. 3. Schools.
4. Suicide--in adolescence. 5. Suicide--
prevention & control. HV 6546 J69s]
HV6546.J64   1987   362.2   86-23085
ISBN 0-398-05302-2

To Ernst and Steve and Sylvia Fay.
If only I had known then . . .

and

To Mom, who gave us as many chances
as we needed.

"Do not go gently into that good night,
Rage, rage against the dying of the light."

Dylan Thomas

PREFACE

THERE ARE several reasons why we elected to write this book. First and foremost probably is our own personal concern with the problem of suicide in today's society, especially as it appears to increasingly impinge upon our young people.

Both of us are involved in professional careers which though more broadly focused than upon suicide as a single concern are certainly enmeshed in both the training of people to work in the area of suicide and in active involvement in the field ourselves.

We are busy with counseling, research, training and management activities related to suicide. Each week we come face-to-face with people who are experiencing the effects of suicidal thought or behavior. And during some weeks it happens every day. We live in a community and state which experiences far more than an average share of suicide. We are closely familiar with communities and subsets of our state's population which suffer more from suicide than perhaps anywhere else in the world. Even if we were so inclined, it would be impossible to ignore the problem in our own environment.

We do not perceive ourselves as crusaders. Neither of us are "crusader-type" personalities. We do have, however, a strong personal concern about suicide and firm professional commitment to work toward lowering its negative effect in our society.

We have been particularly impressed with the dramatic role the schools may play in suicidal experiences. Where prepared and dedicated, the school offers assistance perhaps unmatched by any other resource including both the home and the professional therapist. Where the school is unprepared or reluctant to become involved, it is apparent to us that the tragedy is markedly compounded.

We have found very few school personnel who are emotionally disinterested and many who express fear, insecurity, worry and anxiety over what to do, how to do it, and how to prepare for the eventuality of being called upon for help. In such situations we have found that school personnel, perhaps because of their background and training but also perhaps because of their close association with youths' problems, learn willingly and quickly how to increase their own capabilities to help youth in suicidal crises. We chose to write this book because we wanted to help those who are interested in helping others.

The problem of suicide in school children of all ages is addressed, and much if not most of the material we present is relevant to adolescents and younger children, as well. Most of the behavior dynamics that we discuss are directed toward the adolescent age group. This is a deliberate and not altogether arbitrary decision. Even a single suicide of a pre-adolescent youngster would be one too many, but we are aware that there are far fewer suicidal risk children in the elementary grades than in junior high and high school, and generalizations which can be applied to groups of youngsters are much more difficult in the younger age groups. So we have oriented much of the book toward the older youth. Certainly, basic principles of prevention and intervention apply across the entire age range and would be equally applicable to college and university students.

We have only briefly touched upon the problem of suicide among school personnel — staff not students. Such an event is very traumatic to school children and is worthy of attention. The chapter on survivors is very relevant in such instances, and much of the material on prevention, recognizing risk, and intervention can be applied to a teacher as easily as to a student. Our choice of emphasis has been based primarily on space limitations.

Too many people have helped for us to list them individually. We do wish to note with appreciation the cooperation of a number of the educational and social service agencies of our home community and other communities where we have worked, as well. They have offered ideas, critiques, and both emotional and conceptual support. Our professional colleagues have been equally as supportive and helpful. A special thank you is extended to the graduate students of the Counseling Psychology program at the University of Alaska-Anchorage for their willingness to share ideas, act as pedagogical guinea pigs as we tried out ideas and approaches, and for their enthusiasm in wanting to help people, an enthusiasm and sincerity which has constantly bolstered our motivation and spirits. Other students in seminars and workshops have also been very helpful. Ms. Amy Beth Johnson's care in working with bibliographic resources is noted and appreciated. Ms. Debbie Whitmore has given many hours to the more mundane tasks of library searches, manuscript typing, and similarly unglamourous but absolutely vital contributions to this book. For this we thank her.

S. Johnson and L. Maile
Anchorage, Alaska

CONTENTS

SUICIDE AND THE SCHOOLS

CHAPTER ONE

ROLES AND RESPONSIBILITIES FOR SCHOOL PERSONNEL

"He who will not risk cannot win."
John Paul Jones

THE PROBLEM is inescapable, so is the responsibility. Despite the unpleasantness of having to face the reality of potential self-destructive behavior among our youth and the fear and anxiety experienced when we consider that such problems may occur in our school or on our campus, our responsibility is clear. Indeed, having to deal with such a tragedy may be more than a possibility. It may, instead, be a probability if any of the nationally reported statistics are correct.

How severe, how widespread is the problem? Since suicide has long been a taboo word in our society, raising issues unpleasant and frightening for many to consider, exact numbers and case data are difficult to obtain. Most experts in the field and epidemiologists suggest that the reported figures are probably too low. In many instances suicides go unrecorded, listed instead as accidental deaths, death from natural causes, or other less disturbing labels due to the tendency to protect either the "good name" of the victim or the "feelings" of the survivors. In addition, it is noted that only about 2.5 percent of all suicide attempts actually succeed (Perr, 1979). Apparently far more people attempt suicide than the number of reported deaths would indicate.

With this protective buffering, this "conspiracy of silence" in mind, and cognizant that reported figures are likely to be too low rather than exaggerated, what do current statistics tell us about current suicide rates in the United States? Here are some sample figures:

3

• For every death by drowning there are 3 by suicide.
• For every 3 homicides there are 4 suicides.
• For every 2 auto deaths there is a suicide.
• For every tornado death there are 273 suicides.
• There is a suicidal death in the United States approximately every 20 minutes.
• Suicide is the second or third highest cause of death among college students (depending upon the data examined).
• Adolescent suicide rates have risen almost 400 percent since 1957.
• Threat of self-destruction is the stated reason for referral for psychiatric help of between 8 and 10 percent of child clinical patients (Associated Press, 1985; Fujimura et al., 1985; Science, 1985; Shaffer, 1982).

The problem is ubiquitous and certainly not limited to the United States. Canadian teenage suicide is reported to have increased 32 percent in the past decade (Duraj, 1984). Diekstra (1985) states that in the European economic community, suicide is the second or third most frequent cause of death in the adolescent-young adult age group and accounts for 10 percent of all deaths in those countries.

ISSUES FACING THE SCHOOLS

Suicide is no respecter of person or status. Individuals of all types, races, socioeconomic classes, geographical locations, levels of intelligence, and virtually every age group are found among its victims. It is obvious that despite our best efforts to improve the mental health of our general community, children and teenagers of today are "at-risk." As a consequence, it is equally obvious that those who regularly work day-to-day with and among our young people are going to encounter the effects of suicide, either through directly facing the grim event itself or by encountering the ever-widening ripple of emotional involvement experienced by those who are left behind, the survivors of suicide. In some instances, whole classrooms of students or even entire schools—their student bodies, faculty and staff—are suddenly included among those survivors, with immediate need for support and help. It is estimated that the number of directly affected survivors may be as high as twenty times the number of actual suicides. The effects range widely.

Considering these facts, school personnel are faced with several important issues which cannot be safely ignored.

Personal Feelings

Death and dying are unpleasant and difficult concepts for almost everyone. When the loss of life comes as a result of self-destruction, the concepts are even more complex. When such an event directly involves a young person supposedly in the happiest, most carefree part of life, feelings run extremely strong, and ready answers which both comfort and alleviate fear are difficult to find.

In such instances, the tendency is to turn to other community resources, the home or the church, expecting these to bear the major responsibility. School personnel prefer to think of their community responsibility centering more closely around the traditional 3 R's with affiliated responsibilities with which the school becomes involved primarily because they facilitate or expedite the learning process. And such has been the accepted role of public schools in the United States ever since education began to become more of a community than religious or extended-family responsibility.

Future teachers in training and their on-the-job role models do not typically perceive of themselves as being deeply involved in more than peripherally supportive mental health activities. And, as a result, when asked to consider being faced with such emotionally "heavy" tasks as providing meaningful answers for a classroom of youngsters who have experienced the suicide of a peer, the most immediate response is often one of fear, denial of personal responsibility, expressions of feelings of insecurity and lack of competence or all of these.

School administrators express similar doubts. Such questions as allocation of time for training, conflicts of interest with existing community institutions, and doubt as to role performance and purpose abound.

Yet, the need is high, and those who have had to face the reality of "calls for help" express their concern for adequate training, preparation, and role definition. Rosenthal (1981) cites 87 percent of respondent school counselors reporting that they had faced the need, within their school-counseling role, to provide some sort of comfort and support for grieving students (an important aspect of suicide-survivor work). While over half of the counselors felt they had adequate counseling skills for such important tasks, 93 percent felt that formal training and preparation should be provided to prepare them for such instances.

A 1981 study of Canadian schools commissioned by Ottawa (Duraj, 1984) noted that the suicidal intervention of school personnel had proven to be a helpful contribution to the battle against this killer of youth. But it was also noted that the most important factor leading to such success was a carefully constructed quality relationship between students and teachers which facilitated such intervention.

No one can deny that feelings run high in face of the specter of suicide. School personnel and students are no exception. But the presence of these feelings, which if unheeded can be debilitating to any program of prevention, intervention or rehabilitation, cannot be ignored. The problem is present in high numbers. Schools must accept responsibility for some part of a community-wide response and at the same time seek to alleviate the fears and anxieties present in their own teachers and students. The most obvious answers to solving the problem of personal feelings of fear and insecurity lie in the direction of clearer role and task definition, specific training, and the clear presentation of task-related and problem-solving information, all of which are topics specifically addressed in later chapters.

Increased Training and Workload

Undeniably, today's educators are faced with an increasing array of knowledge, techniques and skills which they are expected to master to some degree or another in order to be adequately prepared for the classroom. The addition of another task, particularly one as clearly significant as working with and for suicidal youth, easily appears to teacher and administrator alike as presenting workloads and time-demand expectations beyond reasonable expectations for even the most dedicated educator. Faced with the apparently immovable object of the reality of suicide among school-aged children and the irresistible force of limited time-availability for school personnel, what can be said?

First of all, it would be blatantly dishonest to suggest that becoming adequately prepared to be an effective member of the task force against youth suicide would generate no extra time demands. But, at the same time, it should be reiterated that when faced with the actual presence of a need for crisis performance, the teacher's and administrator's time is going to be consumed in prodigious gulps whether or not they are prepared. And, if they are prepared, operational and functional effectiveness in themselves are time-savers, are major assets in the reduction of job-performance stress thereby leaving more time for everyday tasks and demands.

It should also be noted at this early juncture, though elaboration will follow later, that it should never be expected that school personnel are faced with the task of becoming on-site substitute clinicians with all the necessary prerequisite knowledge and skills to handle any type of emotional crisis. This is not so. Some training is necessary. There is an important body of knowledge to be acquired. And some specific types of personal feelings and sensitivity must be individually recognized and then cultivated. However, as the successful contribution of thousands of crisis-center volunteers across the nation testifies, sufficient training, knowledge, and sensitivity can be garnered in a relatively short period of time to be useful and effective.

For those who become highly motivated and wish to be more deeply involved, there are always further steps that may be taken. But it would be foolish, unrealistic, and unnecessary to suggest that each and every teacher and school administrator must become a resident expert capable of doing all things for all types of suicide crises. Such is neither necessary nor expected. Instead, ways and means of establishing a school- or district-wide preparation program will be suggested, along with methods for calling upon better prepared and more professionally involved resources. Implicit in such suggestions is the assumption that school involvement can be on a time and intensity level commensurate with the wide range of such demands all school personnel face. Critical points for making inclusion/exclusion decisions will be noted along with some useful criteria for making such decisions wisely in consideration of other factors peculiar to the individual situation.

Identification of Teaching and Training Objectives

The blanket goal of trying to prevent suicide and rehabilitating recovering attempters and/or survivors is far too broad to be useful in conceptualizing any specific programmatic design. While there are a wide number of responsibilities with which the school, depending upon staff and situation, may choose to become involved, there appear to be five major tasks that can be accomplished with demonstrable success through a reasonable amount of planning and effort. Each of these, of course, may be subdivided into smaller tasks, and each has a training or preparation phase and an ongoing operation phase, as well. The following chapters of this book address these tasks and offer program planning and participation guidelines. These major tasks include: (1) recognizing the "at-risk" signs in an individual, (2) responding to a crisis, (3) providing a supportive environment for recovering attempters, (4) providing support and help to survivors of a suicide experience, and (5) providing ongoing informational and training workshops for both staff and students.

Networking with the Community

Suicide is something no one wishes to face alone, and school personnel are no exception. Nor is there any reason to suppose that in the typical community the school should be expected to provide the major support resources or assume commanding responsibility for meeting the community's needs. Virtually everyone writing in the field recommends and supports the concept of "networking" when facing problems of suicide. Networking may be formal or informal. Duraj (1984), for example, suggests that there is a strong parallel between the function of the family and school system in terms of suicide risk and social relations. As a result, their functions informally become intertwined and mutually supportive.

In preparation for the school being ready to handle crisis situations, should they arise, it is strongly suggested that parents and professional consultants be involved in both the training and the actual crisis and post-crisis follow-up activity. Some others (Johnson, 1985) suggest that networking concepts be taught to teenagers themselves so that they may become familiar with both the need for networking and the available resources for help in their own community. Since evidence indicates (Snyder, 1971) that potential suicide victims typically turn first to family and everyday friends and to the more traditional and perhaps formal sources such as clergy, psychiatrists, social workers and lawyers only later, the need for the school to be more ready to play the role of referrer to other established sources of help is apparent.

On the other hand, schools are traditionally viewed as sources of helpful information, literal depositories and dispensers of information, and as such may be turned to themselves by others seeking assistance or information as to where and how to obtain help. Preparing staff and students alike to play such a role by providing them with clear, unambiguous and up-to-date information and procedures can without question save lives in times of crisis. The amount of time and effort expended in teaching both children and adults how and when to use the 911 emergency number is proof of the acceptance of this principle in action. It works just as easily and effectively when applied to suicidal crises.

IS THERE ANY CHOICE?

Given the magnitude of the problem and the very likely possibility that school personnel and students will be personally touched by problems of suicide, one might very well ask, "Is there any realistic choice?" Personal experience in working with school personnel who have experienced suicide in their schools or which has touched the lives of those connected with their school would suggest that the answer is in all probability, "No, there are no acceptable options."

Any type of disavowment of responsibility, excuses of lack of time or competency fade into insignificance when one must face an actual crisis. Those who cry out for help, who turn to us as someone who is expected to give surcease from pain, or protection from hurt, or sheltering from a terrifying reality do not inquire about adequacy of our credentials, our availability of time, or our feelings of personal adequacy.

One can almost certainly expect to be confronted by the need. The only choice really is whether or not to turn one's back on someone needing help. Few who have already dedicated their lives to serving others through education would elect to refuse.

In realistic terms, the choice is whether or not to be ready to do one's best in such instances or to gamble our own peace of mind and perhaps someone else's life on our own lack of preparation.

There are some good, sound reasons for arguing that intentional preparation makes sense in a number of specific ways.

Reasons of Practical Efficiency

One of the best arguments is that efforts by school personnel are effective in working against suicide. As mentioned earlier, the Canadian study (Duraj, 1984) is an example of evidence in favor of this argument. Professional peers, after years of working in a university health service, remind us that in many instances those cast in responsible roles other than psychiatry may do as much or more than the formally trained clinician.

School personnel experience both the advantages and disadvantages of being cast in the role of knowledgeable authority figures. Teachers are **supposed** to know the answers. It comes as a surprise to many students to learn that answers sometimes escape the teacher, too. Despite such feet of clay, school personnel are in a role position to expect people to turn to them for help and assistance. Couple this with the added reality that teachers may be aware of more personal characteristics about their pupils than anyone else in the community, save the children's parents (and in some instances even more than parents), and you have a group of trained professionals to whom people are apt to turn to for help and who may, through their own powers of perception, be in a position to see and note critical behaviors.

As will be noted in some detail later, warning signs of impending suicidal behavior come from verbal, behavioral, and situational cues. In each instance, school personnel (including fellow students) are in an excellent position to be among the first to become aware of such important precursors of actual suicidal behavior.

Because of the status that school personnel hold within the community, they carry an especially effective networking credibility. They are depositories for and dispensers of information. They are knowledgeable about children and trained to denote and explain a child's behaviors. They are in the business of observing and evaluating students' behavior. And, as a matter of principle, schools are perceived as defenders and protectors of our youth, advocates in a real sense. Because of this, when the school speaks about children "at-risk" there is a very strong tendency for other professionals and community institutions to listen. Consequently, using the schools as a major cog in the networking process is an extremely effective way to make community resources readily available to those of school age who may desperately need them.

Educational Reasons

Using the school to provide help in preventing suicide and rehabilitating those touched by it also can be effectively argued from a pedagogical standpoint. Slaikeu (1984) has noted that crises times provide the school with a unique opportunity to exercise its educational role. He points out that crises require (and schools are in a distinctive position to provide) established, dependable procedures conceived for the purpose of helping institutions and individuals meet and cope with crises; physical resources for some of the necessary behaviors requisite with tension reduction in the face of crises; and, above all, specially trained personnel who know how to train, teach, and help people acquire, improve, and maintain problem-solving skills.

This is an important point, for crises are frequently characterized by a breakdown of what were previously adequate problem-solving or coping skills (Caplan, 1964). One of the both immediate and long-range goals of crisis intervention is to help the afflicted individual discover and utilize any presently available coping mechanisms while in the process of building more effective skills in order to assist in the avoiding of subsequent or repeat crises.

Hoff (1984) has noted that there are social, cultural, and environmental precipitators of crises in addition to personal origins. Her crisis model stresses this fact and emphasizes that, in the case of suicide, prevention of destructive crises outcomes or the worsening or perpetuation of pathology, if it exists, is a major goal. Social support and the effective management of crises are important in attaining this goal. The school, by virtue of its already accepted role each day, faces crises of one type or another. The school also directs much of its educational efforts towards helping individuals learn how to recognize and resolve crises. Whether the specific efforts center around economic or geo-political issues in political science classes, environmental problems in biology, or personal concerns in health and hygiene curricula, the school already has occupied a broadly perceived crisis training and management role in our society. Broadening of this scope to the lifesaving techniques of good coping skills, and, when necessary, suicide crisis intervention, logically follows.

The school is in the position to make a definitively effective contribution by virtue of this acquired role. Not only is the school seen as the dispenser of information about and provider of skills relevant to the meeting and solving of crisis issues, it is also a regularly encountered, virtually "natural" part of the students' day-to-day experience. And, as Hoff (1984) also points out, "prospects for positive crisis resolution by individuals, families, and peer groups is enhanced and negative complications are reduced when crisis management and intervention occur as close as possible to natural settings."

On a final note, schools have a unique opportunity for crisis intervention because of three particularly important aspects of their normal function and curricula (Nelson & Sleikeu, 1984). First, they are in regular, ongoing, and lengthy contact with the crisis-experiencing child. Second, there is a high compatibility between the problem-solving orientation of crisis services and the normal approach to meeting the demands of living as espoused by the schools. Third, principles of sound growth and healthy development are all based on effective learning: schools are in a position to help people learn about crisis solving because they are already teaching people to learn, and people are used to learning in the school situation.

Social and Moral Reasons

It is in the schools that most young people first begin to clearly experience a growing sense of maturing individuality. It is while involved in the process of learning that students begin to recognize the power of knowledge and the importance of becoming their own person. That our school systems in general foster and abet such growth is to their credit. It is far too important an asset to be ignored. Gill (1982) has called our attention to an important truth: "Perhaps most important in eradicating suicidal impulses is the profoundly validating experience of being empathetically understood and accepted by another human being."

Though suicidal individuals and frequently those touched by others' suicidal behaviors may require long-range treatment and help, immediate psychological first aid is of paramount importance in saving lives and maintaining some semblance of ongoing personal effectiveness. As Slaikeu (1984) has outlined in detail, crisis intervention requires both crisis therapy and psychological first aid. The former is typically the province of professional help-givers specially trained and practiced in the nuances of treatment. The latter is the responsibility of and generally within the competency capability of most of us who are apt to be in a position to respond to a call for help.

School personnel are consistently in a position to expect such calls and should be prepared and ready to respond. Ray and Johnson (1983) have outlined the critical steps in preventing adolescent suicide. The first four on their list sound like a carefully prepared description of the trained teacher. These include:

1. Using people who are close enough to be alert for signs of increasing suicide risk (they mention teachers as one of the typical subsets of people who meet this criterion)
2. The most critical intervention behavior is good listening
3. The next most critical behavior is providing assistance in getting professional help
4. Being willing to be involved, to be contributory

As Hoff (1984) reminds us, social isolation only promotes suicidal tendencies. Personal and social resources in addition to material resources must be provided.

The school is also in a distinctive position to provide some of the vital psychosocial evaluation of the individual's behavior, assist in the development and implementation of a meaningful crisis-reduction plan, and finally to aid in the very important follow-up evaluation of the effectiveness of any developed strategy and activities.

From a quite different perspective, the school and its personnel have the responsibility to respond to broad as well as specific community needs. Suicide is a very real problem, but it is an assailable one. It is not a problem that the schools may ignore with moral impunity. Genuine professional role integrity can be maintained only by attempting to respond to the challenge.

In a more individual sense, the school also owes something to its own personnel. Facing suicide-related crises is as potentially emotionally shattering as experiencing a catastrophic fire, a burglary, assault, or any other event which assaults our personal life space. Relatively uncomplex training experiences, the dissemination of some accurate and useful information, and the outline and simple practice of a few crisis management techniques will go a long way toward providing our school personnel with the type of personal preparation they most need to meet this type of stress. When pupils and staff alike are devastated by a suicide in their midst, there is no time for fence mending or after-the-fact remedies. In many instances, our children will need the ready assistance of mentally healthy teachers who have learned themselves how to handle such stress and can, in spite of their own grief or anger or anxiety, be help-givers to our youth.

The challenge is one of moral integrity, and there is no reason to suppose that most school personnel will be less responsive to this challenge than they have been to others in the past.

SCHOOLS AS PART OF THE SUICIDE PREVENTION AND INTERVENTION NETWORK

The functions of the school as it becomes involved in the suicide problem are varied. While often interactive and overlapping, these three important functions are most easily viewed through three separate and distinct aspects of suicide work: **prevention, intervention,** and **rehabilitation.**

Preventive functions are concerned with both primary and secondary intervention.

Primary intervention focuses directly on preventing or at least lowering the incidence of suicide among students and school personnel. When involved in primary intervention, the school is addressing preventive measures that clearly and distinctly are involved with and related to suicide. These include outreach networking, information dispensing, parental involvement, and crisis management training.

Secondary intervention focuses more generally on broad issues and typically is concerned with creating and sustaining good general mental health, building adequate problem-solving skills, fostering constructive and supportive family and peer group relationships and all aspects of the students' lives which can and do affect their overall mental health. Suicide, as a specific topic, may be involved as a segment of these activities but probably to no greater extent than other social or mental health topics such as drinking, safe driving, building of communication skills, and similar areas.

Intervention functions are always concerned with interrupting a maladaptive sequence of behaviors or events. In the event of a crisis, the focus of effort is upon maximizing the probability of positive and helpful outcomes and minimizing the opposite.

The term "crisis" should not be considered to always mean a time of dangerous peril with predominantly negative overtones. "Crisis" literally means "turning point," and solidly conceived and well-executed intervention programs invariably operate following the basic assumption that even traumatic episodes can be turned into profitable growing experiences. It is true that individuals in crisis are probably more vulnerable and at greater "risk" than others. But the presence of risk offers possibility of growth and improvement, and every crisis, as opposed to a situation with affirmed negative prognosis, has hope as well as threat.

Intervention is comprised of three levels of function. Which level is operating depends upon the immediacy and intensity of the crisis or threat. In suicide, of course, the level is determined by the imminency and lethality of the individual's behavior. The levels are: (1) direct first-hand support and guidance, (2) activation of a system or systems of support networks which provide help and assistance of potentially greater depth, duration and intensity, and (3) in the presence of life threat, direct lifesaving or lifeline activities ranging from emergency medical care to primary crisis intervention of a very personal and one-to-one nature.

Rehabilitation functions come into operation after the fact. These functions tend to be more long-ranged in nature, less crisis-oriented, and often are subsumed under a design which combines a new and more easily perceived need for long-term crisis prevention along with some activities directed toward rebuilding personal, social and everyday problem-solving behaviors in those already afflicted.

Rehabilitation activities may involve working directly with those who have attempted suicides. In such instances, rarely does the school work alone. Typically, such children, or adults, have been and are receiving other kinds of support and help, often of a very professional and involved nature. It may even be in the form of ongoing professional psychotherapy. The school does not, nor should it have, the responsibility for the same functions as a help-giving social agency or an individual psychotherapist. However, the school does have a very important social-support role to fullfill in terms of helping individuals regain or achieve a sense of personal self-worth. The school also is in an excellent position to almost routinely provide a sense of predictable, sustained involvement through the regular process of being active in studies, extracurricular experiences, and the wide range of personal interactions these and other school-related activities provide.

In many instances, perhaps even more often, the rehabilitative function of the school will be concerned with those who are in a very real way the "victims" of suicide but who have not been attempt-perpetrators, themselves. These individuals, the **survivors of suicide,** are less apt to have professional or regular support services than the perpetrator. Because of this possible void in support resources, the school has a very special function to play. The school's involvement may be concerned with providing support and care for a single child whose parent or some other loved one has been a suicide, or it may be working with an entire classroom of students who have lost a teacher or peer.

Grief work, "death education" in some curricula, silent-support networks, special staff training workshops each offer the school an opportunity to fullfill its post-suicide or suicide-attempt responsibility.

Subsumed under the structure of these three critical functional areas are many opportunities for staff and students to play very important and highly contributive roles.

SPECIFIC ROLES FOR SCHOOL PERSONNEL

Some roles may be more clearly the responsibility of certain individuals than others by virtue of their specialized training. However, it is a fallacy to assume that the interest, skillfulness, motivation or even the ultimate effectiveness of an individual will be due automatically to specialized, formal academic training for certain crisis situations. While a few schools occasionally may have such personnel on their staff, their presence is more apt to be a serendipitous event than related to any specific recruitment strategy.

While it is true that administrators would seem in most instances to be more apt to "administrate" and counselors to "counsel," crisis situations are likely to elicit functional roles far different than job-description-defined responsibilities. In a crisis, those who can, "do." Those who cannot "do" may be more in the way than anything else. And, since crises do not follow carefully preconceived organizational patterns and expectations, the need for someone who can "do" is likely to occur in unexpected times and places and in many instances in situations where formal help and support lines are not quickly available.

The elementary teacher who, while taking his or her turn at noon playground supervision, answers the screams of children who have found a playmate hanging from playground apparatus has no option but to take immediate and responsible action. Calls for counselors and administrative help are unavailable luxuries for the moment.

Consequently, the training of personnel for crisis-intervention roles makes the initial assumption that the responsibility may fall upon anyone's shoulders at any time. Training and preparation should be universally applied with general disregard for position or assigned responsibilities.

Crisis prevention, an equally important objective for the schools, and post-suicide experience rehabilitation, also an important task, offer more opportunity for matching individuals to tasks and for taking advantage of specialized training and interests. However, if prevention and rehabilitation are to be effective, some level of widespread information familiarity and involvement is necessary. Individuals may play more specialized and deeply committed roles, but the general attitudes and atmosphere of involved concern must permeate the entire school population.

The range of roles through which school personnel may assist in the assault against the suicide problem is wide and varied. It is likely that few schools will become involved in all of them. However, the very wide scope of possibilities in itself is a positive factor, in that it facilitates schools of varying types and sizes in defining roles which fit the needs, capabilities and motivation of their own personnel, school body and community.

A number of these roles are easily identified. They may be easily perceived through the application of the three facets of suicide work: **prevention, intervention,** and **rehabilitation.**

Prevention Roles

Everyone would rather prevent a crisis than have to deal with one. Fortunately, there seems to be adequate consensus that suicide is a problem amenable to preventive measures. The school can make a very strong contribution to such an attack on this significant social problem by deliberately developing some of these preventive roles.

Outreach Networking

This role is comprised of both formal and informal efforts by school staff and personnel (including administrators, teachers, support personnel, and students) to link the school to other community resources. This linking, or "networking," is designed to help the school in building an atmosphere of good mental health, solid trust, mutual respect, and an open and declared commitment to helping people in need of assistance. Networking efforts can range from simple school assembly and bulletin board informational programs to the mutual sharing of names and phone numbers of trained or professional people interested and willing to be of service. These preventive activities, undertaken in advance of the appearance of a crisis, not only create a better situation for handling actual crisis intervention and rehabilitation when the need arises, but they also help prevent the development of crises through the deliberate creation of an atmosphere conducive to effective ongoing personal problem solving and stress reduction.

As Fujimura (1985) has pointed out, even those personnel who have been professionally trained to meet and handle suicide crises will profit from knowing where their appropriate referral and support sources lie. An important component of the psychological first-aid approach to meeting suicidal crises (Slaikeu, 1984) is the willingness and the ability of the first-aid provider to assist in taking concrete action. The weight of such responsibility is eased and the concomitant increase in feelings of security, self-confidence, and preparedness makes a strong positive contribution to the general mental health of a school.

Information Dispensing

Dispensing of accurate and helpful information is an intrinsic function of the school. Providing staff, students, parents, and to a certain extent the community, with factual information about suicide fits easily into this traditional role. Through the application of normal operating functions (e.g. health classes, community school activities, PTA and other joint school-home involvements, bulletin board and special program and visiting speaker offerings), the school makes a substantive and important contribution towards preventing the tragedy of suicide.

Crisis centers and other mental health agencies and organizations invest a significant amount of staff time and energy in their community-education programs. These efforts can be richly augmented through a cooperative involvement with the schools. In most instances, these agencies with specialized resources are more than willing to assist the school by providing relevant literature, speakers, films, and professional consultation. But, at the same time, school personnel have much to offer. Schools are staffed by professionals trained in the effective dispensing of information. Teaching is their strength. It should be strongly utilized.

In addition to being the place in the community where effective teaching is most easily accessed, the school brings the traditionally granted position of conferred authority. The public expects the school to know the facts, to have accurate information on hand or know where and how to find it, and to be willing to share it with all. These attributes, earned by a long history of public service, can be effectively used in respect to a suicide-information program.

The topical subject of programs designed to provide preventive information can be varied. Most professional efforts along these lines typically focus upon three major areas when dealing specifically with suicide prevention. These areas include: (1) providing information about the long-range and immediate precipitating causes of suicide (Ray & Johnson, 1983), (2) restructuring people's ideas about suicide in order to replace myths with facts (Johnson, 1985), and (3) making sure that the public is aware of the signs of distress, signals for help, and nature of distress that a suicidal person may display (Giffen & Felsenthal, 1983; Jacobs, 1971; Madison, 1978). The school can easily offer meaningful help in each of these three areas.

Parents should certainly be a major target for the type of informational programs mentioned above. They should be contacted as a group and offered opportunities for the same kind of informational training as is offered to staff, students, or the community at large.

In addition, parents should be individually recruited for the purpose of forming outreach information and support-giving calls throughout the community. They should be consulted on the ways and means whereby students may be most effectively involved. They should be recognized as an important source of contemporary information on where and how to network with the community.

But in addition to this focused extension of the school's informational program, the school has potential for other richly rewarding joint roles with parents.

Parental Involvement

Too often, a focus of blame and responsibility shines upon parents and the family as the possible or even probable cause or precipitator of adolescent alienation and its related problems.

While it is true that an unhealthy family situation does increase the stress level and therefore the vulnerability of all involved, the other side of this argument is frequently overlooked. Probably, the best, the most reliable, the most easily accessed, and potentially the most efficiently applied source of preventive mental health and personal support in a crisis is the family. For every deteriorated family situation which has contributed to the suicidal risk of an individual, there are dozens of other instances where the strength and resiliency of the family, and the productive coping and problem-solving skills learned from the family, have provided a foundation of good mental health and an effective barrier to the threat of suicide.

Healthy relationships, effective parenting, and a sound, knowledgeable understanding by children and especially parents of human behavior as it functions in both good times and bad, is probably the best anti-suicide weapon that our society possesses (see Fig. 1-1). There can be no doubt that the absence of these does increase the "at-risk" factor for a wide variety of mental health problems, including suicide (Cohen Sandler et al., 1982).

The school has a natural role to play here, since the development of these attributes contributes not only to the prevention of suicide but to many positive aspects of growth, development, learning, and effective living. As a part of its everyday function, the school teaches about effective learning and living. Deliberate extension or enrichment of this program to include these three important aspects of a psychologically healthy home environment is easily and naturally accomplished. The importance of such a preventive contribution is virtually immeasurable.

TRIAD OF FAMILY EFFECTIVENESS FACTORS

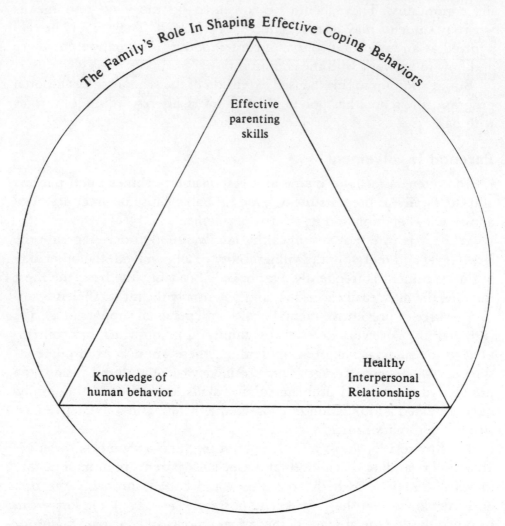

The Family's Role In Shaping Effective Coping Behaviors

Effective
parenting
skills

Knowledge of
human behavior

Healthy
Interpersonal
Relationships

Figure 1-1. These three factors are largely responsible for maintaining the effective mental health of the family unit, the best anti-suicide weapon we have.

Crisis Management Training

Every crisis invites, in an epidemic-like fashion, the spawning of more crises. Students and teachers having gone through a crisis will experience an aftereffect which includes feelings of guilt and depression, anxiety and concern for unfinished or unsuccessfully completed tasks. Such a response is normal and to be expected. Still, the better a crisis is managed, the less severe is the effect and the more easily is it understood that the reaction is largely a temporary emotional rather than a lasting cognitive response to a deeply disturbing situation.

An ounce of prevention truly is worth a pound of cure in such instances. It is difficult, if not impossible, through training to teach people not to strongly react to having experienced a severe crisis. Crisis management does improve through preparation and training, however. One can be trained to handle a crisis more effectively and to better deal with one's own behaviors during a time of crisis as a result of such preparation.

TABLE 1-1

EXPERIENCES OR SITUATIONS WHICH CONTRIBUTE TO THE ELECTION OF SUICIDE AS A RESPONSE TO STRESS

1. An extraordinarily threatening event, particularly if it is seen as a long-term threat to happiness, status or self-esteem
2. Linkage of negative experiences to feelings of personal vulnerability
3. Inability to produce what are perceived as minimally adequate or average-quality coping responses
4. Unusually strong demands for personal competency, particularly in a mode or situation which is perceived as "public"
5. Any severe stress which occurs when or where there are no perceived people or institutions to provide support or understanding
6. Past experience in situations or a subculture which has placed some form of implied approval on suicide
7. Chronic depression or physical illness
8. Loss of a significant other
9. Alienation from family or friends
10. Behavior which is perceived as disorganizing or destructive to the happiness or well-being of significant others
11. Confusion over role-expectancies and the criteria for acceptable performance in these areas
12. Public ridicule or blame or experiencing loss of faith in self by others, humiliation
13. Compounded stress factors, such as any of the above, plus being a substance abuser
14. Unrequited love or unanswerable attack
15. Inability to communicate feelings or problems due to poor communications skills or absence of listeners

Adapted from Madison (1978), Ray and Johnson (1982), Rosenbaum (1975).

As Rosenbaum and Beebe (1975) have wisely noted in their examination of the occurrence of and treatment responses to psychological crises, such crises are produced by a number of different factors. Certainly, both long-term and immediate extraordinary threatening events or experiences can precipitate a crisis. But it is also important to realize that in many instances even such extraordinary occurrences fail to evoke crisis responses in most individuals. Those most apt to succumb to the crisis threat are those who feel most vulnerable, least well prepared, and least adequate to respond effectively to severe stress and its accompanying demands for personal problem-solving response.

Crisis management activities help decrease vulnerability and prepare teachers, staff, and students for effective responses, thereby reducing the probability of minor crises evolving into major ones.

Specific roles include simulation training, providing of response-option information, awareness of one's own emotional response style, and general stress-reducing techniques. Each of these is very compatible with the learn-by-doing approach so prevalent in contemporary education. And, it is important to note that the rewards for such involvement are high and immediate. "Be prepared" is more than a scout motto. It is a functional confidence-giving component of good mental health and makes people feel better immediately.

Building a Positive Mental Health Environment

This is not merely an important role, it is a vital one, since only the school and it's personnel can accomplish it for that part of the student's and teacher's day which is spent in the school environment.

Though it is obvious that the individual in crisis needs the support that a healthy environment can provide, it should never be forgotten that the same healthy environment which provides this support is also substantially responsible for the prevention of many other crises. In healthy school environments participants learn the everyday skills which give them the strengths necessary for coping with those "extraordinary events" which can precipitate crises. Those whose coping skills are less effective, and who may find themselves treading precariously along the treacherous edge of personal disaster, are more quickly noticed in a healthy and involved environment. Help comes more quickly and more effectively. McBrien (1983) has said it well: "The key to a suicide prevention program based on situational clues is the network of concerned school personnel who keep the school counselors informed of students who experience the life crises known to be danger signals" (p. 77).

It has been wisely suggested (Ray & Johnson, 1983) that the network supporting and treating youth experiencing suicidal crises in their life must consider a wide spectrum of the victim's lives. Certainly, the **biophysical** aspects of their problem must be considered and problems of physical health, psychopharmaceutical treatment of clinical depressions and similar medically oriented responses are well-known.

But as Ray and Johnson remind us, the psychological and sociological aspects of life should not be ignored, either. The environment can make positive psychological contributions by attention to the tasks of dealing with reality, the presence of opportunities for observing and learning problem-solving skills, practice in effective communication (both the speaking and listening aspects), and through a general social modeling of effective living.

The sociology of healthy living also involves the school and its personnel. Developing regular habits of productive social interactions, group and family informal networking, as well as peer-group and student-faculty interaction patterns all add an important asset to the individual's reservoir of defense against crisis-producing stress.

Sheehy (1976) has reminded us that "marker events" (and the school experience provides many of these) cause changes in our internal perception, our concept of self and others as they relate to us. The importance of having a balance between security and danger and an inner awareness of our own vitality should not be underestimated. Mentally healthy individuals are capable of and frequently practice dealing with the "NOW," the "HERE," rather than dwelling on an unassailable "BEFORE" or a fantasized and unproductive concern for the "LATER" or "AFTER." A healthy school environment reinforces attention to the present.

TABLE 1-2

HEALTHY VERSUS UNHEALTHY PROBLEM-SOLVING FOCUS

Healthy	Unhealthy
Here and now	Before and after
Alternatives considered	Single solution fixation
Sharing of problem and responsibility for finding solutions	Going it alone
Willingness to compromise	Perfectionist, all or nothing
Satisfaction from effort	Satisfaction from accomplishment
Breaking large problems into modular bits	Emphasis on the total problem
Prioritizing of sub-tasks	Random selection of problems to attack

A significant aspect of the positive mental health environment is the presence of readily available, easily experienced, and personally rewarding emotional support.

The general value of support and the important role it plays in both the prevention of and recovering from crisis has been stressed by many. Relative to the problem of suicide, the contributions of support to prevention, intervention, and rehabilitation are quite specific. Among these are:

1. The reduction of anxiety through the development of feelings of security and comfort.
2. Feelings of worth and being loved and respected, which are created by the emotional presence of others.
3. Assurance that help with problems is not only available but that realistic coping and planning are possible.
4. A broadening awareness of different perspectives as experienced through interaction with others and the very important corollary which follows; namely, that every individual has the right and may choose to change his or her mind.
5. Close group relationships and interpersonal sensitivity tends to reduce impulsive and abortive solution attempts of which suicide is a paramount example (Brammar & Shostrom, 1982).

Sensitivity to one's relationships with others, to the fine nuances of others' behavior, and to our own emotional response and responsibility is an important part of many of the workshops designed to help those potentially at "high risk" of suicide (Johnson, 1985; Steele, 1983).

While somewhat less specific than some of the other tasks defined here, the role of promoting an atmosphere of positive mental health is clearly a responsibility of the school. Attention to the components of such a helpful ambience cannot be ignored by any school that wishes to minimize the number of emotional crises among faculty and students.

Intervention Roles

There are three major facets or phases in suicide intervention. The roles which school personnel are called upon to play are closely dependent upon which of these three phases is involved. A suicide crisis situation elicits a particular phase based primarily upon the amount of imminent life threat present. As a consequence, those who would carry such roles must first of all possess appropriate information and necessary prerequisite skills for judging the life threat present.

If life threat is very low or nonexistent in terms of the immediate situation, then intervention roles focus primarily upon personal sensitivity and support with networking and more involved help resources being of concern but with considerable less sense of urgency.

If life threat is obvious or if there is any ambiguity about the absence of life threat, then intervention roles focus first on networking and only subsequently on personal support.

If life threat is high with threat of imminent suicidal behavior, or if there is ambiguity about the level of identified life threat, then emergency lifeline responses are warranted.

TABLE 1-3

LETHALITY LEVEL AND INTERVENTION RESPONSES

Lethality level	Intervention stance	Tactics
High risk	Very directive	Act on behalf of victim, mobilize resources, seek help, take total control as necessary to effect intervention.
Some risk	Facilitative where productive coping is present: Directive where apathy or ineffective behavior is present.	Listen and give advice, encourage and abet constructive behaviors, present and discuss options, help victim prioritize.
Low risk	Facilitative	Listen and empathize, be ready to respond to call for help, encourage victim taking action, share feelings and ideas.

As Brammar and Shostrom (1982) have cited, crises have certain identifiable characteristics. These include (1) the presence of severe stress, (2) disruption of everyday routine, (3) acute frustration, (4) feelings of anxiety — both referenced and free-floating, and (5) feelings of helplessness. Any support roles which tend to reduce the amount of any or all of these negative characteristics can be helpful in reducing life threat and suicide.

Sensitivity and Support Roles

These roles can be far more subtle and indirect than the naive help-giver might at first suppose.

Rosenfeld and Prupas (1984) suggest that the individual in need of support requires at least two levels or phases of sensitivity and support before or in addition to the more traditional support-giving interactions. These two, often overlooked types of support include, first, the granting of personal distance, tolerance, and a type of help or support which does not infringe upon the person's privacy and sense of individuality — a sort of "non-impinging" type of help. When and how to use this type of support, and, most importantly, when to move to other types of support because the situation warrants a move, are important discriminations that require careful consideration and probably some specific training. The second phase, also often overlooked, involves the offering of a wide variety (in terms of presentation methods) of safety, acceptance, non-reciprocating giving where the support person is willing to give without an expectation of receiving, and other types of largely atypical personal relationships.

In a sense, such support approaches offer the inviolate acceptance of the worth of the individual which is sought for within the confines of the private therapy room. The difference is that in this case the support must be extended in open, public, and often unusual circumstances and without time for the careful development of person-to-person empathy characteristic of the therapy room. While many individuals without clinical training possess the personal capability and personality structure to feel comfortable about extending such support, it is often necessary to spend some time in training the individual to recognize the cues for granting these or other levels of support.

Another aspect of support lies in the role of the empathetic and understanding gatherer of relevant information. Rosenbaum (1975) offers a checklist for analyzing the crisis situation and the individual's call for help. He suggests that the potential help-giver consider these four factors:

1. The personal characteristics of the individuals involved and the setting in which the call originates or in which help must be rendered.
2. The event or situation which apparently has precipitated the call for help.
3. Points or loci of points of greatest stress or tension along with the correlative vulnerabilities of the person in need.

4. The individual's desired solution and/or expected outcomes.

Sometimes, such important data is difficult to obtain, particularly in a quick and accurate fashion. The development of a role of recognized empathetic interaction, high credibility, dependable and predictable responses, and acceptance for the importance of personal privacy and personal space facilitates the successful gathering of such data. Every school usually has some individual on staff who has already developed a reputation in the students' eyes for being the students' friend, potential confidant, source of aid, and comfort in times of trouble. Such individuals can offer a very effective support role in times of suicide crisis and, at the same time, be the vehicle for gathering information vital to important decision making about subsequent support or even lifesaving activities.

There are certainly instances, however, when sensitivity, empathy, and simple one-to-one support are inadequate to meet the severity of the crisis. In essence, the decision whether to treat or not to treat the victim in the current environment should rest upon professional and often outside assistance. Moursand (1985) says the help-giver must consider four aspects of the crisis situation in arriving at such a decision. These are:

1. Who are the "significant others" in this person's life and how available and useful are they for help?
2. What other personal support systems are available and accessible to this individual?
3. What tangible and emotional resources does the individual have?
4. How available are other outside sources of help if the need should suddenly arise?

Ultimately, as Moursand underlines, the ultimate question has two main segments:

- Does this person need me, or can he/she go it alone?
- Does he/she need more or different help than I can provide?

The answers to these questions provide the data for making the decision regarding moving onto the second level or phase of intervention work. If the answer is to look for more help, then other roles are suggested.

Networking

Networking takes place on many different levels. At its simplest and most direct level, networking consists mainly of primary person-to-person intervention through the providing of immediate and personal attention and support. Such intervention can occur very early in the sequence of behaviors, which sometimes leads to suicide. In such instances, it usually involves mostly the development of personal sensitivity to the need others may have for personal support, unqualified acceptance, and relief from self-defeating cycles of loneliness, despair, and unhappiness. If it occurs late in the sequence with suicidal risk higher and the possibility of the actual occurrence of self-destructive behavior more imminent, it may involve more direct support and active intervention.

Emotional "handholding" may be replaced by more active involvement, calls for outside help and the involving of others. In really high-risk situations, networking may involve less private person-to-person activity and be of a more formal nature with deliberate and clearly defined calls for help to outside sources, or very active and direct referrals. The handholding may become a reality with joint journeys to help-providing sources occurring with the support person providing emotional and physical assistance in reaching help.

There are several aspects to networking that involve school personnel in intervention roles.

1. The school should collect and be a readily accessible repository of accurate and up-to-date information regarding available help.
2. The school should have specifically trained people who react well in crisis situations ready to "take charge" and visibly assist in the decision-making and implementation phases of networking.
3. The school should serve as a publicist of the availability of help sources, the ways and means of contacting them, and all other information relevant to finding the right help quickly when it is needed.
4. The school should assume the responsibility for training staff and students in the recognition of danger signs which suggest the need for networking to be instituted.

The various roles are not particularly difficult, but they are vital to saving the lives of school personnel and students.

Some trainers of school personnel (e.g. Fujimura, 1985) feel that these decision-making and implementation skills are so important that they should be included in the regular training of school personnel if maximum benefits are to be received. Such an approach certainly seems warranted. However, in the absence of such formal training, the individual school can go far towards providing in-service training along the same lines.

Emergency Lifesaving Roles

Perhaps less need be said about these roles than some others, not because they are unimportant, but because they are so worrisome and obvious that we may have already attended to them more than some others less immediately frightening.

It has been suggested (Johnson, 1985) that personnel who must face the grim reality of life-threatening crises, especially those dealing with suicide, be prepared to follow the 3A's as guidelines.

> **A is for Accessibility:** Those whose situation provides the likelihood that they will be called upon to save lives must make themselves easily and readily available. When lifesaving intervention is required, help must be quickly available by applying a predictable and standardized method of summoning and obtaining help.
>
> **A is for Appropriateness:** Those who are called upon to save lives in emergency situations must know what to do under the given circumstances and the most efficient means for discriminating the available options as quickly as possible.
>
> **A is for Accuracy:** Those whose actions may mean life or death to others must strive to be error-free in their responses. Quick, decisive, and accurate responses maximize the probability of the individual in need receiving the needed help in time. Not only must choices be appropriate in nature, they must be carried out well.

Certainly, the roles that school personnel should play are affected by these three-point guidelines.

Every school should have specific personnel who are categorically designated as emergency-response personnel. These should be individuals who have demonstrated capability, motivation, and personal effectiveness. Though responding to a fire as opposed to a suicide threat may involve different types of emergency responses, certainly each demands that the school have people at hand ready to respond in an appropriate and accurate and effective manner.

In the case of suicide, there should be a widespread attempt to build these skills in the entire school population to some extent. Unlike many other emergencies, suicidal emergencies very often give us warning. It is true that the signs are not always totally clear, sometimes subtle, and sometimes achieve visibility in unusual sites and situations. But it is equally true that a large majority of people who seriously contemplate suicide do give warning. The ability of a large segment of the school's population to note and recognize these signs, no matter when or where or from whom they appear, provides a broad accessibility to emergency help. This is an invaluable community resource.

Consequently, the ability to respond appropriately and accurately by this same large proportion of the school family, if only in terms of knowing where and how to get more help, is a way in which the school can responsibly respond to the **Accessibility-Appropriateness-Accuracy** guidelines.

Those who work with youth may face the need for a more prompt crisis response than those who work with adults. Though it is a popular myth that suicidal individuals cunningly plan to avoid all types of intervention help, the truth is quite the opposite. Most suicidal people seek help and make active calls for help. This is especially true of adults and to a large extent of adolescents, as well. Along with their maturity, adults are apt to display more ambivalence and deliberateness even in their suicidal behavior. On the other hand, adolescents are far quicker to read everyday problems as being of devastating and unsolvable magnitude, and existence becomes perceived as a black or white decision that is far too often misjudged in the negative. Children appear to kill themselves far more impulsively and with less rational motivation than adults (Husain & Vandiver, 1984). The amount of time one has to recognize danger signals and make emergency responses may be far less for children than adolescents and less for adolescents than for adults. This disturbing possibility presents another major argument for the school being ready to meet the demand for quick and efficient lifesaving responses.

Rehabilitation Roles

When a suicide or suicide attempt occurs, the resulting effects spread throughout the lives of those touched like ripples spreading from a stone thrown in water. Some recuperative or rehabilitative effort needs to be devoted to assist and support those affected. Under the circumstances it is far too easy to focus almost exclusively upon the perpetrator or the immediate family and friends of this person. In truth, the need for rehabilitation is much broader, reaches far more lives, than we might casually consider.

A suicidal event connected with the school, a teacher, or student, for example, leaves many survivor victims. Strong feelings and potentially severe emotional problems may be experienced by broad groups of people. In some instances an entire classroom, or grade level, or even the total student body and staff may need help. The negative effect of such feelings on the educational-learning process are severe. The school cannot, on either a moral or pragmatic basis, ignore the mandate to help solve the problems.

Rehabilitative or recuperative roles are usually of two main types. The roles serve to create or re-create a school-wide, positive, health-giving, strongly supportive atmosphere which facilitates individual efforts. They also may function to provide direct, individually designed support for specific individuals or groups.

In a sense these efforts actually bring the school back full circle to basic preventive measures. A major difference may be present, however. The initial assumption, in a school environment which has not recently experienced a suicidal crisis, is that the school population is an essentially healthy one. The emphasis is upon building skills and feelings that are crisis-prevention oriented. It is also assumed that the major task is to tap already available personal resources, provide modeling and information, thereby facilitating the normal, expected growth in mental health.

When rehabilitation is needed, these same assumptions still may be valid up to a point. But the task of the school is made more complex and difficult by an awareness that many involved may be starting from a minus rather than a neutral or positive position. Some negative effects of an unhappy situation may need to be undone. Feelings of self-confidence and security may be down; feelings of fear and anxiety may be up. Individuals may need encouragement and reparative experiences, in addition to information and modeling. Specific fears and doubts must be squarely faced. Feelings of high vulnerability, including a sometimes frightening awareness of one's own mortality, are likely to be present. A casual, indirect, business-as-usual approach is not the answer.

Reparative and Recuperative Atmosphere Roles

Post-suicide experience has much in common with other types of grief. Kubler-Ross (1975) has noted the progressive stages through which many pass when faced with the concept of tenuous mortality. She notes that the typical progression is from denial and personal isolation to anger to bargaining to depression to acceptance.

Working through these steps, possibly a necessary process if one is to regain productive mental health, is often difficult and lengthy. The school's task is compounded by the fact that there will typically be wide differences among the individuals of the school family in terms of where they find themselves in this vital process.

Experience has taught us that the task is most successfully accomplished when faced squarely and honestly. The feelings involved cannot be ignored in the hope that they will go away. Undealt with, such feelings may have negative effects for years, carried as a heavy baggage of unresolved problems and fears.

Schools can work through small seminar experiences with teachers and selected students, outlining the process and ways in which problems may be resolved. In some instances, a school-wide assembly is necessary and helpfully cathartic. Professional help-giving agencies are often willing to provide assistance in the form of speakers, printed handouts, or short-term curriculum or workshop guidelines.

Separate tasks or roles may include teaching responsibilities, a reaffirmation of the importance of internal-support networking, a focus on meaningful long-range planning designed to (1) reduce the probability of subsequent crises (essentially a preventative approach) and (2) increase the ability of school personnel and students to manage any crisis that does eventuate.

Atypical use of personnel is often warranted. Traditional teaching or administrative responsibilities may be temporarily altered as the school matches the most effective individual to the task.

A common error to be avoided is the tendency to focus heavily upon the issues for a short time and then abruptly stop, returning to normal routine and curricula. There is certainly something to be said for a return to normalcy, and such a return does indeed help recovery by providing predictability and familiarity to the situation. But the school should not overlook the possibility of those individuals who may still need help. These should not be forgotten, and some relatively long-range opportunities for assistance should be provided. It is also hoped that the school personnel will have gained insight and acquired a deeper sense of commitment from the difficult experience. Important facts can be learned from the experience. The school should have a better awareness of its strengths and weaknesses and how the system handles a crisis. Recuperative experiences often prove to be so helpful to students that they become incorporated as part of regular, ongoing non-crisis activities.

Specific Support Roles for Survivors

These roles will usually center about two different support systems. One of these is directed toward survivors left behind due to a successful suicide attempt. The other is meant to assist the individual whose suicidal experience has not resulted in death.

To a large extent, survivors can be assisted through the general recuperative programs suggested above. However, in most instances there will be a nucleus of survivors whose experiences and reactions will be more intense. Sometimes, these individuals are easily identified due to their obvious close involvement with the perpetrator (e.g. siblings, classmates, or the student's teacher). It is not uncommon, however, to find severely affected individual survivors who are not as easily noticed because their relationship is less obvious or because their reactions are subtle and less-focused.

Not only must the school accept the responsibility to assist individuals in need of help, but it should also be clearly pointed out that if such individuals are ignored or allowed to struggle through the rehabilitation process unaided, their efforts may well indeed have a desultory or even debilitating effect upon the recuperation of others. The school has responsibility towards both, of course.

Individual needs often require individual attention and planning. However, some generally helpful role functions may be developed. The school should have individuals ready to deal firsthand with problems of fear and guilt. Questions such as, "Why didn't I see this was going to happen?" "Could I have prevented it?" "Did I (we) cause it to happen?" are common (Madison, 1978). When they arise there is a need for personal support and understanding, presentation of honest and accurate information, and the application of sensitive networking both within the school and by utilizing outside sources.

As noted previously, crises are times of potential change. The school's willingness to deal directly with individuals experiencing survivor reactions may provide the impetus for solid mental health growth from that point forward. As Slaikeu (1982) has pointed out, one can and should link questions about the past to opportunities for change in the future. A number of important, helpful questions may be asked through individual and group sessions, health and vocational planning curricula, and many other regular school activities. These include, "What has been done?" "What can be done in the future?" "What alternatives for help and growth exist?" "What personal and environmental changes are possible?"

At the same time as the school works towards being of assistance to the individual, it should be noted that in no sense does the school have either the right or responsibility to act as a surrogate professional therapist. Some individuals will need specialized outside help, instead. Knowing that some problems are too intense and too complex for the school to handle and being able to offer assistance in finding appropriate help is in itself a supportive and healthy contribution to the individual's mental health.

Specific Support Roles for Perpetrators

Most recovering perpetrators will be currently experiencing or will have recently had professional help. The school has several role responsibilities in this respect. One is to be ready to support and augment individual treatment plans as requested; another is to be sensitive to the need of the individual to return to a feeling of normalcy as soon as possible. The difficult problems connected with effecting that delicate transition is addressed in some detail in a later chapter.

The school also must be sure to neither abdicate nor overdo its responsibility for monitoring the individual's progress. Sleikeu (1984) has noted that there are three important sub-goals in psychological first aid in suicide situations:

1. Providing support
2. Reducing the life threat or lethality of the situation
3. Providing linkage to helping resources

These are also important goals for the rehabilitation process. The school should be ready to help the individual return to a successful and productive life-style, to learn and apply coping mechanisms which prevent the development of life-threatening stress, and to make sure that the individual's re-assimilation into the mainstream of the school experience is supportive, warm, accepting, and as uneventful as possible. The process is delicate and needs careful planning and preparation. Major issues involved in the process are discussed later in this book.

Suicide is a problem that is very much with us in our current educational scene. The school occupies an important place in the community-wide network seeking to lower this threat to our youth.

The roles that school personnel and students can and should play are quite varied and offer many opportunities for effective interaction with those experiencing or in threat of experiencing the risk of stress which is capable of precipitating self-destructive behaviors.

Effective application of these roles requires effort to obtain essential information, to develop teaching and modeling strategies effective to the individual school situation, and the recruitment and training of those who are in the best position to help: the staff, the teachers, the students, and all who share the problem and the solution.

CHAPTER TWO

PREVENTION: THE ULTIMATE CURE

"There are times in every life when we would like to die temporarily."

Mark Twain

S UICIDAL THOUGHTS and the crises which follow are not generated in a vacuum. Though the urgency of a crises experience often precipitates feelings and expressions of surprise, some of the most common reflections one hears expressed in post-crisis recovery work include:

"I guess we really shouldn't have been surprised."

"If we had been more alert we probably would have seen it coming."

"The signs were all there. We just didn't recognize them."

It is not necessarily true that more alertness and increased sensitivity on our part will invariably deter, delay or eliminate suicidal thoughts and actions in those around us. Some of these expressions noted certainly stem, at least in part, from a sense of guilt, which, though sincere, may not be realistically warranted. Though it is estimated that approximately nine out of ten suicidal individuals do present recognizable calls for help, one cannot depend that these pleas will necessarily be directed toward individuals intimately involved with the potential victim's life. Sometimes, they surface in obscure or unusual circumstances. Sometimes, they are directed towards individuals who could not reasonably be expected to be quickly alert to such distress.

Though increased alertness, sensitivity, and knowledgeable awareness does pay off in decreased suicidal risk, as will be stressed extensively in the rest of this book, it is this simple fact of not always being in a position to hear a call for help which is the best argument for a solid program of prevention.

LEVELS OF PREVENTION

Since Caplan's (1964) monumental work, crisis management techniques and activities have usually been conceptualized within a framework of levels, layers, or stages of prevention (Slaikeu, 1984). Though these different levels have some obvious overlap and often each may be occurring at the same time in a given situation, there is value in noting the difference in emphasis each level presents and noting its usefulness in alleviating the social evil of suicide. The approach used here follows Caplan's theoretical model, though others might be applied, as well.

Primary Prevention

Primary prevention, the initial level or approach to the problem, is based on two significant assumptions:

1. Hazardous situations or experiences often occur because the potential threat is unrecognized or unheeded.
2. Individuals and groups have the potential for living a healthy life if afforded the opportunity and resources.

Consequently, **primary** prevention strives first of all to help the individual, organization, or community eliminate, avoid, or modify potentially hazardous situations.

Realistically, we know that some potentially hazardous situations are difficult, perhaps even impossible, to totally eliminate and avoid. New experiences, even in such supportive environments as the school, are stress producers and new experiences cannot be totally avoided by a developing person. Unavoidable trauma strikes many of us. Friends and relations become sick, some die. Others move away or find new friends. Our fondest wishes and expectations do not always come true. In such instances **primary** prevention will try to reduce, limit, or soften one's exposure to the hazardous event or situation. Newness is softened by friendly faces and enjoyable experiences. Trauma is responded to with support, sharing, intimacy and personal warmth. Defeats are demoted by the recognizing of new goals, objectives, and achievable challenges.

And in a very important contribution to individual and group mental health, **primary** prevention strives to help the target of the "slings and arrows of outrageous fortune" become less vulnerable to such attacks, stronger in the face of adversity, more capable in dealing with whatever may come their way.

Secondary Prevention

Sometimes, despite our best efforts, disaster falls. **Secondary** prevention is concerned with helping the individual or group prepare to handle crises with a minimum of cost and a maximum of efficiency. Two main concerns become the targeted objectives for this level of prevention:

1. Limit as much as possible the intensity and duration of any disability (psychological or physical) which results from the crisis experience.
2. Involve the resources of others, both individual and group, formal and informal, in intervention, assistance, and support.

The emphasis is obviously on facilitating recovery. This is accomplished primarily by directing efforts toward ameliorating both the duration and intensity of the negative or unproductive, anxiety-producing experiences. When a crisis does occur, this type of social interaction is invaluable. Its effectiveness is, of course, dependent to a large extent upon the pre-event status and preparation of all involved. When individuals have been made less vulnerable through **primary** prevention, then **secondary** prevention becomes far easier and more effective. The two processes are closely related.

Risk recognition and crisis-intervention organization and techniques are **secondary**-prevention activities. They are very important to the school system attempting to effectively deal with the problem of suicide. Each will be addressed in detail later in this book. However, it is very important at this point to specifically note that even the best of **secondary** prevention plans can be improved by effective **primary** prevention. Failure to carry out effective **primary** prevention very seriously handicaps the effectiveness of any **secondary** intervention.

Tertiary Prevention

Every crisis experience, even when successfully resolved, extracts a price, carries a cost to the individual or group. **Tertiary** prevention is directed toward alleviating these costs. Activities are aimed primarily at recovery, establishment of effective coping behaviors, and returning to the everyday business of living.

Tertiary prevention is designed to make sure that the long-term effects of crises do not permanently handicap those who have experienced them. The assumption is that the victim(s) can, with proper direction and assistance, successfully resume the business of living, perhaps never forgetting the crisis experience but not having to carry an unnecessarily heavy burden of unresolved conflicts and worries.

It is obvious that this final level of intervention is equally dependent upon what has gone before in terms of early preventive measures. Clinicians readily agree that the single best predictor of recovery rate in an individual experiencing mental health distress is the pre-experience resources and health of that individual.

Those who have had a strong and healthy pre-crisis life are least at risk for permanent emotional handicaps. Rehabilitation, as the word clearly denotes, is directed toward rebuilding. Recovery and rehabilitation is far easier accomplished when a strong foundation of healthy experiences and meaningful preparation has preceeded the crisis.

Indeed, in the area of suicide prevention there is absolutely no questioning the old saying, "An ounce of prevention is worth a pound of cure."

PRINCIPLES OF PRIMARY PREVENTION

Primary prevention activities are based upon several fundamental principles. Probably the most basic of these is the assumption that the human organism has far-reaching resiliency in dealing with stress. It is assumed that most people will respond effectively if given the opportunity to be healthy, to make rational choices, and to deal constructively with one's problems.

The major goal of primary prevention is to provide the individual (and the group or community in which the individual resides) with some basic resources. These include:

1. Basic knowledge helpful in solving the problems of everyday living
2. Practical experience in healthy living
3. An environment which facilitates rather than hinders coping with and tolerating stress
4. The ability to accurately monitor one's own adjustment status skills
5. Awareness of and access to support and assistance when individual resources alone appear to be inadequate.

In process terms, these resources essentially translate into three significant segments: first, learning the "how-to's" of mental health; second, acquiring the ability (and the habit of regularly doing it) to assess one's own situation in terms of levels of stress, options for coping, and readily available personal resources for solving or tolerating personal problems; and third, learning when, where, and how to find help when introspective assessment indicates the need for assistance.

The term "crisis" has a frightening ring to most of us. However, it should be remembered that it essentially means "decision point" or "time of decision making leading to one direction or another." At the time of "crisis" an individual is in a position to go forward or to retreat, to make progress or regress. Primary prevention assumes that it is possible to provide the individual with preparation designed to increase the probability of the crisis turning-point resulting in favorable, productive outcomes.

Wilhem (1967) reminds us that the Chinese word for **crisis** is written by using two separate characters blended together — one signifies danger, the other signifies opportunity. It may also be helpful to remember that, by definition, **crises** are relatively short-termed, and what is most needed is immediate help specifically addressing the issue in focus rather than long-term treatments. It is this aspect of crises which underlines the importance of having resources available in the natural environment of the individual experiencing the crisis, ready at hand and easily available when needed.

It should be remembered that most individuals experiencing crises, even such dramatic crises as suicide, are essentially psychiatrically normal in terms of their overall capabilities. It is true that these individuals may be in a position of extreme tension, high anxiety, and often constricted perception when it comes to perceiving adaptive options, but giving the individual the extra resources necessary to rise to the high demands of such precarious situations is one of the main arguments for primary prevention. People experiencing suicidal crises, though they may feel alienated and isolated, still live in and to a very large extent reflect the mores and traditions of their cultural surroundings.

Primary prevention fully endorses the principle that it is easier to be individually healthy if one's learning of coping behaviors has taken place in an essentially health-producing culture.

A very typical component of the suicidal individual's ambivalence about suicide is that part of him or her which says, "I do not want to die: I merely want to be relieved of these worries, this stress, this unhappiness." And in this respect, most suicidal individuals really do want to help themselves and have an available reservoir of capability to help themselves if they can become aware of how to do so. The community or school environment that applies these primary prevention principles takes the all-important first step toward making it easier for the individual to tap that important reservoir of successful living behaviors when crises arise.

The schools obviously have many opportunities for meaningful interface and involvement with each of these segments.

PRIMARY PREVENTION IN THE SCHOOL

The school environment offers some special, perhaps even unique, opportunities for primary prevention. Nelson and Slaikeu (1984) point out that some of this uniqueness comes from the serendipitous fact that the school has more regular day-to-day contact with the developing child than any other institution in our culture, with the possible exception of the family. This longitudinal contact facilitates the application of coping skills to a wide variety of adjustment and adaptation situations and thus facilitates the child's ability to generalize these skills to new and different experiences.

They also note that primary crisis intervention shares a basic common goal and process with the school. It is directed toward the objective of developing useful, applied personal and individual skills. It assumes that the most effective process for acquiring these skills is through the blending of normal growth and development with progressively involved learning experiences.

If the acquisition of coping abilities occurs in settings that are natural and familiar and which additionally may represent or model the scenes and circumstances where real-life application of those abilities is needed, the possibility of successful application is increased. This proves to be true regardless of which level of prevention is involved. As Hoff (1984) has said, "Prospects for positive crisis resolution by individuals, families, and peer groups is enhanced and negative complications are reduced when crisis management and intervention occurs as close as possible to natural settings."

Berkovitz (1984) notes, "Schools are agencies where the behavior and feelings of the majority of children first come to the close attention of professionally trained adults outside the nuclear family, more even than come to the attention of pediatricians or family practitioners."

Awareness of the opportunity for and importance of school involvement in the three-stage prevention process is increasing and the results are very encouraging.

Several states (the leaders have been California, Louisiana and Florida) now require schools to incorporate suicide prevention programs in their curricula. Model school-based programs can be found in such widely different locales as Colorado, Ohio, Texas, Connecticutt, Virginia, and many others. The attention of the federal government has been drawn to the necessity for attacking the problem of youth suicide at least in part through the schools. Some significant suggestions for adequate programming have been formally presented to the congress (see Table 2-1).

TABLE 2-1

GOALS FOR A SUICIDE PREVENTION PROGRAM

1. To increase awareness of the problem of suicide among youth through education of students, teachers, counselors, principals, clergy, juvenile justice workers, mental health professionals and families.
2. To educate as to predictors of the signs of suicide so as to prevent attempts and reduce the numbers of completed suicides.
3. To educate as to crisis-intervention techniques.
4. To promote awareness of community and statewide resources, including mental health centers, private and non-profit agencies, poison control, tie lines, etc.
5. To educate as to the grief process following a suicide for friends, family, teachers, peers, clergy, etc. so as to support grieving individuals and minimize the stigma and frequent "contagion" effect of suicide.
6. To develop a program within the schools which deals with:
   a. Positive self-esteem
   b. Communications skills
   c. Relationships — getting in, maintaining, and getting out appropriately
   d. Process of grief around loss
   e. Positive failure/positive success
   f. Life skills, i.e. decision making, values clarification, problem solving
   g. The meaning of life and death
   h. Avoiding loneliness and isolation — by building support networks
   i. Stress management
7. To develop a training package to be replicated statewide to mobilize communities to preventive efforts against the incidence of suicide through:
   a. A trainer of trainer's manual
   b. Audiovisual aids
8. To conduct statewide workshops using manual and audiovisual aids to leave communities with resources of their own.*

*Statement of Iris Bolton, Director of the Link Counseling Center of Atlanta, Georgia before a special subcommittee of the Select Committee on Aging of the U.S. House of Representatives of the 1984 Congress (Bolton, 1985).

A variety of individual approaches have been instituted ranging from training students to man a "hot line" for fellow students (Winters & Modine, 1975) to a combination of peer counseling, parent education, and a "hot line" for students "out of control" (Neill, 1977). Not only have special training materials directly relevant to suicide been developed (Barrett, 1985; Johnson, 1985), but additions to the traditional curriculum have included dealing with such related topics as **death education** (see Table 2-2) (Schvanaveldt, 1982).

TABLE 2-2

REASONS FOR INCREASED SUICIDAL RATE AMONG THE YOUTH

1. Increased competition for employment in the work world
2. Family life in disarray
3. Increased divorce rate
4. Both parents employed
5. Anger displacement generated by stress
6. Role model among family or friends
7. Substance abuse

Adapted from Maris (1984).

What is required of the schools if they are to contribute effectively to the primary prevention of suicide? Berkovitz (1985) has suggested five separate activities or goals:

1. A healthy general mental health atmosphere of the individual school and school district
2. Optimum psychological services staff
3. An organized and active suicide **prevention** program
4. An organized and active suicide **intervention** program
5. An organized and active suicide **postvention** or **rehabilitation** program.

The validity of applying primary suicide intervention in the schools is well-supported. The major problems seem to be two-fold: raising the consciousness level of those who must endorse and implement these programs, and establishing and putting into action various successful strategies and program paradigms.

SELLING THE IDEA

If primary prevention is so necessary and the schools such an obvious place to apply these important principles, why is it that more programs are not already in place? The fact of the matter is that the subject of suicide is still largely a "taboo" topic in today's society, and schools and school personnel reflect the inhibitions of the public at large.

Cowgell (1977) has suggested that rescuing behavior itself does not appear to be the normal response of the average citizen. One might indeed point at some of the well-publicized examples of witnessing public refusing to intervene or assist a citizen in distress. Despite the fairly pervasive cultural value that we are, at least to some extent, "our brother's keeper," the average person is at best often slow to respond and in many cases highly reluctant to do so. When the situation is highly emotional and relatively strange to most of us, as is certainly the case with suicide, the reluctance becomes more obvious and the latency of our response more apparent.

The answer seems to lie, at least in major part, in education and desensitization. To feel comfortable in meeting an emergency situation, we need to feel capable and adequate. The need for primary prevention becomes involved in a circular process. Primary prevention is needed to help those in crises as well as to those who would help those in crises. Where does one start?

Why the Fear?

There seem to be several major fears or roadblocks to immediate and enthusiastic personal involvement in primary suicide prevention by school personnel. Most school personnel have virtually no training and little information regarding either the problem of suicide or the role and function of prevention at any level. This is a phenomenon shared of course with the general public. The facts of the matter are, of course, that the school and its personnel are in a position of special responsibility and opportunity. Consequently, when they elect to ignore the issue, the moral dilemma is more apparent.

Lack of Information and Training

The term "gatekeepers" is frequently used to describe those in positions most apt to meet, recognize, and respond to the potentially suicidal individual. School environments and processes certainly place school personnel in "gatekeeping" situations. Smith (1976) is among those who strongly suggest that teachers should be given special training to assume the role of gatekeepers among their other functions. It is Smith's assumption, and most clinical professionals would agree, that training itself would alleviate a substantial portion of the fear and resistance that may arise primarily out of the understandable insecurity that accompanies confronting the unknown.

Others, including Shneidman (1976), strongly endorse training programs for "gatekeepers" and would go farther than merely training those most likely to hear the cries for help. Shneidman would involve the general public in programs designed to address the taboos on the subject of suicide so as to give "a greater permission to citizens in distress to make their plight legitimate reason for treatment and assistance."

Most recently, a nationwide panel of experts on suicide have been involved in a progressive refinement of recommendations on exactly what should be taught to various school personnel, how school policies should be structured to facilitate and support intervention at all levels, and principles for both pre-professional and on-the-job training (Lennox, 1986). The panel outlined guidelines for training and in-school programs for many different school personnel. The problem is complex, and the need for education encompasses broad areas of information and knowledge. There was, however, unanimous consensus that the necessary information is generally readily available, reasonably easily taught once content and goals have been identified, valuable to the consumer, and of a nature as to generalize helpfully to other areas of concern for those working in the schools.

There is no doubt whatsoever but that experiencing such training and acquiring the important information would increase individual prevention and intervention skills in the training participants, thereby saving lives. Enriched skills and informational resources would help alleviate fears and doubts about being gatekeepers.

In part, the answer lies in providing training and fact-learning opportunities.

Lack of Structure and Organization for Application. The issue has been succinctly stated by Allen (1976): "The problem is that factual information acquired from programs of education somehow is not translated into lifesaving behavior. Knowledge can go hand-in-hand with deep-seated fears that influence behavior even when the conscious mind is well aware of what ought to be done. . . ." The nationwide study cited above directed considerable attention to the need for an appropriate more-or-less formalized organizational structure, which, though perhaps peculiar to each different school setting, would lend collective support to individualized efforts at suicide prevention and intervention.

Roles and responsibilities should be clearly defined. Useful strategies and operational procedures should be available, and specific support and backup resources should be clearly identified before the fact. The individual is much more apt to step confidently into the vortex of a crisis if he or she knows that substantial help and group endorsement and support is quickly and readily available.

Primary prevention interfaces directly with this issue. Forewarned is forearmed! Primary prevention is designed by intent to anticipate problems and provide in advance of any emergency for the availability of needed resources and assistance. Organizational plans need not be compulsively detailed, but they should be sufficiently operational as to provide easily apparent assurance to the individual that he or she does not and will not stand alone.

Issues Relevant to the Suicidal Situation Itself

The so-called "flight response" is based on an instinctual drive for survival.

Just as we are apt to reflect seriously on our own mortality while facing the loss of a friend or loved one, so are we likely to experience a fear of survival ourselves when involved in working with the suicidal individual. The emotional burden is not light. Reluctance to shoulder its weight adds to the general resistance often encountered when recruiting for volunteers to assist in prevention and intervention. To want to avoid some of the heavier emotional responses of suicide work is a natural and expected response.

Ross (1985) has identified four specific concerns which may account for a considerable proportion of the lack of popular advocacy for educational programs regarding young people and suicide.

Fears of Possible Contagion or Epidemic. The press is quick to notice and publicize what appears to be "clusters" of suicides, where individual suicide seems to be modeling on others or happening in groups. In actuality, the fact seems to be that epidemic suicides, except in highly distinctive situations where atypical value or quasi-religious factors may be involved (e.g. Kamikaze suicide pilots in World War II), the risk of this happening seems to be slight.

The fear is based on an honest but mistaken acceptance of the wide-spread myth that talking about suicide with a potential suicidal individual will precipitate the act. The opposite is true. As every crisis-line worker knows, talking is a primary form of suicide-lowering intervention. To the extent that awareness of another's suicide may precipitate like behavior in a high-risk individual, it appears in fact that failure to intervene at some level of prevention does not lower but may indeed increase the at-risk level of the victim due to loss of support and alternative avenues of coping.

Manipulation By Others. No one likes to be used by others, and each of us have experienced sufficient instances of such behavior as to develop strong aversions. A common fear of those who first consider working with suicidal youth is that threats or gestures of suicide will be used as a means of taking advantage of them. There is fear and resentment of attention-getters and borderline psychopathic youth who might use the gatekeeper's immediate response style and emotional vulnerability for devious ends.

It is very true that something as serious as a suicide threat does yield such an immediate response that it can easily be used as an attention-getter (and crisis-line workers do deal everyday with chronic threateners who may not really be at-risk). Still, the categorization is not clear-cut and absolute. Some of those who manipulate by threat may be, in spite of their deviant coping mechanisms, genuinely suicidal if the threat is not heard. Some who threaten and gesture, with no intent, make errors in judgment and a gesture becomes life-threatening. But, many, many more — far too many to risk ignoring to even a small degree — are calling for help in the face of considering an act which often is a permanent and irreversible response to a temporary problem.

The risk of being manipulated to any great degree in reality is relatively small. To whatever extent it is present, it appears to be worth it when measured against the number of lives that may be saved.

Ambivalent Emotions and Feelings. Witnessing the potential destruction of a young life is a solemn experience, and emotional impact is typically very strong and personally upsetting. One of the most common reactions is increased introspection and consideration of one's own life situation. If such reflection is done with some degree of tolerance and acceptance for our own personal inconsistencies, we frequently find that our feelings are mixed.

For those who either threaten or act out we often discover compassion, though it may be mixed with wrath or hurt over having to expose our own vulnerability and uncertainties. We find our sympathetic behaviors intertwined with anger. Such ambivalence can be very discomforting. When trapped between two polemic sets of feelings, our immediate tendency is to attempt to remove the conflict as quickly and parsimoniously as possible. If an effective solution is readily at hand, we will use it. If not, our tendency is to quickly remove the stress in whatever way available. Very often, the most immediately available adaptation is to flee. When considering the possibility of such ambivalence and confusion occurring in the future, the easiest response is to lessen the probability of avoiding the precipitating event or situations. Resistance to preparation which will almost certainly lead to greater involvement in such situations is easily understandable.

Fortunately, these fears like many others, can be lessened and more easily handled by foreknowledge and acquired coping mechanisms — another argument **for** rather than **against** primary prevention.

Denial. Refusing to recognize or accept the extent or immediacy of the problem or the need for one's self to become involved in it is really only another example of the flight response to ambivalent feelings. The most common denial encountered is: "Suicide is not really relevant to youth (or schools, or teaching, or educational curricula, or non-clinically trained individuals, etc)." Some resistant individuals will admit the topical relevance but resort to personal exclusions: "I'm just not good at talking to people"; "I'm too high strung to be of help to those in crises"; "I can't handle stress myself, let alone help someone else"; "I'd like to help, but I can just barely manage to find time to do my own lesson plans as it is."

The fact is that in virtually all of these instances, the main culprit is fear and personal insecurity. Uncertainty and feelings of inadequacy are not only honestly and widely shared: they are, in an interesting way, helps rather than hindrances in suicide intervention. The person in crisis needs not only support but acceptance. To receive support from those who admit to having fears and inadequacies themselves is a powerful message. It says, "To be frightened is not necessarily to be defeated. To be troubled is not necessarily to be alone. To be in need of help from others is not necessarily to be devoid of the ability to be of worth to others."

Careful and thorough education and training, becoming aware that prevention and intervention is at its most basic level a task requiring humanity rather than clinical training or personal invulnerability, recognizing that personal acceptance and assistance is a shared, reciprocal

process involving compassion and patience more than high proficiency
and specific performance criteria, is one of the major goals of an effective primary prevention program.

WHAT ARE THE GOALS?

Field research following the *Yom Kippur War* in 1973 yielded some
useful findings (Neill, 1977). A primary focus was upon the needs of the
children and youth who experienced cataclysmic disruption of their life
space and personal lives. The events were devastating to many. It was
subsequently determined that prevention and intervention of incapacitating crisis responses in children required three different sets of process
strategies: (1) those directed at primary prevention through before-the-
fact education, (2) those directed at ameliorating non-productive behaviors in response to a crisis itself—secondary prevention, and (3)
well-planned situational and tactical response to the need for rehabilitation after the fact—tertiary prevention.

The three-tier model of primary, secondary, and tertiary prevention
was strongly supported. It would follow, then, that a similar model
should be effective if applied to meeting crises in the lives of school-aged
children and youth in a variety of circumstances, including suicide.

Psychological First Aid

Slaikeu (1984) has written extensively and effectively on the topic of
crisis intervention. A fundamental concept that he repeatedly reiterates
is that of the necessity for having both an organizational network and
personnel prepared and trained for immediate response to crisis
situations—first aid responses as it were. The preparation of organizations and personnel is a primary prevention approach.

Slaikeu presents five major components of efficient psychological
first aid. None of these can occur consistently by serendipity. They result from forethought and anticipation, organization and training, preparation and readiness. Slaikeu's work is highly recommended for those
who wish a broad but thorough knowledge of crisis intervention. For our
purposes here it is important to briefly note these five components and
underline the absolute necessity for primary prevention in preparing for
adequate psychological first aid. Individuals administering such first aid
need to have the knowledge, training, and organizational support to do
the following:

1. Make close, immediate and meaningful psychological contact with the crisis victim
2. Accurately and carefully explore the dimensions of the problem
3. Explore for, recognize, and examine possible solutions
4. Assist the victim in the taking of concrete action toward crisis resolution
5. Follow up to see that immediate intervention interfaces adequately with a longer-termed and broader-based rehabilitative network

Effective Teaching Skills

Primary crisis prevention requires effective teaching skills. It is obvious that school personnel should, by virtue of their training and experience, be in an advantageous position to make strong and effective contributions of this nature in an institutional setting designed for facilitated learning experiences.

Trained educators are particularly prepared or can be readily trained to offer the following important contributions:

1. Specialized knowledge of relevant subject matter
2. Specialized knowledge about children and youth and their developmental processes
3. Specialized knowledge about the learning process, including:
    a. How to introduce and help the learner absorb difficult material
    b. How to facilitate and improve not only acquisition but the recall and application of useful information and skills
    c. Skills of generalization and divergent thinking which help the individual seek out new or alternative solutions to problems
    d. How to reduce the exacerbating effects of narrowed perception, constricted thinking, and too intensely focused problem solving which accompanies the anxiety of stressful situations

Sergiovanni (1975) has reported four factors important to good teaching. These are a sense of purpose, accurate perception of the learner, knowledge of content material, and mastery of technique.

Each of these are characteristically present in far greater amounts in the trained educator than anywhere else in our society. Each of these is vital to primary prevention.

Does It Work?

In those situations where careful planning has been blended with broad-based support and developing enthusiasm, the answer is an unqualified, "Yes!" Anecdotal reports in support of extensive primary prevention are broadly based. In locales such as Fairfax County, Virginia and the **Cherry Creek Project** in Colorado (which has subsequently grown into a broader statewide project which involves professionals and volunteers alike), progress continues with useful new materials being developed for sharing with other locales (see e.g. Barrett, 1985).

In San Mateo, California, a substantive part of the demonstration program, fostered by and worked out in cooperation with the county crisis center, concerned itself with the establishment of evaluative criteria and measurement of effects and results. The criteria used (and results obtained) were:

1. Changes in the number of potentially suicidal students identified through the school system:
   The number identified tripled.
2. Changes in the number of students calling the crisis center:
   An increase of 8 percent to 21 percent was reported.
3. Frequency and types of request for consultation regarding suicide issues by school personnel:
   Teachers have requested that the training become part of their regular in-service training.
4. Requests for the program from other schools not in the original program:
   All schools in the contacted area have so requested.
5. Evaluations by actual participants:
   Overwhelmingly positive evaluations were received.
6. Observable community reaction:
   The program was publicly and formally commended by the Board of Supervisors and the Parents and Teachers Association (Peck, 1985).

The answer is clear-cut. Primary prevention, carefully conceived and executed, **does** work.

STRATEGIES FOR PRIMARY PREVENTION

Secondary prevention, concerned with effective intervention in an immediate situation, focuses largely upon successful tactics for reduction of an ongoing or developing crisis. Primary prevention, on the other hand, must consider strategies that involve longer-ranged planning, interaction, and prevention. The success of primary prevention programs in the schools rests upon three solid cornerstones: carefully planned strategies, committed and motivated participants, and broadly based ongoing support. The necessary strategies, though vital to success, are not particularly difficult either to understand or put in effect.

Schools are in a position to establish primary prevention in several different ways, each of which fit logically and easily with regular ongoing school activities. As Robbins and Conroy (1983) have noted, in order to be genuinely effective, specific goals and strategies need to be established for each step of primary (and, subsequently, secondary and tertiary) prevention.

Strategy One: Creating a Healthy Psychological Environment

Perhaps the most effective place to initiate basic primary prevention may be in the original personnel selection and hiring activities. While it may not always be feasible to screen potential new personnel for attributes relative to primary prevention, the school can certainly make it clear that the establishing and maintaining of a healthy psychological milieu is an important aspect of the school's function and involvement and that contributions are expected of each employee. Slaikeu (1984) has suggested that, "It is important for administrators to include crisis services in the job description of teachers, counseling personnel (guidance, school psychologists, social workers) and administrative personnel (including secretaries and office staff), as well as principals, deans, and others in higher administration." Such a policy would, if nothing else, create a "set" for all employees, a personal awareness that the school considers a healthy environment essential to its everyday operation and that meaningful involvement is expected of each employee.

Such a pervasive attitude has many advantages. It creates an atmosphere of normalcy when mental health and/or crisis issues are discussed and a basic readiness to be involved, and to both receive from and give help to others when the need arises. It has been noted that the best preventive measure, particularly for older students, is to engage them in a "helping system" from the beginning of their formal education experience (Albert et al., 1973).

Characteristics of a Psychologically Healthy School Environment

There is no shortage of helpful guidelines towards establishment of the psychologically healthy environment in the school. Principle components and basic structure, atmosphere, and activities which facilitate creating and maintaining such an atmosphere are all easily identified. Fortunately, these components fit very well with the major goal of every school, efficient education, and facilitate rather than complicate traditional ongoing classroom activities.

According to Berkovitz (1985), consideration of a positive mental health atmosphere should include attention to both the ethos and specialized services of the school. He suggests that a healthy ethos reflects four characteristic attributes:

1. Deliberate attention to aspects that enhance positive growth in individuals
2. Flexibility and sensitivity in teachers
3. Receptivity of staff and students to attitudinal input
4. Academic expectations that are positive in nature

As for the specialized or "psychological" services or activities that enhance the mental health atmosphere, he includes:

1. Counseling services
2. A student-helping network
3. Adequate teacher discrimination of problems and referral responses
4. Availability of interview and diagnostic activities (at all levels of sophistication as the need arises)
5. Availability of professional assessment of situations suggesting problem status or high risk
6. Opportunity for individual creative expression

A more specific set of proposed approaches or activities has been outlined by Blomquist (1974). These approaches focus heavily on the primary prevention of problems through emphasizing before-the-crisis preparation and crisis-preventing or crisis-coping skills. They include:

1. A broad offering of remedial reading opportunities due to the strong relationship between reading difficulty and educationally related stress
2. Encouraging children to become participants in extracurricular and community-services activities as a deterrent to withdrawal and feelings of isolation at times of crisis. Such activities also promote a

commitment to becoming involved in the improving of poor societal conditions

3. Structuring the curriculum to include a more positive study of society, with an emphasis on problem solving and the building of a society that is interdependent upon each other for support and assistance

4. Development of personalized rather than institutionalized teacher-student relationships

5. Creation of a "friends network," where everyone in the school has at least one friend upon which to call for help so that everyone may expect assistance to be available in time of need

6. Allowing school counselors to practice their counseling skills instead of being surrogate administrators

If the purpose of creating a positive mental health environment is specifically directed at the primary prevention of suicide, specific advice and guidelines are available. Most of this volume is directed toward that objective, but there are other sources, as well. Berkovitz (1985) has approached the task from the orientation of the school psychologist and offers an eight-point set of objectives designed to create a "suicide-prevention climate" in the school. He suggests that program and organizational decision making should consider these objectives as important criteria if suicide prevention is a substantive goal:

1. Good student and school-staff morale

2. Effective student-to-student relationships

3. Effective student-to-teacher communication and relationships

4. Parental involvement in school activities (especially at the elementary level)

5. Neatness and attractiveness in the classroom and overall school physical environment

6. A present and functioning professional school-support staff including counselors, school psychologists, social workers, and nurses

7. Presence and easy availability of curriculum and library materials designed to help students with life-coping skills

8. Existence of extracurricular or community-supported activities open to all students, and a school staff willing to follow up on students' involvement

The individual personal characteristics that enhance positive interpersonal relationships between the troubled student and the adult help-giver are simple but vital. Motto (1985) cites the characteristics of the effective adult as presented by a group of stressed young people currently undergoing therapy or counseling. These youth look for and respond to individuals who, in their words, are "really interested, concerned, natural, act like a real person, understanding, honest, do not talk too much, willing to listen but do not criticize."

Any program that creates or strengthens these attributes in school personnel is going to increase effectiveness in the primary prevention of suicide.

Adjustment Versus Adaptation

The vast majority of suicidal individuals do not wish to die; instead, they seek escape from problems and stress too difficult or painful to bear. As Shneidman (1985) has so succinctly stated, "One of the main functions of personality is to reduce tension. In this view, suicide is (only) an extension of normal personality functioning, albeit in an extreme circumstance."

As is frequently stated, the suicidal individual is making an adjustment to stress, which is in most instances permanent, though the stress itself may be only temporary.

Adjustment, as a concept, assumes that the individual is largely in a response mode to stress and must personally yield, reshape, give in, or otherwise redo the self to accommodate the stressful factor(s). While this may be reality at times, and learning to make effective adjustment in the face of unchangeable facts is both helpful and healthy, primary prevention is based on a much more creative and farther-reaching assumption—the principle of **adaptation.**

Adaptation, as a principle, assumes that the individual often does have options available which can alter the nature, extent, or effect of the stress and that learning to develop and exercise such skills is the most effective way to combat severe stress even before it arises. Certainly, when working with an actively suicidal individual, the principle is clearly applied when the most significant query being presented in all intervention approaches is, "Isn't there some other way?"

To assure that emphasis is upon **adaptation** rather than merely upon **adjustment,** four major contributive factors to adaptive success must be kept in mind as programs are organized and activities planned. Awareness of these factors and strengthening the individual student's resources in regards to them helps assure the formulation of an effective primary prevention atmosphere and program.

Factor One: Successful Adaptation Is Related in Part to Both the Duration and Intensity of Stress. Stress can incapacitate or even kill if either of these two aspects exist in amounts beyond the individual's ability to handle. The extensive work of Selye (1976) in the cost of stress is an important resource of information for the primary prevention program planner.

Unfortunately, the tendency of the untrained person is to equate the impact of stress with the single factor of intensity. The insidious, strength and reserve-sapping effect of ongoing though relatively low-level stress is too often ignored.

Schools can make a substantive contribution to the mental health of students and staff alike by deliberately moving to remove sources of regular ongoing stress in the immediate school environment and by developing a sensitivity to the presence of ongoing stress in individuals. Major stressors of high intensity should not, of course, be ignored. But too often an individual fails to cope with these crisis stressors due to a depletion of stress-handling reserve brought about by ongoing but lower-intensity stress.

Factor Two: Individuals Do Not Have Unlimited Reserves of Energy for Combating Stress. Therefore, the impact of stress is related both to the energy costs of the stressors and the available resources of the individual. Much of the strain of stress can come from fear and worry. Pre-education can substantially reduce the intrinsic cost of stress by limiting it to the stressor itself rather than the broader cost of stressor plus fear plus worry. The widespread effectiveness of pre-birth educational programs for expectant parents is evidence of this. Pregnancy and delivery includes unavoidable physical stress. The probability of a normal and essentially uneventful delivery is greatly enhanced by helping the expectant mother and father learn the truth about what to expect and how to deal with it.

When an individual's resources approach depletion, motivation, intentions, and knowledge play only a marginal role. There is a point in stress experience for **every** individual, regardless of strength or training, when additional successful coping is not possible without assistance. To recognize this, seeking help and yielding individual responsibility temporarily to others becomes the only rational and dependably effective response. Knowing when help is necessary becomes a sign of strength, rather than weakness, and an avenue of hope rather than a cul de sac of despair. Providing opportunity to learn this can be a very important contribution of a primary prevention program.

Factor Three: An Individual's Vulnerability to Stress Can Be Modified. It follows, of course, that if an individual may become less vulnerable to stress, then the cost of stressors may also be modified. Though some stressors are very real indeed, others are created or magnified in the anticipation, worry, and non-productive "belief patterns" of the individual. Learning to accurately anticipate genuine stressors, to ignore or appropriately downgrade those stressors which have little real impact upon us apart from what we delegate to them, significantly decreases an individual's vulnerability to stress (particularly the ongoing type of stress). Therefore, a greater reserve of available energy is available when legitimately unavoidable stressors come along.

Individuals tend to have their own style of perceiving and dealing with stress. Research indicates that this is only partly defined by innate or covert physiological processes. A significant part of one's stress vulnerability (or lack of it) is learned. It is the basic assumption of almost every therapeutic approach that the individual is in part the victim of his or her own thinking and may in turn be the recipient of the important attributes of productive, effective thinking and perceptual habits. A good example of this, applied to many everyday problems, can be found in the approach of Rational-Emotive therapy techniques (Bernard & Joyce, 1984; Ellis, 1971; Ellis & Grieger, 1977).

School curricula and environments can easily assist in decreasing the vulnerability of the individual through well-planned primary prevention.

Factor Four: The Best Defense Is a Good Offense! The major resource providing the individual with access to adaptive rather than simple adjustment options is the presence of broad options of well-learned, tried-and-true coping mechanisms. Earlier in this chapter we cited the suggestions of Blomquist (1974) regarding the ideal parameters for preparing the individual to cope with life's stressors. The natural "fit" of this approach with the traditional school curriculum and activity pattern is patently obvious. Just as we teach kindergarteners to look both ways at the school crossing, so can we teach our youth how to recognize, accurately evaluate, and subsequently cope with identifiable potential stressors.

As a result, many potential stressors will never achieve a stress-producing stature. Others will be remarkably reduced in their cost to the individual. Individual vulnerability can be dramatically reduced.

Many of life's most basic coping skills can be taught. The majority of the ineffectual and non-productive coping patterns we tend to develop and then harbor as reality can be recognized and amended before they become ingrained habits. Just as we teach the responsibilities of good citizenship through participatory government, and all students' attention to the rights of individuals, so can we help youth become effective managers of their own psychological environment.

If primary prevention can be established as an integral segment of our regular school curriculum and activities, the suicide rates of youth (and of adults too as the results generalize to post-school years) will drop automatically. And, as an immediate pragmatic benefit, the need for extensive efforts in secondary and tertiary prevention will also decrease.

Individual and Group Prevention

Extensive experience with patterns of suicide in those who are or were "significant others" for suicidal individuals strongly supports the concept that suicidal behavior is at least in part subculturally transmitted. Certainly, the principles of practical application of suicide intervention and suicide-survivor work equally support the opposite positive side of the coin, that effective recovery and meaningful recuperation can and is transmitted through interpersonal contacts in the subculture.

A number of workers in the field have authored useful materials for creating a healthy group atmosphere in order to facilitate reaching the individual in need (see Chapter Seven for material sources). O'Roark (1982) cites a list of four coping skills that should be, according to school psychologists, part of the school curriculum in order to bolster the stress-resisting capabilities of the subcultural milieu and therefore of the individual student:

1. Development of an individual's self-esteem so each student has an internalized intrinsic value because of who, not what, he or she is
2. Communication skills necessary to communicate feelings as well as concepts
3. The concept of positive failure, i.e. that success comes from effort as much as accomplishment
4. How to deal with and recover from grief or loss (see also Viorst, 1986).

It is for precisely this reason that the Samaritans, noted worldwide for their activity in suicide prevention, suggest that the most effective suicide prevention environment is one which provides regular and ever-available access to on-site peers for "call-in" or "drop-in" calls for support and help (Lawton, 1978).

As Slaikeu (1984) has noted, most schools have the physical facilities generally necessary for effective suicide prevention due to the high compatibility of educational strategies with crisis-intervention strategies. Added to the need for appropriate physical space and time allowances are simply the establishment of formally organized policies and procedures (essentially, a declared and visible commitment to prevention), along with personnel and staff, trained, available and involved in this important process. These components go far toward creating the type and quality of group milieu, or subculture, conducive to meaningful prevention of suicide among our school-age youth.

Strategy Two: Prevention Through Anticipation of Likely Problems

Cataclysmic events and circumstances often serve as precipitators of suicide among youth, due in part to the tendency of young people to be more impulsive in suicidal acts than adults. However, the significant problem areas that really give birth to and feed the syndrome of suicidal feelings and thoughts are apt to be more incipient, chronic, and very often about the same as those encountered by non-suicidal youths of the same age or level of development.

In other words, the problems of many suicidal youth are not much different in nature and type than those experienced by their non-suicidal peers. The victim's reactions, coping reserves, support systems, and general psychological health may vary from those of more successfully adapting individuals, however.

Creation of a generally healthy environment contributes substantially to the coping behaviors necessary for adaptation rather than maladjustment. At the same time, it should be realized that it is impossible, probably not even desirable, to totally buffer youth, psychologically healthy or not, from a wide range of difficult situations, stressful experiences, and personally vexing problems. Many of these, as the saying goes, "come with the territory."

It is helpful to be able to anticipate these; to be aware of when, how, and sometimes why they may arise; and to have some insight into the ways in which youth react and work the problems through to resolvement.

Many of these problem areas might be labeled as "normal developmental problems" in the sense that they are broadly experienced by many youth in our Western culture and are not the distinctive province of the inadequate, troubled, or high-risk individuals alone. Slaikeu (1984) has said that, "The common theme in developmental crises is that their precipitating events are imbedded in maturational processes."

Many of these maturational processes are involved with what is perhaps best described as periods of transitions in a person's life: times when one's roles, or self-perception, objectives in life, or even one's personal philosophy of life is changing. The concept of "passages" is common in today's thinking. Such works as *Passages* (Sheehy, 1976) or *Male Mid-life Crisis* (Mayer, 1978) deal extensively with this concept. Indeed, a crisis itself can be viewed as a transition between two potentially more stable and less self-disturbing periods of life as Levinson (1978) has noted.

The "passage" or the "passage process" can become unusually difficult, it may occur in a fashion or manner that makes it difficult for the one experiencing the stress to perceive that the stressors are also common among peers. An individual's reserves may be so low as to fail to provide the necessary strength with which to handle stress or, if the individual is surprised by transitional demands, facing them unexpectedly. In such circumstances, the crises may assume dangerous levels and/or potentially disasterous forms.

Fortunately, many of these transitional or developmental problems are predictable. Primary prevention steps may be taken to share awareness that the experience is typical rather than atypical, to build reserves, to remove the surprise factor. This helps diffuse the problem, capping it at a level where it can be safely handled without entering the realm of "high-risk" ideation or behaviors.

To a certain extent adolescents are all alike: they face similar stressful demands and many of their crises are predictable. This is useful in primary prevention work. However, as Hafen and Frandsen (1986) stress, useful as knowledge about these common denominators is, one should not forget the **individuality** of the adolescent person at the same time as one deals with concepts common to a group described as **adolescents.** The transitional problems are shared, but individual perceptions and reactions may vary greatly. Much of the earlier literature, for example, including some of the hallmark concepts still very useful today, was primarily based upon consideration of data drawn only from males. Even gender, as Gilligan (1982) and Peck (1982) have warned us, can play an individualizing role.

Primary prevention provides protection against disasterous crises developing. It cannot, however, offer total protection. It must be mixed with the effective leaven of personal warmth, sensitivity, interpersonal alertness, and knowledgeable involvement by human beings who are accessible to those of our youth who need help in time of crises.

Perhaps one of the most effective ways to combine a sensitivity to the individuality of the troubled youth with the common factor of developmental problems is to look at some of the shaping factors that mold both individual and stereotypical behaviors, particularly those affecting adolescents in our society.

The Vulnerability of Youth

One reason why adolescents are especially vulnerable to isolation and loneliness in their problems is that they have a tendency, despite their often overpowering concern for conformity, to view themselves as individuals, as being "different," somehow set apart (often in an unrealistically ego-centered way) from their peers. Ellkind (1974) reminds us that adolescents often perceive themselves, their feelings, and their ideas as being "exceptional." Such "separateness" lends self-assigned importance to their passage experiences. Preoccupied with new and increasing demands for career orientation, values clarification, and newfound intimacy demands and opportunities, it helps to feel a little "special," perhaps a bit "extra important."

What this results in is a self-promulgated aura of invulnerability, almost amounting to a non-pathological example of a delusion of grandeur. When problem-solving techniques don't work, when coping skills break down (and these things do happen to everyone), the tendency is to further self-delude by generalizing one's exceptionality to include the amount, type, and importance of failure as well. Adolescent group culture contributes to this potential alienation by establishing what amounts to a powerful, though fluid and relatively short-lived, class-conscious society not consistently overtly tolerant of individual differences.

Adolescence can be a lonely period, frequently laced with feelings of alienation. In part, the problem arises from cultural expectations for change, passages as it were; in part, the problem is self-created and self-perpetuated by the individual adolescent. Whatever the reason, being special means being alone; being alone means being exposed. Vulnerability is then increased exponentially.

Some of the major transitional crises, common to all, contribute to this heightened vulnerability.

Identity and Role-Diffusion Stressors. Historically, this concept has been brought to our common awareness by the extensive work of Erickson (1968). He has identified a series of transitional or developmental crises which seem to be experienced by many if not all of us in Western culture. In Erickson's conceptualization, the process of making transitions, of facing critical "turning points" or "developmental crises," is with us from birth until death.

Adolescence is not a fixed-year period, the age of its occurrence varying from individual to individual and blending and intermixing, overlapping, with childhood at the beginning and young adulthood at the end. Consequently, care must be taken to examine what may be unresolved childhood crises carried over into adolescence or young adult crises precipitated into the life of one still chronologically and experientially an adolescent. There are indeed problems of adolescence. It is true, however, that many adolescents also face the need to solve problems of childhood and/or young adulthood at the same time. The entry and exit portals of passage sometimes are confused and poorly defined.

Erickson has examined a number of potential troublemaking critical crises. Three of these contribute to adolescent vulnerability and are of primary concern to those concerned with the troubled adolescent.

1. The Childhood Task of Resolving the Conflict Between Industry and Inferiority. Erickson points out that a major developmental task of childhood is to resolve the conflict encountered in the demands of society for the individual to become industrious. The child is faced with the need to acquire information and academic skills, while at the same time trying to meet expectations by contributing to the culture and becoming productive and self-actualizing. All of this must be achieved in a culturally predefined and accepting way. At the same time the growing youth is facing the reality of personal inadequacies yet to be removed, and effectiveness shortfalls which are frequently demonstrated and underlined in interpersonal conflicts with peers, parents, teachers.

Though described by Erickson as primarily a problem of childhood (i.e. pre-adolescence) in actuality, many youngsters move into the adolescent years and environs with these crises still unresolved.

2. The Adolescent Task of Resolving the Conflict Between Identity and Role-Diffusion. Adolescence, defined both physiologically, and culturally, brings with it new tasks, new conflicts, new crises. The adolescent must face and master the challenge of physiological growth and changes and accompanying social correlates. New challenges for a more demanding type of intimacy with unavoidable positive and negative consequences are encountered. Values and moral reasoning undergo change as well (Kohlberg, 1969). Cognitive behaviors evolve to more abstract levels which though exciting in possibility and offering far broader horizons for the future still bring with them an awareness that one's own hypotheses about life and living may not be viable or in harmony with the ideas of others (Kohlberg & Gilligan; 1971). Vocational and career-choice problems become part of the individual adolescent's immediate life space rather than mere indefinite speculations and play-like role explorations of an undefined future status.

Each of these developmental tasks presents a crisis in the sense of being a transitional turning-point. Each places the individual in the position of struggling to establish his or her own individuality, exposed and vulnerable as it may be, while at the same time achieving acceptance by others, and facing the need to be an integral part of the culture, safely secure in the anonymity such goodness-of-fit offers. Each may, if ignored or handled without sensitivity, grow into a genuine personal crisis with far-reaching implications.

3. The Young Adulthood Tasks of Resolving the Conflict Between Intimacy Versus Isolation. At this stage of development, the individual finds that the new tasks which loomed so large upon his or her horizon in adolescence are indeed only the forerunners of still greater demands and challenges.

Physiological growth has matured into the capability and responsibility for marriage and parenthood. The challenge of intimacy versus isolation becomes unavoidable in adult social relationships and the probability of impending mate selection and marriage. Morals and values are no longer abstract concerns but now become cornerstones for critical personal decision making related to a host of life-defining choice points, vocation, marriage, career objectives, etc. Cognitive styles are now the *sine qua non* of one's existence. How one conceptualizes and solves problems firmly affects one's life. The responsibility for one's own life becomes blatantly obvious and this realization can be a lonely and frightening experience. Vocational choice is no longer a task for which one must prepare. It is a task of the "here and now," unavoidable, critical, and often with foreshortened time pressures.

It is impossible to grow without some risk taking. The developmental periods spanning the school years are times of risk taking. If those who interface with developing youth are knowledgeable about the potential crises which naturally accompany these transitional tasks, major primary prevention steps may be taken. This knowledge, if deliberately applied, suggests an awareness of incremented alertness, more sensitivity, activities and relationships which share information with youth and communicate to them acceptance of their critical problem areas.

Probably most of all, such a program establishes, a priori, a supportive network ready to note and help those who are hurting. And at the same time, youth growing in such an environment are given an all-important "set" toward their own feelings of uncomfortableness. They learn to expect difficulties, they become aware that virtually everyone struggles with the same problems, that virtually no one solves all the problems alone, and that not only is assistance and support at hand, but that to seek out, accept, and use help is in itself an indication of insight and maturity.

The myth that one must walk alone is not allowed to exist.

Continuity Versus Discontinuity: A Special Problem

Though it is a common denominator to most if not all of the developmental tasks mentioned above, the special problems of continuity versus discontinuity deserve special attention in any primary prevention program.

The impacts of growth and development are many and far-reaching. A frequent dispairing query of parents is, "Why do they act that way?"

It is helpful to have some common "umbrella" concepts at hand which cover wide ranges of individual behavior in terms of responding to the request for explanations and the identification of some of the causal factors.

These impacts stem from a wide variety of changes occurring in the youth's life which encompass aspects of their lives related to temperament, cognitive problem solving, moral reasoning, physical growth and change, gender and role identifications, values, and personal objectives. A major truth of "growing up" is that it is a repeating process of making and breaking bonding relationships with others. There are two major reasons why this apparently self-defeating behavior occurs.

First, there is a biological reality to be faced. The family bonds of childhood cannot be indefinitely perpetuated. Mothers and fathers die. The individual must achieve some status of individual independence and self-sufficiency or perish. As obvious as this seems, facing the reality of establishing individual identity causes many youth (and parents) pain and distress.

Second, if the requirements for developing self-sufficiency are to be met, it is necessary to acquire experience, to practice the difficult task of building relationships. Since the still developing youth has not yet established a stable temperament-value-cognitive-moral basis upon which to build lasting relationships and insufficient experience for making use of what viable foundations may already be established, the process is essentially one of trial-and-error. To try something new can be frightening. To fail is most often so, particularly if the goal is important and satisfactory development of an effective process is critical to happiness and a sense of well-being.

Bonding behavior is natural, healthy and obviously helpful in adding to one's sense of security. At the same time, reaching for the goal of individualized and mature bonding relationships carries with it the automatic assurance of experiencing a sense of insecurity. This insecurity, an awareness that the comfort of the past may not be applicable in new situations and surroundings, confronts the youth with **discontinuity**. It is exciting to "be on your own." But just as the small child's early threats to run away usually carry them only as far as the neighbor's backyard, so is there a conflict between hanging on to the increasingly non-functional bonds of past years versus the need to move on to the potentially longer-lasting bonds of new relationships.

All youth are forced into experiencing the conflict. Typically, there is a shift in bonding behavior from the home, to home surrogates, to peers and others outside the home. This is very often accompanied by a crisis of feelings of discontinuity.

The youth feels alone and without ties from either the past or the future. Extreme, sometimes bizzare, and occasionally dangerous acting-out behaviors may result. The progressive points on the continuum of alienation-rebellion-estrangement-acceptance-independence are not well-defined or always easy to identify. Many developmentalists feel that these apparently different vectors of reaction to the stress of continuity-discontinuity are merely different facets of the same behavior, varying only in their reflection of the ease with which the individual youth (and parents) meet and handle the developmental crisis.

There is strong reason to consider many adolescent runaway behaviors as essentially being a dramatized call for help, for rescue, for a chance to return to the less frightening and confusing continuity of childhood with its lesser demands and less critical acceptance.

It has been strongly suggested (Erickson, 1968) that in many instances there is a plea for a form of temporary reprieve from growing up — a period of grace at the point of merging of adolescence and young adulthood — when the youth requests and is given permission to "linger in childhood" yet a little while longer, delaying the traumatic acceptance of the reality of discontinuity accompanying a new identity. This period, sometimes labeled **social moratorium,** at best offers a delay in crisis resolvement. Though commonly observed in the rationalized delays in far-reaching decision making, e.g. choice of a career orientation in college, it is never helpful in the long run and seldom even does much to reduce present stress levels. Ambivalent behaviors, though allowing one to avoid facing adversive decisions, also rob the individual of any of the rewards of accomplishment and the satisfaction and comfort of eventual stress reduction by effective problem solving.

The school can take substantive crisis prevention steps by helping the individual come to grips with discontinuity and by providing support and acceptance without creating requirements for perpetual bonding responsibilities.

Strategy Three: Prevention Through Awareness of Critical Situations and Events

Not every problem area is common to all youth or unavoidable. There are some situations and problem areas which, though not experienced by all youth, do seem, when experienced, to carry the risk of heightened vulnerability and greater risk for crises of dangerous proportions. These are worth noting.

Problems Precipitating From Groups

"Why is suicide of the young apparently on the increase?" Invariably, professionals in suicidology are asked this question by the media, by parents, and even by young people themselves. The answer is not immediately obvious. But even a casual survey of the most commonly expected causal factors indicates the importance of group membership and effects (see Table 2-2, p. 44).

Of primary concern is the need for the individual to be able to offer a workable reciprocal relationship in group activities. To feel comfortable in a group, one must be able to both give and receive in a fashion meeting group and individual expectations.

Sometimes, the individual does not yet have these skills in hand. In other instances, the group itself is in such disarray that unreasonable expectations are put upon the individual. The unhealthy or disorganized group may be in no position to contribute to the individual. Consequently, the relationship becomes one-sided and of little benefit to the individual group member. Families with parents whose problems are so self-consuming that they have little time or sensitivity for their children are prime examples of this type of dysfunctional group. Sometimes, even healthy, functional groups will cause stress for members. This is especially true if the individual member has not yet established sufficient confidence in a well-defined personal identity to withstand stressful and uncompromising demands of the group.

The developing adolescent and young adult is especially vulnerable here. Developmentalists have isolated this process, called **foreclosure**, as the root of difficult problems for the individual youth (Newman & Newman, 1978). Foreclosure is the stabilizing of one's personal identity too early as the result of outside pressures and the demands of others. There is an apparent advantage to the youth in doing so, as there is a sense of security in "belonging" and not having to go through a longer, self-sustained process of establishing identity. But, as Janosik (1984) points out, the danger for the adolescent in crisis is that a sense of personal accomplishment and satisfaction is lacking.

The schools can offer specific assistance in this area. The educational environment can alert the developing youth to this tendency of groups. It can help establish the habit of exploring for options. It can facilitate the building of identity formulation and the acquiring of skills so the individual need not depend as much upon the demanding group for security in seeking personal identity. Providing the youth the opportunity to achieve a functional independence in achieving identity is a major contribution. As Gordon (1985) wrote in his dedication, "I write to encourage you to stand for **something**; otherwise you may fall for anything."

In those instances where the individual youth is deprived of healthy group learning experiences and support, the school can offer surrogate functions through staff and peers so that a safe and less demanding group-learning environment is at hand.

Personal Motivations for Suicide

Shneidman (1985) has adopted Henry Murray's **needs** classification as a means of categorizing the varying motivations for suicide. Many of these apply to the youth as well as to adults. The assumption to keep in mind is that suicide is perceived to be an intentional behavior designed to meet needs or remove the frustration experienced from failure to do so. Primary prevention intervenes in the process by helping the individual to (1) develop rational and reasonable types and levels of needs so that frustration is experienced less often and less severely, and (2) find viable options less severe and irreversible than suicide when severe need frustration is encountered. Among those need areas noted by Shneidman as motivational factors in suicide are these (Examples are taken from the authors' experience with real-life cases):

1. The need to avoid distress and pain, to protect oneself from having to experience these feelings.

   Example: **A high school student elects suicide in preference to being exposed as a dishonorable person after being caught in a locker theft.**

2. The need to defend oneself against assault and to vindicate oneself in the face of loss of ego strength.

   Example: **A student, accused by peers of being cowardly, a sissy, subsequently kills himself while attempting a risky bluff in a game of Russian roulette.**

3. The need to abase oneself, to atone or take punishment for deserved wrongs, to submit passively to outside forces.

   Example: **A non-married pregnant teenager loses her baby and takes poison leaving a note that she is unworthy to live, as "God has proven."**

4. The need for succorance, to be loved and cared for and receive sympathetic attention.

   Example: **Rebuffed in attempts to be recognized by an idealized lover, the victim of unrequited love, a teenaged boy hangs himself in the school auditorium.**

5. The need for autonomy, to be free of restraint and independent.

   Example: **A high school girl, grounded at home for three months because of a curfew violation, runs away and cuts her wrists in an urban "flophouse."**

The important point to remember is that we all have established hierarchies of needs which strongly influence our behavior. To feel frustration at the deprivation of such needs is also a universal reaction as is an attempt to find workable ways to circumvent the difficulty.

Primary prevention in the school can focus on an open awareness and assessment of how the student's individual set of needs influence him or her. Knowledge that need frustration is universal helps avoid feelings of helplessness and hopelessness. Learning about tolerating frustration, tolerating the delay of gratification, and finding eventual means for need gratification reduces much of the cumulative pressure and the tendency for impulsive, cataclysmic responses so typical of even the healthy young person. If the youth is potentially suicidal, such developed tolerance and lessened impulsivity can be of lifesaving importance.

Identified Contributory Causes in Youth Suicide

Finally, there are some situations or circumstances that have been clearly identified as adding significant stress to the youth's life and as a consequence resulting in an increase in both suicide risk and actual behaviors (see Table 2-3).

TABLE 2-3

UNIQUE FACTORS IN ADOLESCENT SUICIDE
COMPARED TO ADULTS

1. More often revenge motivated.
2. More anger and personal irritation involved.
3. Greater impulsivity.
4. More negative interpersonal relationships.
5. Have more non-fatal attempts.
6. Come more often from families of origin which have experienced divorce and suicide.
7. Less likely to have financial, work or marital resources.
8. Involve more risk-taking behaviors which eventuate in death.
9. More often involved with substance abuse.
10. More romantic and idealistic.
11. Have lower self-esteem.
12. Fewer life accomplishments to use as fallback options.

Adapted from Maris (1985).

These are worth categorically noting, since both primary and secondary prevention approaches merge to focus on these prime contributors to loss of adolescent life. In a preventive mode, the school can focus on the building of an environment and the teaching of information and skills that help prevent the occurrence of such events or successful handling of them when they do arise. There are many that appear to have definitive causal effects; only the major ones are noted here. Some of the materials cited in Chapter Seven direct the reader to more specific information along this line.

Family Dysfunction

Dysfunctional families include not only those experiencing death, divorce, and separation but also those apparently intact but experiencing internal problems that are disruptive and non-productive (Peck & Litman, 1974).

Such a family, distressed as it may be, is a major source of support and a symbol of permanence to the adolescent. The family assures the developing youth of the continuity of generations, a link with the past and an available handhold when future stresses are encountered. Dysfunctional families not only deprive the youth of the traditional contributions families make to the individual, but they also force the youth into a position of isolation and high vulnerability: feelings of alienation are accompanied by feelings of helplessness, a sense of being adrift without mooring or hope of rescue. In the worst of all scenarios, the developing child actually learns patterns of maladaptive coping behavior from his or her dysfunctional family members. This unfortunate circumstance is not limited to a single social class or culture. Adolescents from families of every social class and status are vulnerable to the negative effects of a dysfunctional family just as is true of suicide.

It is true that young people are remarkably resilient. Given a little space and time in which to react, their recuperative and regenerative powers are tremendous. But a dysfunctional family deprives them of space and time. The dysfunctional family draws energy rather than sharing it or contributing it. It forces the young person into positions of exposed self-dependency, which leaves little room for safe experimentation in the process of living or tolerance for frustration, failure, or defeat.

Faced with the negative influences of a dysfunctional family, the youth must expend all reserves and sometimes find themselves without apparent options, hope, or the energy to search for solutions. Shneidman (1985) notes the wish or need for cessation of pain as being one of the common characteristics of the suicidal person. At such times, suicide may be viewed as a logical escape route.

The school must be particularly alert for such situations. The natural reluctance of the adolescent to share intimate personal problems, coupled with the embarrassment of being in an apparent atypical family situation, may cause the youth to hide and disguise a potentially explosive situation.

Farnsworth, in the foreword to Shneidman's collection of college students' essays on death (1972), writes, "Private hopelessness or despair, rather than public distress . . . shared with one's peers, is the paramount motive for suicide **(among college students)**." The best overall solution is to provide a consistently supportive environment and a functional network of peer and adult support figures. These two maximize the troubled youth's personal resources and may increment the possibility of either the youth sharing problems or others noticing them.

Personal Loss

We've already mentioned how the typical adolescent feels "exceptional." Part of this exceptionality self-concept comes from a defense which protects the youth from dealing with problems by picturing himself or herself above and beyond such threats. It is far safer for the adolescent to ignore threats to invincibility than to face them. The excitement and energy of youth does not easily settle into considerations of mortality or even less severe indications of personal vulnerability. Death of a close friend or loved one, or sometimes even separation, carries a twofold impact. The youth must face the reality of the traumatic event. And, one's own lack of invincibility, one's vulnerability, and, in the case of a death, one's finite mortality cannot be ignored.

Crook and Raskin (1975) point out that mere loss by natural death alone does not typically predispose a child to attempt suicide. In family death-related juvenile suicides, the negative effect of a dysfunctional family is frequently apparent. Indeed, as Ray and Johnson (1982) have reported, sometimes irreversible losses such as the death of a loved one are easier for the youth to handle than an apparently avoidable loss as in a marital separation or breakup.

For those youth whose life-style and coping patterns are carrying them already periously close to crisis, the traumatic episode may be too much (Cohen-Sandler et al., 1982; Shaw & Schelkon, 1965).

In most but not all cases, school personnel will be aware of such situations. Adolescents need to work through the same grieving patterns as others (see Chap. Six). Fortunately, their abundance of energy and natural enthusiasm for life is frequently a major asset, but there is no guarantee that the troubled youth will be able to handle these problems alone.

Usually, the need for support is relatively transitory. The recovery rate can be and often is rapid, and what is most often needed is support, acceptance, and understanding during a brief crisis period. In other cases, the school may need to apply not only intervention but rehabilitative networking to provide deeper or longer-lasting help.

But, as in so many of these issues, preventative measures make the task easier. The youth who is regularly used to seeing people give and take support will more easily avail himself or herself of it at times of crises.

Depression

Depression is frequently cited as a cause of adolescent suicide. This may be debatable in some instances, since it is sometimes difficult, especially after the fact, to accurately determine when depression is part of the cause or the result of other suicide-precipitating problems, more of a symptom. There is total agreement though that depression is a commonly observed part of the personality pattern of the suicidal person, and the young person is no exception.

It is equally true, however, that depression as observed in adolescents is not necessarily the same phenomenon as that seen in adults. Its effects may be similar, but its outward characteristics are often sufficiently different as to warrant special consideration by school personnel. As Ray and Johnson (1982) remind us, the adolescent may be much less free in sharing his or her down moods. Covert depression, with indications allowed to surface with only an occasional close friend or in carefully selected situations, are quite typical.

In general, depressives are clinically categorized either as agitated or passive. Active, acting-out behaviors seem to be more typical of adolescents, and with suicidal adolescents these behaviors often become more pronounced. Peck (1985) has suggested that "acting-out depression" might even be listed as a major category of adolescent suicide.

The school is in an excellent position to both note and deter the development of such behaviors. Faced with the frustration of closed options, the depressed adolescent may display behaviors that others characterize as disruptive, directly aggressive, angry, threatening, hostile, and even deliberately dangerous (Cohen-Sandler et al., 1982). Since adolescent depression often displays surges of feeling, despair that seems too great to contain within the constrictions of so-called "normal" or "acceptable" behavior, atypical, anti-social behaviors result. One of the clues to the real essence behind such behaviors is that they can be seen to be atypical of the regular behavior pattern for a given young person, an anomaly noticeable to those who know the individual well. Because everyday association provides a good baseline against which to evaluate behavior changes, it may be the school that is in the best position to note such early alteration of behavior patterns. This can frequently be done long before precipitous suicidal activities ensue.

On a broader basis, young people can, in the process of everyday learning about mental health and adjustive behaviors, acquire useful skills in evaluating their own mood state, electing to find support when necessary, turning to options with less threat than suicide ideation. They can also be taught that mood swings are part of the normal variance of life. Armed with this information they can then accept their "down" periods for what they are, temporary deviances from normal feelings, and be less inclined to feel insecure about their own mood, worrying less about its permanence.

It would be unreasonable to suppose that any school program can even come close to eliminating depression. But there are many opportunities for better preparing the adolescent for the shock of such feelings. Recuperative and recovery skills can also be prelearned in many, many instances. Certainly, whether depression is a direct cause or a behavioral correlate of crisis-related despair, it offers clues that can serve as stimuli for positive preventative measures.

Substance Abuse

There is total agreement on the serious impact of substance abuse on suicide rates. This is demonstrably true for virtually every age and socioeconomic group, but the effect on teenagers is especially serious. This was evident over a decade ago (Peck & Litman, 1974) and it is equally apparent today (Cohen-Sandler, 1982; Hafen & Frandsen, 1986).

There are several important reasons why substance abuse significantly raises the suicide-risk level of teenagers.

1. Those who develop substance abuse habits or addictions often are seen to have personalities that reflect a sort of generalized dependency. They perceive themselves as innately inadequate and fail to

have self-confidence in their own ability to perform adequately in important situations without the support of drugs or alcohol. Turning to the substance for support, they in fact reaffirm their own negative self-appraisal. Their hypotheses become self-fulfilling as the toxic effect of the substance on behavior lowers their personal sensitivity and effectiveness. In the more rational interludes, when the substance's effects are not present, they then must face the double self-condemnation of being inadequate **and** substance-dependent. At such times suicide, seen as an escape from the unhappy reality of the dual problem, becomes more appealing.

2. We have already noted that impulsivity, action without careful forethought, is very typical of the young. Impulsive suicide, for example, is much more common among adolescents than adults. Faced with crisis-producing stress, the adolescent is in what often appears to them to be a critical situation. Extreme behaviors, such as acting-out, or even suicide, are very apt to be the young person's impulsive response, given without taking time for rational consideration of available options. The presence of a toxic substance in the brain lessens the effectiveness of rational considerations when they are made. In fact, it decreases the likelihood that they will even be considered, and increments suggestibility, a state of mind that tends to greatly increase the tendency toward impulsive behavior.

   If spontaneous, ill-considered behaviors involve lethality, the results are, of course, disasterous. Quite apart from the chronic high-risk status that addiction and habituation fosters, even psychologically healthy, single-instance substance abusers must be considered at higher risk when under toxic influence.

3. Suicidal behaviors run the gamut, from casual consideration to attention-getting gestures to attempts flavored with "call for help" attributes to specific and deliberate self-destructive actions. Even when in full possession of their faculties, some successful suicides appear to fall into the category of those who misjudged either the lethality of their situation or the probability that help would arrive in time to save their life. Couple this danger of miscalculation with lack of experience and accurate information (about the lethality of mixed drugs, for example). Combine it with the uninhibited impulsivity, decreased judgment, and slowed reflexes that accompany drug or alcohol intoxication and you have a life-threatening timebomb set to explode.

The teenager is extremely vulnerable to such a threat. Inexperience with alcohol, for instance, leaves him or her little margin for error. The real danger is that the person under the influence of a toxic substance responds to all life-threatening possibilities exactly as does the drunk driver: there is a mixture of decreased physiological response capability along with a deteriorated ability to accurately judge or even recognize one's own impaired judgment and behavior.

Whatever positive action the school may take towards substance abuse education without a doubt contributes in a major way to the primary prevention of suicide. There is no satisfactory, fast-acting antidote for the negative effects of substance abuse. Prevention is the only viable solution.

Extreme Performance or Accomplishment Demands

The growing years provide an emotional experience which is a two-edged sword:

- It is exciting to become an adult; it is frightening to be alone and on your own.
- It is exciting to learn new and exciting information; it is frightening to be constantly publicly evaluated on your achievements.
- It is exciting to see your own body sexually mature; it is frightening to face the responsibilities of marriage and parenthood.
- It is exciting to emulate your parents; it is frightening to have to replicate the successes of someone who has already succeeded.
- It is exciting to contemplate a career; it is frightening to witness the savage competition of the working world.

It is consensually agreed that strong demands for an individual to display competence can "trigger" suicide potential, particularly in situations that either have perceived criticality to the youth or which obviously reflect areas of self-perceived inadequacy (Madison, 1978). This seems to be true in many different countries and cultures.

Certainly crisis-level stress stemming from the pressure to perform knows no favorites of age or capability. Low performers suffer from pressure to improve. High performers suffer from pressure to maintain or broaden their performance. Suicide can and does result from such pressures for the average and the atypical, the young and the old.

The paradox is that the adolescent's reality world does stress growth, improvement, goal-setting, achievement and accomplishment. There is a narrow line between motivating encouragement and the production of threatening stress:

- "Congratulations on the "B" in Geometry. Now, let's try for the "A.""
- "Not many freshman make the junior varsity as you have done. Just think, by the time you are a senior, you may be team captain!"
- "Two more inches and you'll be as big as your older brother."

Who can say which of these represent simple challenges and which may become a critical overload? The answer is, of course, that it is probably impossible to always tell for sure.

This is why primary prevention in the school is so important! Young people in the midst of a world of challenge can learn to take satisfaction in effort as well as achievement. To learn this is to learn the reality most of us will experience all of our lives. There are many competitors in a race but only one winner. No high school class will have more than one or two valedictorians. The football princess can date only one boy at a time.

Learning these truths, acquiring the skill to fairly evaluate one's own efforts, to appreciate one's self for what one is rather than what one **has done,** are all lessons that can be learned to a very large degree in the school environment.

Teachers' attitudes and the administration's recognitions go far in shaping the individual student's philosophy regarding effort and achievement. To provide youngsters with the opportunity to develop positive self-concepts, even in the face of marginal achievement performances, is primary prevention at its best. And, in many instances, these lessons will provide valuable emotional resources for the individual many years past the school days.

Intimate Experience with Suicide

Anyone exposed to or affected by a suicidal experience is considered to be at greater risk as a result. Children of suicidal parents are at greater risk. Parents of a suicidal child are at greater risk. Individuals who have had a friend, acquaintance or fellow worker involved in suicide or a suicidal gesture are at greater risk (Diekstra, 1985; Matter & Matter, 1984; Tishler & McKenny, 1982).

The reasons are varied and may differ considerably from individual to individual, depending upon their own coping patterns and vulnerability.

The most commonly feared aspect—that one suicide may serve as a model or precipitate another—is probably less common than thought.

But if affected individuals are especially vulnerable, the experience certainly adds significantly to stress levels and may carry an individual beyond the stress threshold that he or she can easily handle. At such times almost everyone experiences an increase in introspection. This results in heightened consideration of one's own problems, vulnerability, mortality and similar heavy and potentially stress-producing topics.

If the perpetrator was a close significant other such as a loved one or intimate friend, there may be an implied permission to reflect on adjustive options (i.e. suicide) that may have never been given consideration before. This is not to suggest that such reflection and consideration in and of itself presents or creates suicide risk. It does mean that the individual has moved farther along the continuum of suicide ideation than perhaps might otherwise have been so.

Schools should not be paranoid about the matter. Tragic as any suicide is, it is entirely possible, if properly handled, that the experience may result in even stronger and more resilient adjustive capacities than before. Chapter Six deals extensively with suicide survivor work. Though survivor work may most often be thought of as a rehabilitative measure, it also carries clear preventative messages, as well. It is a preventative responsibility and contribution that the school should not shirk.

The Bottom Line

Primary prevention requires considerable effort. Careful planning is necessary. Consistency is vital. Momentum must be established and maintained to assure that the participants' motivation and commitment remain high.

Is it worth it? The answer is an unqualified yes. All the odds are in primary prevention's favor!

Primary prevention is built upon the positive assumption of a healthy organism. Every principle of adaptation and survival suggests that given the opportunity, the human being is capable of effective behavior and productive accomplishment. Certainly, the adolescent in particular is clear evidence of the validity of these principles. Full of energy, models of the broadening and strengthening effects of growth and development, adolescents bring every positive attribute to problem solving that could be wished (see Table 2-4).

Primary prevention merely takes advantage of these capacities. It facilitates growth, expedites problem solving, strengthens adjustment, and reinforces the natural adaptive attributes of the young person. It is a sound investment in a positive future. It saves lives!

TABLE 2-4

PREREQUISITES FOR AN ADOLESCENT TO SERIOUSLY CONSIDER
SUICIDE AS A VIABLE PROBLEM-SOLVING OPTION

---

1. Be faced with a problem which is unexpected, intolerable, and apparently unsolvable
2. See this problem as one more in a chain of problems which can be expected to continue
3. Believe that total escape, i.e. death, is the only answer
4. Arrive at this conclusion essentially in social isolation with little or no sharing of the problem with others
5. Be able to go against all the social norms and mores so far internalized
6. Be able to do this (#5) because you feel that you are not a functioning part of society
7. Be able to formulate perception of self in such a form that behavior contradictory to social norms fits the self-description
8. Do this by defining the problem situation as not of your own making, unresolved despite your efforts, unsolvable except by suicide
9. Remove all other viable options but suicide so that social onus and "sin" or wrongdoing aspects are removed
10. Be self-assured that after death will not be a recapitulation of the problem situation

---

Adapted from Jacobs (1971).

CHAPTER THREE

RECOGNIZING THOSE AT RISK

"Befriending is being able to share the unshareable, bear the unbearable, accept the unacceptable . . ."

The Samaritans

APPROXIMATELY 5,000 young people in America kill themselves each year. That statistic alone defines the enormity of the problem. It represents a tragic waste of human life which in most cases could have been avoided had someone, anyone, recognized the signs of impending trouble before it was too late. Far too often, the family and friends of perpetrators cry in anguish, "If only I had known . . . if only a sign had been given . . . a word dropped . . . even a hint."

An equally tragic statistic is that it is estimated that about nine of every ten of those lost youth did communicate their pain and intentions but were not heard, recognized, taken seriously or responded to effectively enough to save their lives. Or, as is often the case, they did not cry out to those who knew them best because of a misperception of others' interest, concern, or capability to help.

"We thought he was a normal kid" was the pained statement of fact made to us by the parents of a high school student who, because of personal stress and hopelessness, elected to become one of the lost five thousand. Their reflections about their son were revealing. "We did notice that he had become more quiet lately, rather reflective, and stayed in his room a lot. He didn't seem to want to be with his friends much either, but we never . . . ."

This young man had indeed presented some unmistakable signs that things might not be going right for him, but the signs were not interpreted as signaling suicide or even as indicating anything more serious

81

than a passing change in mood. The parents should not be blamed. Without the benefit of some education about suicide potential in youth and concomitant warning signs, many possibly significant serious mood change indicators may easily and understandably be overlooked as they were in this instance. The normal mood swings of adolescence are confusing and can easily obfuscate the genuine issues and concerns. Parenting youth with normal problems requires a great deal of expertness and finesse. Correctly tuning-in to the signs of serious problems is a special challenge, and parents should not be expected to carry the entire burden alone and uninformed.

It has been facetiously said that parenting is the most difficult task in the world for which we are willing to calmly accept untrained workers. The skills necessary in this special facet of parenting are not ones expected to be acquired without some help.

The school has a twofold responsibility in this regard. First, it must help prepare individuals (students before they become parents, and parents of those students already being served) to take a more active role in preventing the loss of so many young people to this dreadful outcome. And second, where it is at all possible, take an active role itself, acting as a source of sensitive significant others who are prepared to actively monitor the coping behaviors of students, being able and ready to recognize signs of impending trouble, hints of distress, and, in extreme instances, desperate calls for help.

Suicidal behavior is an extreme effort on the part of the young person to cope with the stresses of existence. Tragically, it often leads to cessation of pressure in the worst of all possible ways, by ending one's life to avoid the causes and experience of pressure. The tragedy is compounded. It is devastating, not only because of the loss of so much human potential, but also because there are so many positive alternatives to this fatal option. Suicide need not be the final solution, and we all need to be in a position to recognize when our testimony to this truth is needed to support a youth in trouble. This is certainly a responsibility of parenting, but it is also a responsibility borne by others, the schools included.

As broad a base as possible is desirous when creating a protective network for such a serious consideration as loss of life. It is one thing to say that nine of ten cry for help; it is another to consider that the calls for help will not always be to loved ones or knowledgeable and sensitive friends, close neighbors or long-term friends.

WHAT CAN BE DONE?

The tragedy experienced by the parents mentioned above might well have been averted had someone in the young man's social network been cognizant of the developing crisis. There seemed to have been indications of the need for help presented at home in this instance. But we cannot always be sure that such will be the case. Without a widespread sensitivity borne of knowledge, the cries of the potentially suicidal too often go unheeded. The school is in a powerful position to help.

It should be noted that the absence of help does not usually arise from a lack of caring or unwillingness to help. In our work with a community crisis center, we have found a number of the center's callers to be friends and family of those who are considering or seeking to end their misery through suicide. To receive a third-party call expressing concern is a very usual occurrence. Very often the center is in a position to help even though it is at a distance, so to speak, through a third person. The following case is an example.

> Jennifer, an older teenager, called to express her worry about a friend. "I don't know what's wrong, really," she said. "It's just that something doesn't seem right."

Sometimes, a friend can pinpoint specific bits of troubling behaviors; sometimes not.

> "The two of us have double-dated a lot . . . she's very popular, more than I am. She's been active in a lot of school activities, has a good personality, and everyone thinks of her really being where it's at. But lately, she's been, ah, just different sort of."

The crisis worker was able to elicit the information that Jennifer's unidentified friend had recently dropped out of several activities and expressed little interest in others, slowing her dating pattern to almost nothing.

> "I've asked her to go out with me and some old friends, guys we used to date right along, and she just says, 'Oh, you go. You can find someone else. I'm not up to it.' She really worries me," Jennifer shared fearfully. "I'm afraid something really awful is wrong."

While there was nothing in the reported concerns to strongly suggest suicide per se, there were indications of changes in behavior patterns that suggested the possibility of some new or different stress patterns operating in a young person's life. The major asset that an unidentified young woman had at the moment was a concerned friend.

"Are you worrying that she might be suicidal?" our crisis worker asked, coming immediately to the point. "Yes, maybe, oh I don't know," was Jennifer's anxious response.

In response, the crisis worker took the time to do three things: (1) carry on a general discussion about the various signs and behaviors that may indicate suicidal consideration or risk; (2) help the caller quickly practice some rudimentary active-listening techniques so she could be more closely involved in helping her friend; and (3) suggest to Jennifer some ways in which she could put her friend in touch with easily accessible and always available support resources.

Jennifer's school was identified, as well as her general neighborhood. From a list of available resources, the crisis worker gave Jennifer names of people at the school and the names of a physician and a clergyman in her section of town, each of whom had received suicide-intervention training. The caller was also encouraged to make further use of the center's crisis line for either her friend or herself if the situation further worried her.

Such an example is not atypical. It has been our experience that a brief explanation of empathy-based listening techniques is often sufficient to initiate successful attempts to gather more information and provide better assistance to a friend in trouble. While formal professional training certainly goes farther in the developing of helping techniques, even some minimal training and practice is often sufficient to initiate a process of personal interaction which can lead to a successful and healthy outcome.

We firmly believe that non-clinically trained individuals, friends, and family (and certainly school personnel) can go farther toward creating an atmosphere of credibility and trust in the therapeutic support process, which definitely lessens the probability of extreme impulsive behaviors and increases the probability of successful longer-term and perhaps deeper involvement with professionals initiated at a later time if necessary. In summary, then, we are completely convinced that two major lifesaving tasks are possible at the family, friend or acquaintance level:

1. Observations can be made and information gathered that may yield critically important information about the level of suicide risk in a troubled individual.

2. The process of relating closely with an individual, in part to facilitate the gathering of such information, is in itself a significant step toward establishing a possible life-giving support network for individuals experiencing extreme stress. For those with high suicide risk, such action often helps lower the level of risk dramatically. For those not yet at risk, these types of relationships are very valuable in helping prevent the risk ever developing.

We can think of no better setting, no richer environment for such activities than the schools.

Shouldn't It Be Done at Home?

From the beginning through to the completion of their education, children spend the majority of their waking hours in school or school-related activities. As the young person matures, areas of interest and focus increasingly shift to loci outside the home. Independence grows and the proportion of time and even the significance of family activities changes. Other influences vie for equal importance and significance in the life of the developing adolescent.

This shift is related to and in a large part the result of increasingly important relationships with family friends and peers and influential authority figures outside the family. The school environment is a major forum for the development of these relationships.

Up to relatively recent times, there has been a tendency for educators to place the burden of education in certain "delicate" or "uncomfortable" content areas on the home. This reluctance to share the burden has essentially been a not-always-defensible extension of assuming that the intimacy and privacy of the home is the logical, best, and in many instances only place for such learning to occur. Avoided areas have included such apparently taboo areas as sex education (still a hotly debated issue in many areas), child abuse, substance abuse, and often many more general topics of mental health.

However, the trend has been changing across the United States. While sex education is still approached very carefully and with some varying degrees of acceptance and success, most schools and communities now accept the principle that other similar topics, such as drug and alcohol use, should be included in the school curriculum. Anti-abuse campaigns now regularly involve segments of the community far broader than the home, and schools are frequently the site of special

speakers, workshops, and other public awareness and education activities. The nucleus of our argument is that suicide prevention should be as
much a part of such home-school-community programs as these other
important issues. The concept already has strong support in many communities, and clear evidence of efficacy is available in terms of measur-
able positive results of such programs.

To suggest that the school carry a major responsibility is in no way
intended to be an indictment of family role or function. Nor is saying
that schools need to consider greater involvement than present an indictment of the schools. Rather, it is to clearly underline the need for a preventive program that permeates all aspects of our culture, thereby
assuring that every developing young person will have the opportunity
to be forewarned, forearmed, and prepared to successfully handle the
problem if and when it does arise.

We maintain that such programs are really only clear investments in
the resources which represent our society's hope for the future, our developing youth. The immediate tragedy of the suicide of a youth is profound. The loss in human potential that such a death portends is
awesome. Future costs are untold.

Mental Health as a Part of the
School Program

The educational system represents a comprehensive and multi-
staged approach for broadly disseminating information and facilitating
the acquisition of knowledge. Ranging from an introduction of number
concepts which grow into the ability to handle personal finances and
mathematical careers to an introduction to letters and words which
eventually develop into great literature, stirring addresses, and meaningful ideas, the school is a prime shaper of our country's future from a
learning standpoint.

Inclusion of a systematic component of the curriculum dealing with
the fine art and appropriate skills for effective personal mental health is
a logical decision which only strengthens all other aspects of the curriculum. The growing person needs to develop a sensitivity to the meaning
and importance and indications of impending crises which require the
sharing of support and a group acceptance of responsibility for support
of those in need. To suggest that one individual needs another in times of
mental health crisis is totally congruent with the principle now being
more broadly developed and supported across the nation than ever

before. We are indeed, in many ways and in many aspects of our lives, "our brother's keeper." An important prerequisite to successfully implementing this philosophy is to help individuals become comfortable in helping others, familiar with the roles of being both help-giver and help-receiver.

The school's willingness to become involved in this healthy growing process in no way decreases the responsibility or importance of the other institutions of our society. The family, the neighborhood, and the church each represent viable and important sites for helping with the problem. As we have stressed in this area of networking, those communities that find a way to successfully blend the contributions of each of these institutions into a meaningful whole are the most likely to minimize tragedy among their youth and assure a high probability of effective and happy lives for many.

Young people need well-planned and increasingly sophisticated instruction in the skills of effective living in today's complex world. Included should be skills that enhance not only the well-being of themselves but also the well-being of others, the establishment. In reality, these skills become the foundation for a very broadly based peer-support network.

One of the most successful forms of learning occurs when the student may model on an effective example. As a consequence, schools have two types of responsibility: (1) to serve as a major support source in the recognition of those in need; and (2) to also be visible as a model of what acceptance of such responsibility means.

To be truly functional, peer-level support networking can be ultimately effective only if school personnel develop and model a type of individual rapport so that there is ready recognition by all involved and affected as to what it means to be ready to help, qualified to help, available for helping, and involved in helping.

Major Tasks

This is one area in learning where textbook models alone will not suffice. It is important to be a "doer as well as sayer of the word!" To be an effective "doer" as far as successfully intervening in situations carrying high risk of suicide, the school needs to focus on three major tasks.

First, the school must establish both an internal and external atmosphere and reputation as a potential help-giver. Students and staff alike should be able to perceive their school as an environment that is actively concerned about their mental health status and willing to step forward with active assistance and guidance when it is most needed.

Second, to adequately protect the students from the too often incipient growth in stress levels that can grow into a full-scale suicide crisis, they should live and work among individuals who are sensitive to each other's distress, emotional needs, and general coping behaviors. Though adults who are significant others can measurably help establish and maintain such an environment, the single most effective contributor is the students' peer group. Effective suicide prevention programs for young people almost invariably involve the use of some form of peer support or peer counseling.

Third, everyone in a position to observe, to help, and to rescue must be in possession of the necessary knowledge prerequisite to doing so quickly and effectively. The school system serious about suicide prevention among its staff and students will establish ways and means to convey information about the risk of suicide, about the facts and myths regarding those who are suicidal, how to interact with those who appear to be at risk, and about how to develop the sensitivities that facilitate being able to hear and recognize a call for help.

Developing an Atmosphere of Help-giving

It is very easy to assume that the established sources of help in the average school, the nurse or the school counselor, for instance, if properly utilized will provide all that is necessary in time of individual student crisis. While such resources are invaluable and play an imporant role in any suicide prevention program, they simply are not enough. Extensive enrichment of these specialized functions alone will not produce the lifesaving results desired.

The intent may be very good. The specialized student personnel sources are logical places to find help, and when well-functioning student personnel people are sought out by distressed students, the results are often very positive.

The unfortunate truth is that in many instances the troubled student will turn elsewhere for help and go unnoticed, and therefore unaided, by the school's student personnel services. In those instances where the distress leads to such overt deterioration of normal behavior that public attention is drawn to the student thereby eliciting contact by student personnel specialists, the intervention often comes so late that unnecessarily high risk may already have been experienced.

To be effective, the stress of students should be noted when it is at a level commensurate with a reasonable chance to avoid the high-risk concerns. To accomplish this, the entire school needs to be involved. This means that administration, faculty, staff, student peers and parents as well need to become sensitive barometers of students' stress levels and thereby avenues for seeking and finding help. Only by cooperative effort on the part of the entire school population does the lifesaving effect of suicide prevention reach the level everyone seeks.

Operating on minimums, giving what amounts to cursory support, even if it involves extra attention to the student personnel services, is not enough. Cries for help are apt to go in many directions. The family is often the most common target, but friends, physicians, clergy, mental health workers, and lawyers also may be the recipients of such pleas. Ideally, cooperation in recognizing and sharing information should encompass the entire community, but, as a first step, the school can take an important stride toward improving the troubled student's chances. Since the cries for help take diverse directions and present themselves in many different forms, a wide strata of listeners needs to be available. Fortunately, there are many available in the typical school environment.

Natural Help-givers in the School

The ability to detect discomfort or serious distress on the part of another sometimes takes a considerable degree of sensitivity. This can be particularly true if the individual in trouble is an adolescent. The adolescent has neither the inclination nor experience that permits for an easy outpouring of inner feelings. Often, suffering from typical bouts of general lack of self-confidence, to admit to being in the flux of intense feelings and panic-creating frustrations, is more of a threat than the average adolescent is going to risk.

When confidences are shared, they may often be admitted only to individuals in whom the adolescent has already vested more than an average amount of trust, though the investiture of this trust may be done quietly and without the recipient's awareness. Sometimes, these are close personal friends but many times not, since close friends may threaten a special level of vulnerability if allowed to become too close to one's innermost thoughts and feelings.

Adolescents commonly seek out a confidant. These people, usually individuals whom the adolescent has had opportunity to observe in positions which display a fidelity worthy of trust in the adolescent's eyes, have a unique opportunity to be the one's to first see and be able to respond to a troubled adolescent's quiet call for help.

Increasing the Probability That Someone Will Hear

The personal traits that characterize such natural help-givers are difficult to list. They certainly do not fit any stereotype of age, sex, color, creed or most any other individualizing pattern one might mention. However, they are almost always someone with whom the adolescent has come in rather frequent contact or been able to regularly observe. This suggests that in some covert manner the adolescent has observed and measured those about them and found certain individuals who meet the highly personal criteria which allows for such a relationship.

In all probability it is impossible to totally create natural help-givers as resources for troubled adolescents. Still, it is very possible that the school may approach that model by recognizing that such help-givers do exist, that troubled adolescents will use them when they are available, and that it is often possible to identify these individuals and create environmental milieus that are conducive to them being of service in suicide prevention among adolescents. It is also possible to train the effective behavior in those who display the aptitude but lack the experience. Too often we hear the lament, "If only I had known, I might have helped." Far better to work toward placing likely listeners in a position where they might hear and offer help and intervention.

Schools are likely places to find help-givers for adolescents. All the ingredients are present. There are many individuals who regularly interact with teenagers, both on the youngster's good days and bad. The opportunity to display sensitivity and understanding and to earn trust are frequent. Adolescents frequently find themselves in positions of exposed vulnerability, whether reciting in front of a class or having to weather a broken teenage steady relationship. They are highly sensitive to those individuals who respond warmly in such crises situations, offering an encouraging and healing unqualified acceptance.

It is interesting to note, however, that while many individuals who others accept as "natural" help-givers are aware of the peculiar status they hold for some people, such status and self-awareness does not guarantee responses that are automatically right, appropriate, or in the best interests of the troubled individual. Just as some advanced students in counseling training classes display an apparent aptitude for easily creating the therapeutic atmosphere with clients but need training in techniques and skills to effectively utilize this aptitude, so do natural help-givers need similar guidance and shaping.

Cindy was an example of this type of person who tries their best but finds that best painfully inadequate due to lack of knowledge and training. It had been an emotionally devastating experience for Cindy and for most of her high school friends, as well. The suicide victim, a young friend, had been universally liked. Her death came suddenly, apparently without warning, a surprise to all. Cindy's best friend had been dead less than a week when Cindy first shared her story with the school counselor. In the process of working on grief with a group of classmate survivors, the counselor talked a bit about signs of suicide. After the session, with tears in her eyes, Cindy told what had happened.

> She always spent a lot of time with me when she was worried about something. She would talk and I would just listen. It usually made us both feel better. But last week . . . she seemed a little down, but I didn't even think about her killing herself. She gave me two record albums and one of her new outfits, just outright, as a gift. I thought she was just tired of them. Do you think she was trying to tell me what she was going to do?"

No one will ever know, of course. But had Cindy, as a natural help-giver for her friend, been previously taught some of the signs of suicidal risk, she might have wondered enough to ask. And, with the kind of relationship she and her friend shared, she may very well have been told the truth.

Finding and Recruiting Help-givers

In a number of Alaskan **bush** communities, small, rural, isolated villages often with an almost homogeneous native population, we often find small groups of people, indigenous to the village, who essentially serve as grassroots mental health help-givers because they are the people others come to when they are in trouble. In some communities, these help-givers may be the village elders, in others the constabulary, or even some of the local high school students. But whomever they may be, we find that almost every village has them. When crisis training teams visit these communities, they have learned to seek out these local help-givers and to be sure that they are among those who receive the necessary training and information. Being already on site, already identified as those who will listen and try to help, these individuals can effectively apply the information and skills they have acquired to a variety of potentially life-threatening problems, including alcoholism, child abuse, and certainly suicide.

We would certainly not suggest that high-risk recognition and crisis-intervention training be offered only to the natural help-givers. But identifying these individuals, enlisting their help, and providing them with tools to enhance their already effective relationships is often an important first step toward constructing a school-wide network.

It is important to keep in mind that in the school environment any person may be a natural help-giver. It is also wise to remember that there may be many other people interested in being in that role who need only moderate amounts of training in presenting empathetic and sensitive feelings to those around them to be able to function.

In the schools we would suggest starting with the natural help-givers, reinforcing the role by giving it public recognition and appreciation, and by encouraging and supporting those among the student body who seek help through this route. When a school is seeking to increment the number of natural help-givers in its environment, it is in a noticeably nurturing stance. Operating in this way, it is sending the message basic to all help-giving at the time of crisis, a message which says, "There are those around you who care."

Rather than openly solicit the staff and student body for those who play a help-giving role, we have found it effective to start by introducing the concept and offering training to two equally effective but quite different groups in the school: the teachers and the students. Many natural help-givers will seek the training without having been directly recruited. We look for those in each group who demonstrate an interest in help-giving roles and offer them information and knowledge that will start them toward playing a special lifesaving role, that of a **gatekeeper.** Gatekeepers are individuals who serve to keep the distressed student in touch with those who care and can help, and away from an isolated aloneness which so increases the student's vulnerability as to put him or her at risk of life-threatening behavior. Potential gatekeepers are found among staff and students alike.

Developing Gatekeeper Roles Among the Teaching Staff

Every one of us can probably remember at least one teacher who stands out in our memory of school days as a particularly caring and approachable individual. Almost every school seems to have some individuals on the instructional staff who fit this mold in the perception of students. It may be difficult to ascertain exactly why certain teachers are seen this way, since such individuals certainly do not necessarily all fit the same mold. In some instances, the individual displays warm and friendly behavior which obviously invites friendly relationships with students. In other cases, the **chemistry** which seems to be present in teacher-student interaction appears to arise from some less obvious attributes difficult for adults to perceive. But in seeking natural help-givers among the teaching staff, "why" certain individuals seek this role is less important than their level of interest and aptitude for acquiring the necessary behaviors.

Research indicates that teachers are high on the list as individuals whom students seek out when looking for help. However, as Ross (1985) reports, over 90 percent of all student responses indicated that the first person they would approach for help would be a "friend." Because this is so, in helping schools to build internal-support networks we try to maximize the probability of students coming in contact with trained helpers by looking for those teachers whom students also see as friends. The task is not all that difficult. All one really has to do is ask the students. They'll know!

These teachers are usually doubly efficient helpers. They are frequently contacted by troubled students (and training assists them in recognizing which of these may be at-risk), plus they know how to successfully encourage students to seek still further help. They also are often interested in being recruiters of still more helpers and usually are in a position, largely because of information students share with them, to steer any program organizer toward additional interested and capable personnel.

They serve an additional function: they are validators. Students will often accept at face value a new program, such as a suicide prevention endeavor, if it has the validating approval of these people who are special to the students. They are very often the very foundation of a successful program, lending credence and importance to its activities in addition to the giving of their own personal services.

Using Students as Gatekeepers

Student **gatekeepers** serve in various ways. In some schools they are simply those individuals who have high respect and trust from their peers, those who can be used in a general way to dispense information to their peers and give support to those who seek it. Sometimes, these students are aware of their special status with peers and seek only to acquire skills that give them the security of feeling that they are doing the "right" thing. Others may have already developed some skills as leaders in other roles, such as youth groups, student government, church organizations or similar settings. These young people can often profit from special classes and contact with various community organizations which are prepared to use and develop the skills already present to some degree. Some crisis centers use student volunteers to help staff teen-crisis lines. Some serve as volunteers at crisis-relief nurseries or in similar public-service agencies.

In many instances, the basic skills must be taught. And this is an entirely feasible goal in many instances. Students yet to display the overt behaviors which mark a natural help-giver can be given the opportunity to develop the interpersonal skills which can eventually lead to active support roles among their peers.

Not every student will develop into a natural help-giver, but any student may be called upon to be a gatekeeper. We should remember that the major reason a person will be called upon to help another frightened by the thoughts of suicide is because they are a friend. Any broadly based suicide prevention program in the school should give serious attention to teaching such skills and dispensing appropriate information school-wide. An obvious reason for doing so is that it is a good way to motivate and recruit those with potential for more extensive leadership. But it is also important to do it so that every single student, if possible, has accurate information on hand and some idea of appropriate and effective responses to make if signs of suicide risk should present themselves in a peer.

Peer Counselors

We have found many schools having very good success with some form of organized **peer counseling.** This is a peer-support model which formally recognizes certain selected students in a quasi-counseling role with their peers. Such systems usually provide the designated students with some special training, and they serve as conduits of helpful information and as sources of support and guidance on important but relatively uninvolved personal and student group issues. In most instances the student counselors have some constant working arrangement with the regular school counselors or some other staff or administration liaison arrangement. They are neither trained for nor presented as substitutes for professional student personnel workers.

Peer counseling takes advantage of some of the strengths any counselor brings to a troubled individual, combined with an optimum ability to relate on their own level with students who may be at-risk. Many times, where an adult might have difficulty obtaining an accurate picture of a teen's inner feelings, a peer counselor may be openly confronted with the necessary information or recognize the important signs even when they are not openly displayed. Subsequent contact is easier to effect and less threatening to the average student.

Some special training is required, of course, but the motivation level of the learners is usually very high, and the preparation itself carries personal reward and peer group status. The end result, the presence of involved, interested teenagers whom other teenagers respect and with whom they are willing to share their problems and feelings, is a tremendously valuable asset for any school.

Resources for Gatekeepers

The resources needed by effective gatekeepers in any particular school can be most easily ascertained by reiterating the general objectives for which this role and function exists.

One major goal is paramount. The purpose of the gatekeeper is to help people avoid having to experience the ultimate stress by giving them personal support and guiding them to appropriate help-giving resources. In such a role, the gatekeeper serves not only those experiencing suicide ideation but also all the others who may be touched and made more stressed by a suicide-related experience in their life. Hopefully, in most instances the gatekeeper's task is prevention rather than intervention, to prevent the suicidal crisis from occurring.

To accomplish this fundamental purpose, three sub-goals must be met. The gatekeeper must:

1. Be in a social and physical position that facilitates contact by those in need
2. Be able to observe and recognize behaviors which may provide information about the stress level of those with whom they may interact
3. Know when and how and where to direct individuals to help-giving resources

The resources required of the school are directly parallel to these objectives.

1. The school needs to support (and, when necessary, to teach) social skills conducive to gatekeeping roles and provide physical opportunity for these important interpersonal contacts to occur.
2. The school must help the would-be gatekeeper acquire the information and training necessary to be able to adequately observe and discriminate stress-related behaviors.
3. The school must provide information and training relevant to supplying active support and intervention.

It has been our experience that the first objective is most easily and effectively met through the activation of a peer-level support network which has active staff and administration support. Whether this will be a formal peer-counseling program or not depends upon administrative policy of the individual school.

Meeting the second objective requires several types and levels of information sharing and training. Some in-service sessions with staff are a must. Succinct and accurate information about suicide, suicide risk, and everyone's responsibility to be actively involved in lowering the threat to the school population must be widely disseminated throughout the school population and to those on the outside interested in and involved with the school. It must be made clear that the school positively evaluates the helping and concerned role for staff and students alike.

The third objective requires some active networking with outside sources of both emergency and long-range help. It also necessitates the presence of some specific intervention skills. Some of the staff may already have these skills in hand, but the school must take active responsibility for training designated staff for specific emergency intervention roles and provide broad general crisis-intervention techniques for the entire school community to be ready whenever and wherever the need may suddenly arise.

In many school systems most if not all of the resources are already present, sometimes actively functioning. But where this is not so, the initial action step required, once the philosophical position of becoming involved in an active suicide prevention program has been reached, is to make sure the prerequisite resources are or can be made available.

The rest of this chapter addresses the specifics of the first two objectives. Chapter Four is devoted to the third objective and special issues relevant to active intervention where a crisis or near-crisis situation has been identified.

THE PEER-LEVEL SUPPORT NETWORK

Based upon common experiences and research results such as those reported by Ross (1985), there seems to be little doubt that the personal friend of a suicidally inclined teenager is very apt to be a person contacted for help. And although training teachers to be more sensitive to the distress signals emitted by troubled youth probably raises the number of contacts made in that direction, peers are in a position to hear and recognize such calls more often.

There seems to be a tendency for stressed teenagers to become even more isolated, to feel their situation more hopeless, and to call out less often as they enter young adulthood (Peck & Schrut, 1971). As a consequence, it becomes even more imperative to ease the process of calling for help by high school students through providing a receptive and attentive peer group ready to hear and respond.

Organizing and Recruiting

Initial momentum must be achieved through broad and highly visible support of the school administration. The administration controls several variables crucial to success. These include endorsement of the staff-support activities as a legitimate part of regular responsibilities, flexibility in temporary schedule assignments of both staff and students as critical situations may arise, official liaison with a support network, and facilitation of training through provision of time and materials needed for training.

One school with which we have been associated has carried the school-wide support network far beyond the suicide area. At this high school, teachers and students are given administration-approved time off for brief visits to students in the hospital, for example. The philosophy of this school, which has achieved considerable local attention for its high morale and strong school spirit, is that the individual student is an important part of a school community; that community exists to aid, support, and do anything possible to make the student's life a happier and more effective experience. The support activities generalize through all aspects of students' everyday school life, including a student tutoring corps manned by both teachers and students, and a very effective peer-counseling program which directly addresses the recognition of suicide as a problem and suicide prevention as part of its responsibilities.

Administration also must take the responsibility for being the bridge
between parents and the school, fostering and nurturing parental involvement and support, explaining school programs, promulgating peripheral opportunities for parents and community friends to become
active learners themselves through asociation with school suicide prevention activities, and publicly recognizing the value of the service rendered by student-peer gatekeepers.

The attitude of the administration is probably the single most important recruiting tool when seeking student participants. If administration
actively endorses the principle, teachers, staff, and students will soon
follow. In our experience, students do not need to be convinced of the
need for them to help in the battle against youth suicide.

One of the questions we routinely ask of students attending our
school presentation is, "How many of you know someone who has taken
or attempted to take their own life?" It is a rare class in which less than
one-fourth of the class raise their hands. The average is probably closer
to one-third or one-half and in some instances has been as high as two-
thirds. Though this may be reflective of our often being invited to work
in districts which have known particularly severe problems, we are convinced that some experience with severe suicidal or parasuicidal behavior is very common among our youth.

These same students also demonstrate an active rather than passive
concern for the problem of suicide. It is interesting to note that ex-
changes similar to the following are the norm in our experience. "We are
here to help you better understand the problem of suicide as it affects
people your age. What are some of the questions that you would like
answered?" Hands usually go up all over the assembly. The most frequent response by far is, "How can you stop someone from doing it?"
The youth are already action-oriented. Any clear suggestion for organizing an active program of presenting information and learning how
to deal with it in one's own life and others' as well is invariably met with
enthusiasm.

Students are more than willing to take an active role in supporting
their friends in times of stress, but they can't act effectively without some
preparation; of this they are also aware. The questions which follow in
an introductory session are full of "How do I . . .?", "When does one
. . .?" inquiries. Though our young people want to take part, they are
quick to point out their own fear of inadequacies. "I'm afraid I would say
the wrong thing!" they sometimes tell us. This blend of social activism

with reticence because of an awareness of possible personal inadequacies provides all the motivation needed for enlisting students in a training program designed to help make them effective gatekeepers. At this juncture, school-wide staff cooperation and participation in preparing becomes crucial.

The Phases of Staff and Student Preparation

Student-staff support, very important to the success of any peer-support network, goes through several identifiable phases. Though the presence of mutual trust and support is probably equally important in each of these phases, it's actual purpose and function changes considerably as the program develops. To some extent, this passage through the phases goes on continually in a school even though an active program may have been in existence for some time. The arrival, recruitment, and involvement of new staff and students assures the need for each of the phases to be operational over and over again.

Phase One: Initial Recognition and Support

The strengths and weaknesses of each individual who interacts with students in a suicide prevention program must be considered in the development of a viable support system. Though those which have an obvious facility for positive interactions must be utilized fully, homogeneity of personality type, or school position and responsibility level, or style or interaction is neither needed nor even desirable.

In the initial stage, the strongest support the staff can give is to clearly communicate an awareness of people's different interests and skills coupled with an overtly expressed appreciation for the willingness of individuals to become involved.

The school should not only publicly recruit volunteers but also commend the school population's enlistment in the crusade. In those schools where this type of program is most successful, such public recognition takes many forms. Honor rolls of volunteers are publicized, the school paper is encouraged to run stories about the program, and released class time is frequently given for sign up or initial information-giving sessions. In many instances staff and students are treated alike in such announcements. As staff enlist, they are included alongside students' names, with the direct implication that the program is a joint staff-student, school-wide endeavor.

Phase Two: Joint Exploration and Learning

As a cadre of potential gatekeepers is assembled, the school should be ready to take advantage of initial enthusiasm by moving promptly into a learning and training phase. Although it is impressive to have such activities functioning school-wide, we recommend starting some training activity as soon as a small group of recruits, perhaps as few as five or six participants, have enlisted.

From the work of Meeks (1971) and others, we have some idea of what type of therapists work best with teenagers. If we were to generalize these positive characteristics to include some traits which would help gatekeepers, we might find the overall picture to include traits of warmth, open-mindedness, tolerance, quiet self-confidence and similar items. Table 3-1 contains a suggested list of those characteristics that might be encouraged during these sessions. While not exhaustive, such a list gives us some things upon which to work. These traits should be fostered when present, shaped when absent, and encouraged when displayed.

TABLE 3-1

PERSONAL CHARACTERISTICS WHICH MAY FACILITATE
ESTABLISHING A GATEKEEPER RELATIONSHIP

1. Behavior patterns which encourage student identification with the gatekeeper
2. Non-intrusive, tactful
3. Basic belief in the human drive for emotional growth and health
4. Neither pompous nor overvaluing of self-dignity
5. Reasonably confident of his or her own self-image and life or ability to change them
6. Responsible and trustworthy
7. Practical minded and willing to deal in the realities of compromise
8. Accepting of individual differences in philosophy, style, values, and interests

Very often, the initial training sessions can and should include students and staff together. This establishes a team concept and also assures a more uniform data base and consensual understanding for subsequent functions. It is during this period that basic information (as covered later in this chapter) is disseminated, roles and functions are defined, and individuals become acquainted with their own personal interface with the program.

One of the valuable assets of these initial joint sessions is an appreciation for the varying types and amounts of skills, interests, and personal and role-defined attributes that different individuals bring to the program. It is the beginning of the internal network. Staff develop an enriched appreciation for the intensity and value of student dedication to better living for everyone. Students learn a great deal about different role functions of various staff personnel and the usefulness in support roles of different staff personalities. Levels of interaction and stages of crisis become commonly learned and appreciated.

For example, most schools are pretty well-prepared for major student crises even when they are limited to one or two individuals. A student experiencing a publicly observed family disruption or dysfunction of a rather common nature, (e.g. an impending or recently completed geographical move) usually finds the school ready to be supportive and helpful in a more or less formal manner. School counselors, the school nurse, assistant principle, or other special school staff are called into use. Students and staff are aware of these typically available resources. Very often many are not sensitive to the potential support functions of an intermediate nature: the need to have someone understanding at hand when the family dysfunction is disturbing and upsetting but of a nature as to be subtle or not consensually noticed. Or, they may be unaware of the school's varied personnel and material resources for responding to crises of a dramatic and cataclysmic nature such as suicidal feelings.

Students and staff learning together begin to build a mutual respect for their own capabilities and the potential capabilities of the school as a social system united together to protect its members. The payoffs include high morale, a clear sense of and appreciation for networking, building of self-confidence and a sense of interdependence with others. The latter pays off in two ways: (1) it dramatically increments the school's ability to help others in time of impending crisis, and (2) it helps build internal strengths and resiliency in the gatekeepers so they themselves are less vulnerable.

Phase Three: Separation of Responsibility

One of the things which makes a network more valuable than a single resource is the diversity of support and services it can potentially offer. Clearly established separation of responsibilities as assigned to students and different staff independently is important for successful functioning. Another major asset of such discrimination of tasks and roles is that it underlines the point that students do indeed have some specific functions in a peer-group support network which are essentially their's alone. They learn that though their functions are separate, the overall system is dependent upon the cooperative interaction of all involved.

Students (and staff, too, for that matter) need to recognize that they have a unique function and offer unique contributions to the system. When assisting school personnel to build this type of support network, we suggest assignment and training relative to the following objectives as a minimum. Participants must be trained to:

1. Recognize and deal appropriately with the types of information relative to students in distress that may not be easily available to others, e.g. a student athlete's locker room expression of extreme depression over failure to adequately perform, or a coed repeatedly throwing away lunch food and not eating.

2. Willingly and informally share feelings and emotions both with distressed peers and with other members of the network who may be in a position to offer substantial help. They need to learn the importance of assisting those who are in a position to give substantive aid to obtain the "big picture" by giving them what may seem to the naive observer as incidental and unimportant pieces of information. This is actually a sub-set of good communication skills in general, of course.

3. Be familiar with ethical considerations which should go hand in hand with being worthy of trust, close-mouthed, and tactful.

4. Become familiar with resources (written materials, people, agencies) available to the distressed student and knowing how to put the student in contact with them.

5. Have a very clear recognition of the responsibility for seeking help, for not playing the lonely hero in times of emergency.

6. Demonstrate an awareness of the possibility for needing some personal support themselves and where to get it and how to reduce their own stress when the need arises.

There is a major premise that really subsumes all these functional objectives. It is that perhaps the richest source of information about the emotional state of a student is another student who is also a friend and peer. If this is firmly endorsed by the administration and staff and plainly conveyed to the students, most of the other things fall into place relatively easily.

As professional educators, we often overlook students as a viable source of information about their own kind. It is an oversight we too frequently encounter in working with schools.

A high school with which we are familiar recently had a dramatic awakening to this reality. Following an abortive suicide attempt by a socially attractive and popular young coed student, it was discovered that her suicidal behavior had apparently stemmed from guilt and self-devaluation following a complicated and long-term experience with sexual abuse and rape. When school officials were so notified by investigating youth authorities, they were shocked. No intimation of any problem had been noticed by any school personnel even though subsequently related details of the incident indicated that school-related activities had been involved and that several school personnel had been in a position where they might have been reasonably expected to know about the coed's emotional decline. The administration, concerned about its own lack of internal communication flow, addressed the overall problem by setting out with our help to organize a student-support network.

In one of the early training sessions the issues of sexual abuse, rape, and crises responses were discussed. School officials were totally amazed to discover that several of the students had obviously known of the young lady's distress and the reasons for it far prior to the suicidal behavior. Upon reflection it was obvious that the facts were almost brazenly present upon even very shallow and almost incidental inquiry, yet were apparent only to peers of the victim who were not really sensitive to the escalating crisis that the young girl was experiencing.

The clear truth which emerged was that the only individuals to know, before the suicidal behavior caused a massive involvement of personnel from several agencies, were the students. There is little doubt that had a trained peer-group support system been operational in the school before the crisis, the probability of suicidal behavior would have been greatly diminished, perhaps even totally avoided. Certainly, such examples offer clear and compelling reasons for the inclusion of students in the process of supporting other students who are experiencing heavy stress.

Phase Four: Backup and Referral Functions

Though student gatekeepers do bring a unique contribution to a suicide prevention program and operate with a semblance of autonomy, no organizational plans or training paradigm should encourage or endorse the concept that these students are working alone. They are frontline troops, active in a way which faculty and staff cannot always duplicate, but they must be constantly and firmly embedded within an operating support system broader-based, more experienced, and far richer in resources than the students themselves can be.

The last phase of training must deal with both the necessity for such interaction and the ways and means to accomplish it. When holding training workshops, we stress the concept that the student activities and staff activities are parallel virtually all the time and that the two frequently merge into a whole in which the separate functions are not only combined but perhaps indistinguishable.

To exemplify this, we draw up action plans which note typical student gatekeeper activities and the parallel roles and resources that staff have to offer in support. The activities on the list will vary according to the needs and resources of the school, but a typical list might look like the following sample.

Student activity: Getting to know students who may have limited support networks.

Staff resources: Providing peer-counselors with names of students new to the school or those who have just experienced a death or major trauma in the family.

Student activity: Helping a student troubled about personal health but reluctant to seek medical advice because of low family financial resources get in touch with professional medical resources.

Staff resources: A school nurse or counselor who has a list of low-cost medical clinics and who is prepared to help the student or the student's parents make contact with an appropriate source.

Student activity: Trying to determine if a peer's casual remarks about depressed feelings have any crisis significance.

Staff resources: A readily accessible staff member who has the assignment of being an advisor to peer-counselors.

Student activity: Finding immediate help when faced with what the student gatekeeper feels is a genuine suicidal crisis.

Staff resources: Designated staff members trained and ready to give immediate response to a call for help, and physical locations in the school where emergency numbers or promptly responding emergency information resources may be located.

Student activity: Assisting a student who is experiencing panic with an academic problem.

Staff resources: A pre-established procedure for getting a student an immediate appointment with a school counselor and/or teaching staff identified as special academic help-givers.

Student activity: Gatekeeper has personal concerns over his or her helping role and personal functioning level in that role.

Staff resources: Regularly scheduled stress-reduction and information and feeling sharing sessions with a staff leader and other gatekeepers.

The list could be extended almost indefinitely, but a common theme runs throughout. The paradigm is that students take at least some responsibility for making person-to-person initial contact with peers. Those peers who are experiencing stress should already know via school-wide publicity that there are interested helpful peers available. The peer counselor or gatekeeper simply makes the helpful interaction simple and easy to accomplish.

The peer-counselor knows that his or her major responsibility is to be especially sensitive to signs of a student being at-risk; to make contact; offer acceptance, understanding and help; and then move directly to put the student in touch with other segments of the extended support network. The student peer-counselor or gatekeeper must clearly recognize that backup and referral help is always readily available. There is never a need for the student to bear the situation alone except for a very brief period while initial contact is being made.

Besides an awareness that troubled and distressed students very often need resources beyond those available to the average student gatekeeper, another important concept must be taught. This is the need for cross-validation of observations about others' stress status. Unilateral judgments should always be open to reappraisal, with any substantive action depending upon some objective concurrence from other sources. The initial contact function serves primarily to put the system on alert to possible needs. Immediate definitive action without taking time to confer with others should follow only when the observer is seriously concerned about an at-risk status which appears to be very severe and immediate, a threat of what appears to be possibly imminent suicide.

Teachers and other staff are in an excellent position to help with this cross-validation procedure. They bring a different subjective viewpoint, empirical data not always available to students (such as academic grades), sometimes more patience and maturity, and an attribute often sorely needed by the student peer-counselor who has encountered a real crisis: support through the sharing of the decision-making responsibility.

Having staff available and perceived as accessible by the student gatekeepers takes careful planning, training of both parties, and an organization of material and emotional resources that can be accessed quickly with self-confidence by the user.

To establish this broad network of support, great care must be taken to anticipate needs, train all involved, assemble information and support materials, and teach students how to activate and staff how to respond within the system. Students really play two primary roles: they are first and foremost initial contact sources at the student's own level, individuals who have learned to look for and recognize the overt signs of internal stress among peers. Secondly, they are facilitators or expediters whose actions help assure that the troubled student knows help is available, is put in touch with it, and that there are people and materials and organization in place to help with the process as necessary.

INFORMATION AND TRAINING NECESSARY FOR RECOGNIZING SUICIDAL RISK

There is some benefit to be derived from the mere presence of any support system. Knowing that there are supportive individuals at hand lessens the cost of severe stress. However, in the area of suicide prevention, the final efficacy of such a system lies in its contribution to saving lives. To successfully intervene in a potential suicide-crisis situation there are specific decisions that must be made and, when the threat of suicide appears to be at hand, specific tasks to be accomplished (Moursand, 1985).

The gatekeeper, regardless of style or approach, in actuality asks two very significant questions:

1. Does this person need help, or can he or she handle it alone?
2. If help is needed, is more required than I or other non-professional support persons at hand can provide?

The decision is whether to intervene at some yet to be determined level or not. The gatekeeper must consider the availability and relative efficacy of support systems in the distressed individual's life space. These include significant others, formal group support systems, personal physical and emotional resources, and if necessary processes for referral to professional help.

If intervention is elected because of assumed suicidal risk, critical tasks must be promptly addressed. These include an assessment of the imminency of suicidal behavior, an assessment of the lethality of the subject's situation, any unusual idiosyncratic personal or group dynamics working, and the activation of some form of direct treatment initially in the form of immediate intervention. Even the most diligent and caring effort to appraise the self-destructive status of a young person may be in vain without a clear set of criteria to help evaluate the self-destructive potential of the troubled individual's coping behaviors.

An urban crisis center working alongside public health staff recently experienced the difficulty of helping the concerned parents of an adopted Southeast Asian child determine that child's at-risk status. Despite a team of experienced gatekeepers, the differences in culture made it difficult to evaluate withdrawal behaviors, stress-related verbalizations, and self-imposed cultural isolation. Later, upon staff discussion, the staff noted that their problem was very similar to that which any untrained individual faces when attempting the role of gatekeeper. Motivation and intent were unquestionably of the highest caliber. The problem was that the observers were not sure what to look for or how to accurately interpret what they saw in this child of a different culture. Normal everyday communication interactions were ineffective. They felt helpless and frustrated and their own stress and worry added to that of the parents.

It is absolutely imperative that all individuals involved receive this basic training if the system is to depend upon them. Meeting the crisis unprepared does not bode well for success. Even when the gatekeeper is well-trained, it is necessary to have a valid and reliable data base upon which to act. Recognizing the necessary components of that data base and knowing how to assemble them into a decision-aiding cognitive map requires knowledge of some facts and sensitivity about the use of various kinds of observational and situational data.

The Importance of Knowledgeable Observation and Data Collection

Probably the initial step to take in training students and staff as data collectors and decision makers relevant to gatekeeping is to demonstrate to them just how serious the problem really is. Facts and figures about the incidence of youth suicide should be honestly shared. The extent to which recognition and effective intervention attenuates the problem should be clearly taught.

Potential gatekeepers should not be mislead into expecting that their efforts are the ultimate answer or that they will always be totally successful. But the reality of the situation is that their efforts can make a very substantive contribution to lowering suicide risk in their school. This conviction is a necessary prerequisite to all other training. Given an acceptable functioning level of interpersonal skills and techniques, their ultimate success will depend upon how well they can observe others' reactions to stress and collect the data necessary for making at-risk judgments. Knowledgeable observation and effective data collection is a most critical element in any suicide prevention program. In order to develop the skills necessary for adequate observation and collection of data used in prevention-intervention decisions, the prospective gatekeeper must acquire some background knowledge.

We also feel that it is very helpful for help-givers and gatekeepers to understand something about crises in general before they start to learn about suicide. They should learn how crises affect individual problem solving, feelings, perceptions, self-confidence, and the availability of personal resources. Most need some practice in sharpening their own observational skills, interpersonal relations, communications habits and other similar personal attributes which aid the role they are about to assume.

Once the individual begins to perceive the seriousness of the role they are adopting, have a sense for the dynamics of crisis, and an awareness of the various interpersonal skills they'll need to use to be effective, training can begin to focus on the topic of suicide itself. The primary emphasis should be on how to be alert to and recognize the various signs that signal an increased probability of suicidal risk. All subsequent decisions and activities are predicated on the gatekeeper's ability to observe and correctly interpret what is perceived.

A number of important topics regarding suicide must be covered in the training of potential gatekeepers. We suggest grouping these into four main categories:

1. The "at-risk" concept
2. Situations and circumstances which allow or encourage suicidal ideation to grow
3. Facts that are important to know and myths which must be rejected
4. Clues and cues which help the gatekeeper to recognize suicidal risk.

Once these are learned, training can move on to other topics which require this knowledge as a baseline.

Basic Facts and Concepts

The "At-Risk" Concept

The term "at risk" carries the connotation of some outside factor or motivator impinging upon the organism and against which the organism must be protected. While this is true to the extent that no organism is equipped by nature to withstand the effects of prolonged severe stress regardless of its origin, we do not mean to imply that any single factor, experience, trauma or personal style in and of itself leads to suicide.

A common worry of families that have experienced suicide is that there is some genetic component involved. While it is unquestionably true that poor coping skills and maladaptive traits are learned and may be assimilated from a dysfunctional family experience, the supposed genetic factor has never been substantiated.

What then does the term "at risk" imply, and what is its usefulness? "At risk" means that the possibility of self-destruction as an adjustive response to stress has been increased beyond a normal limit. It does not mean that the subject is definitely suicidal, probably suicidal, or necessarily likely to be suicidal. It does mean that the circumstances in which the subject is existing, and/or the subject's coping behaviors, and/or a variety of other interacting variables are such that suicide is a higher probability than normally. The level at which we assume the risk to be higher than we wish to accept or at which we choose to take an active

rather than an observational stance is arbitrarily selected to fit the situation and resource capabilities of all involved, including those helping
and those being helped.

Some crisis centers, knowing that they must often work at some personal distance from the victim (sometimes via the phone call alone) use a
purely operational definition. Under these circumstances, an "at risk"
individual is anyone who displays "suicide potential," with suicide potential being further defined as those circumstances or behaviors or actions
that have been perceived as being common to suicidal situations in other
people.

This approach is a very careful one which often chooses to assume the
worst so as to avoid ignoring anyone who may be in serious difficulty. It is
probably a wise stance for student gatekeepers to assume, as well.

Simply translated for the gatekeeper-in-training, the principle is easily stated:

> **Suicidal thoughts and behavior seem to occur more often when
> certain situations are coupled with certain personal behaviors.
> Such circumstances do not necessarily indicate suicidal
> thoughts or behaviors are present. They do mean that there is
> greater probability than normal, the subject is at risk, and
> those who have an observing, monitoring, or intervention re-
> sponsibility should be alert and ready to act.**

For example: A high school student who experiences defeat in an
athletic context is frequently unhappy and experiences "down" feelings.
To experience these feelings of frustration and unhappiness under such
circumstances is neither uncommon nor suggestive of pre-suicidal behavior. But we know that loss of interest in friends and activities, dropping school performance, and experiencing family dysfunction are each
listed as indicators of increased suicidal risk in teenagers (Leenaars &
Balance, 1986). Gatekeepers, observing the first set of symptoms, learn
to be alert to such feelings being paired with the second set of behaviors
associated with increased risk. If the disappointment is accompanied by
the other symptoms, an **at-risk** situation may be present.

If the principle is thoroughly learned, then gatekeepers can be taught
to recognize different levels of at-risk and support and intervention behaviors which correspond according to the support resources available
and the established procedures of the school.

Shneidman (1985) has addressed the at-risk levels on the simple basis
of making two precise evaluations, namely, what is the level of lethality

involved and how perturbed and upset is the victim? While overly simplistic for use in a school support system using non-clinical personnel, the implications of such evaluative criteria are clear. Gatekeepers need to know when the situation calls for action, how prompt the action must be, and where to find the appropriate help.

Emphasizing the at-risk concept carries several messages which we suggest be clearly emphasized to participants:

1. Suicide is not the end result of an inescapable chain of events. A number of different definable and recognizable (and often modifiable) circumstances increase the probability of suicide.
2. Suicide is not a binary, either/or situation. There are various levels of suicidal thought and action and help-giver and gatekeeper responses may vary according to the level encountered.
3. Successful intervention is always possible even when the at-risk level is extremely high. Different situations call for different responses, but lifesaving responses are always possible.
4. It is important for the gatekeeper to consider the key issues of being at risk: lethality, imminency, and available help.

It is very important that the staff and student support-team members be fully apprised of the actual nature and characteristics of suicidal thought and behavior. This knowledge helps them operate more effectively and also gives them useful information to share with those whom they would help.

The Truth of the Matter: Important Facts and Common Myths

There are a number of commonly held misconceptions about the act of suicide and those who are suicidal. These pieces of erroneous information are often passed on by well-meaning people who are sincerely interested in helping. Such inaccurate and sometimes dangerously misleading information stems from an almost universal attempt to explain or understand the too often frightening and taboo subject of suicide.

There is strong circumstantial evidence to suggest that many suicidal people receive less than optimum responses from those in a position to help due to a lack of information as to what to do or misconceptions about what are and what are not helpful and supportive behaviors.

Every professional clinician working with suicidal people and situations spends more than a little of their professional time correcting these common misconceptions and tries to replace them with a store of useful information which may be applied in circumstances calling for potentially lifesaving responses. It is very important to note that these misconceptions do not cause and abet errors of commission alone. They also oftentimes delay or even preclude alternative necessary intervention and rescue responses, thus creating significant errors of omission where more appropriate action might have helped.

In teaching trainees about facts and myths, we stress the importance of knowing the facts and avoiding the myths for the prime purpose of being more effective as gatekeepers and lifesavers. Table 3-2 notes a number of common myths, all of which are either totally false or grossly misleading in the assumptions they may suggest.

TABLE 3-2

COMMON MYTHS AND MISBELIEFS ABOUT SUICIDE

1. Suicide is inherited, it runs in families.
2. Suicide is a rich (or poor) person's curse.
3. Most suicides occur in bad weather, the spring, at holidays, or at night.
4. Suicidal people are mentally ill.
5. Suicidal people cannot help themselves.
6. The only effective treatment for suicide comes from professional psychotherapists.
7. Once a person is suicidal, that person is always suicidal.
8. Improvement, once a suicidal crisis is past, means that the risk is over.
9. Suicidal people are intent on dying.
10. People who talk about suicide rarely commit suicide.
11. Asking or talking about suicide with a suicidal person increases the risk of suicide.
12. Most suicidal persons never seek or ask for help with their problems.
13. Suicidal individuals are always angry at intervention and will resent you because of your efforts.
14. Suicidal gestures are merely "attention getters."
15. Young people are not often really depressed and seldom actually self-destructive.
16. Nothing will stop suicidal persons once they elect to kill themselves.
17. The person who fails in an attempt will eventually try until they succeed.
18. Only certain types of people commit suicide.
19. Feeling that suicide is immoral will prevent a person from doing it.

Why Are Some Youth More Apt To Be Suicidal Than Others?

There is no evidence that any particular type of individual or group of people is more suicidal than others, unless one brings outside variables into the equation. While certain individuals or groups may be identified as being more at risk than others, this seems to be inevitably the effect of a major psychological or personality breakdown (as in the psychotic suicide), or due in a significant amount to the effects of an identifiable exogenous variable (such as substance abuse), or of the individual's application of ineffective coping behaviors (such as self-destructive withdrawal). Such behavior also results from a combination of these or similar factors.

It is our finding that in a very large majority of cases, suicidal behavior appears to be nothing more or less than an application of ineffective learned behavior. These thoughts and deeds are ineffective or dangerous coping responses learned through maladaptive experience, poor modeling, or some similar cultural instructor. These totally ineffective behaviors come into prominence when other responses fail or when stress elicits an atypical demand for coping, or when no other options appear to be available.

In attempting to identify the threat or onset of these self-destructive response patterns, we look for cues or clues. These may come from an awareness that the youth's experiences have been of the type which often precipitates maladaptive behavior in someone who is vulnerable. Maladaptive behavior may be anticipated because of noticing that those whom the subject has been emulating are less than functional themselves. Cues may be derived from more direct indicators, signs of deteriorating adaptive behavior, displayed in the things that an individual says and does.

Recognizing Critical Cues

There are no signs or clues which inevitably point to a person's intent to take their own life. Even overt suicidal behavior is sometimes open to questions relevant to the motivation to die versus some sort of posturing or gesturing. Indicative of this, the terminology of the field includes such terms as "suicide," "parasuicidal behavior," or "quasi-suicidal behavior" (Shneidman, 1985) due to the uncertainty of either the prediction or post hoc interpretation of behavior.

If signs and clues represent behaviors or circumstances less focused than actual life-threatening acts, then these become evidences of suicide potential, which are nothing but statments of probabilities with considerable chance of being in error. The process of identifying a student at risk is one of sifting through a plethora of observable and inferable behaviors and motivations in one individual and then measuring them against similar patterns observed in others who have carried suicidal behavior closer to an ultimate conclusion. Unlike medicine where suspected symptoms may often be cross-validated via tests or different observations, suicidal-risk diagnosis is very tentative with relatively few satisfactory means for absolute substantiation.

Fortunately, suicide ideation and related behaviors usually are present and often exhibited for some time prior to a terminal crisis, though with youth the final act itself may be impulsive. Sudden onset, immediate stress-precipitated suicides probably represent only a small percentage of the total number of adolescent suicides (Peck, 1985).

It is commonly agreed that most suicidal persons display overt cues and that a preponderance of them even solicit aid by presenting various forms and types of calls for help. However, the signs are not always blatently obvious to the naive. The calls are not always directed at those in a position to know the person most intimately. And, noticing behavioral changes and interpreting subtle pleas for assistance in many instances requires some specially developed observational skills and sensitivity, skills that may not be expected to be present before training in even the most caring of persons.

One of the most forceful arguments for effecting a broad network of support within the school environment is that it multiplies the probability that the at-risk student will come in contact with someone who is both knowledgeable and prepared to respond. Providing training to potential gatekeepers to prepare them for such intervention is very important.

But what are the clues of potential suicide? Three categories of relevant information are available for those sensitive to their importance. Each of these are often readily perceived through day-to-day contact and, when accurately interpreted, provide much information about an individual's at-risk status. They are: situational contexts which contribute to stress and unhealthy coping responses, the things individuals say, and individual patterns of overt behavior.

Situational Clues. These are clues derived from the day-to-day conditions in which a person is existing. Sometimes, the situation is self-created or even imagined by the individual. Sometimes, it is entirely real and may be beyond individual control. Modifying the situation or one's interaction with it is a function of a therapeutic treatment plan. At this juncture our concern is only for being sensitive to those situations that elicit stress or offer little or no refuge, thereby sometimes precipitating non-adaptive responses, including suicide. Of all the situational circumstances that might be considered, social interaction situations seem to be the most crucial. And of these, the family situation is probably the single most important. Dysfunctional families present more than a passive non-supportive problem. They also foster poor coping habits.

Any one of a number of dysfunctional family situations puts a youth at a higher-than-normal at-risk status. A combination of these factors greatly intensifies the problem. Here are some examples of the kinds of circumstances or situations that should alert a gatekeeper to the possibility of special problems for an involved youth.

1. A sudden or traumatic interruption in the functioning of the family unit, e.g. a death, a geographical move.
2. Crises events which prevent the normal flow of even a functional family, e.g. loss of employment, divorce or separation.
3. Separation from the support of the family because of internal friction or external circumstances, e.g. family fights in the first instance, having to live apart from the family because of illness in the second.
4. Dysfunctional behaviors by significant others within the family, e.g. alcoholism, substance abuse, child abuse.
5. Dysfunctional family patterns, e.g. poor parenting skills, lack of or breakdown in communication within the family, extreme sibling rivalry or parent-child rivalry.
6. Modeling of poor adaptive behaviors, e.g. other members of the family experiencing adjustment problems, displaying criminal behaviors, being suicidal.

Youth may signal problems in the home in a variety of ways ranging from direct discussion with selected confidants to more subtle signals such as reluctance or refusal to allow the involvement of the home in school activities. In the latter case, the student may never invite parents to school activities, speak of parents or home-related events, or invite others into the home.

Other types of social situations are also important. Gatekeepers should be taught to be alert to the following types of non-family situational clues.

1. Experiencing humiliation, disappointment or loss of or failure to achieve self-deemed important social aspirations, e.g. failure to make the honor roll, breaking up of a romantic relationship.

2. Any circumstance that creates a real or imagined sense of being alone, physically or emotionally separated from other people, isolated and on one's own.

3. Any circumstance that the individual student feels is a particularly negative experience, e.g. situations which other students may interpret differently such as being assigned to a particular teacher that the student dislikes.

In developing sensitivity to these potentially problem-creating situations, gatekeepers need to clearly understand two important principles. The first is that the presence or experiencing of a circumstance in no way automatically substantiates the presence of suicide risk. These are conditions that make adjustment more difficult, tend to magnify the natural vulnerability of the young person, and therefore make life more difficult in general. Many youth handle these problems quite efficiently, with no threat of suicide and no long-lasting or involved problems. These circumstances are signals to be on the alert and nothing more. They should not be ignored, but they need not be given disproportionate importance, either.

The second is that the reality of the circumstance is relatively unimportant. Perceived stress is just as damaging as stress stemming from concrete facts. The youth that perceives his home as dysfunctional reacts as though it were. Too often we hear, "I know those people. His home is not nearly as bad as he says." The individual, particularly when under stress, reacts first to his own perceptions and empirically checks out the reality of the situation less and less as stress mounts. Stress, like beauty, is in the eye of the beholder.

One final caveat is needed. Precipitating events and contributing situations have some overlap at times but are not necessarily the same thing. Potential precipitating events (see Table 3-3) are circumstances that should be considered for the youth at risk, but they are most often only the final event in a long chain of circumstances, experiences, and situations. Their presence calls for increased alertness, but they usually have far less impact than longer-lasting circumstances, and the differentiation between causal and precipitating is important, especially in a construction of a treatment plan.

TABLE 3-3
SOME COMMON PRECIPITATING EVENTS*

1. A single dramatic event which seems to threaten the individual's happiness or the future of a close relationship with the context (social, geographical or both).
2. Strong demands for the individual under stress to display strength, competence or effectiveness.
3. Refusal of significant individuals and/or institutions to provide the anticipated or expected help.
4. High cultural or subcultural acceptance of extreme individuality in solving problems (this would include acceptance of suicide as a means of coping).
5. Breakdown in communication pattern with significant other.
6. Major family dysfunction, e.g. divorce, separation, death, etc.
7. A major disappointment or humiliation, either real or imagined.

*These should not be confused with basic causes. These are only the final link in what is most often a long, long chain of stresses.

Things People Say. Rarely does anyone publicly announce, "I'm going to kill myself." But the evidence is strong that such messages suggesting suicide, if properly interpreted, are not rare (Shneidman & Farberow, 1976). Many times the messages are verbal in nature. Sometimes, in desperation the message will be direct but very often not. Some interpretation may be required.

We find it helpful in training new gatekeepers to suggest categories of verbalizations or vocalized conceptualizations which may carry suicidal portent, realizing of course that any such grouping is artificial and arbitrary. Verbal indicators of suicidal ideation or intent include:

1. Those which indicate that the student may no longer be concerned with facing the ultimate consequences of some uncomfortable circumstances.
   Example: "I won't have to worry about grades much longer."
2. Statements that carry a threat of or desire for subtle, unanswerable revenge.

Example: "One of these days they'll be sorry they treated me wrong and won't be able to ask my forgiveness."

3. Statements that indicate an anticipated sudden absence of or from stress or trouble.

Example: "Let 'em yell and fight. I won't be having to listen to it."

4. Statements showing a preoccupation or fascination with death or dying.

Example: "I wonder if after you're dead you remember what dying was like."

5. Statements indicating lack of concern over matters that would normally be expected to cause concern.

Example: "I don't have to worry about my father's (terminal) illness. Everything's just fine now."

TABLE 3-4

DANGER SIGNALS OF INCREASED SUICIDAL RISK IN YOUTH

Situational clues:

Unusual acute stress on top of prolonged chronic stress
Loss of loved one or love object
Erratic behavior unrelated to external situation
Change in habitual behaviors (eating, sleeping, studying, recreation)

Things People Say:

Direct Statements:
"I wish I were dead."
"I want to die."
"I want to be forever peaceful and quiet."
Indirect Statements:
"How does one leave one's body to science?"
"Does it hurt to die?"
"I think dead people must be happier than they were when they were alive."

Things People Do:

A history of previous attempts
Sudden making of a will
Giving away of prized possessions

Personality Pattern Signs:

Depression
Disorientation
Extreme atypical defiance or dependence

While there are other very viable reasons for speaking in the ways these categories indicate, each of the categories can represent the use of a style of coping that is commonly seen in suicidal people. As with the situations noted previously, these verbalizations are not in and of themselves signs of impending suicide. But they are signal flags that the trained observer should be alert for, as well as other validating and substantiating clues.

We always encourage our trainees to be honest about their concerns, not worrying over what they might consider as "false alarms." The best policy is always to share the concern with someone else, another gatekeeper, or a support person. If the concern seems to have any sense of emergency about it, we advise the gatekeeper to ask the person involved. Very few genuinely suicidal persons will deny their ideation or intent if asked directly in a warm and supportive way.

Validation can also come in part from knowledge of the situation, as mentioned above, and consideration of nonverbal behavior, as well.

Things People Do. Though verbal clues may be the easiest to interpret, suicidal ideation and intent may permeate even a larger proportion of the troubled individual's nonverbal behaviors. The signs may be observed in both global and specific behaviors. In a broad sense, when suicidal ideas begin to compete with other less dysfunctional problem-solving behaviors, it is frequently possible to notice a general deterioration in the overall quality of an individual's daily behavior. This loss of effectiveness may be seen in many different ways, but some of the more commonly observed losses in effectiveness are:

1. Changes in a youth's social interaction behaviors, e.g. from shyness to acting out or from aggressiveness to withdrawn behaviors.
2. Deterioration in social skills and normative behaviors, e.g. lessened attention to personal appearance, undependability.
3. Changes in social habits, e.g. lessened interaction with friends, atypical emotional reactions to a social faux pas, change in type of friends.

Some specific dysfunctional behaviors also may occur. This may range from poorer performance in school subjects to more atypical (and therefore sometimes recognized more often) behaviors as disruptive acting out, the giving away of personal belongings, loss of interest in activities and objects and people formally highly valued, changes in eating and sleeping patterns, and unusual levels of withdrawal or social expansiveness.

Sometimes, the suicidal adolescent will devote great care to preparing for their forthcoming departure. Though often done quietly and unobtrusively, the youth may write a will, give away treasured possessions, pay off a variety of outstanding debts of all kinds, make social amends, and in a sense appear to be doing everything possible to leave a positive memory behind. This kind of behavior, if noticed, should be taken very seriously, as it very often occupies the suicide victim's attentions shortly before the act itself.

The guidelines in Table 3-5 and Table 3-6 are useful in helping the potential gatekeeper understand both the signs to watch for and some of the human dynamics that cause these signs to be presented.

The Crisis Syndrome

When the life of a person is at stake, no effort should be spared to seek a resolution other than that person's death. But everyone is worried about being cast in the role of someone who cries, "Wolf, wolf!" Almost every workshop experiences someone asking, "But what happens if I make a mistake? How is the person going to act? What do I say then?" We have experienced this concern so often that we now warn trainees of the probability of them experiencing what we have labeled as the

TABLE 3-5

A WORKING LIST OF WARNING SIGNS

1. A dramatic shift in academic performance quality
2. Changes in social behavior
3. Drug or alcohol abuse
4. Changes in daily behavior routines
5. Persistent fatigue
6. Boredom
7. Preoccupation and inability to concentrate
8. Any overt signs of mental illness such as hallucinations
9. Giving away of personal possessions
10. Truancy
11. Breakdown in communication with family, friends, school personnel
12. Isolation and morose behaviors
13. Insomnia
14. Absence of like-sex parental support

Adapted from a list by Hafen and Peterson (1983).

TABLE 3-6

SOME VALID BASIC ASSUMPTIONS ABOUT
THE SUICIDAL PERSON

1. Difficulties, stresses or disappointments that might be easy for one person to handle might be overwhelming for another. The suicidal person feels overwhelmed.

2. The potentially suicidal person has failed to solve by him or herself a problem self-perceived as intolerable.

3. The potentially suicidal person has directly or indirectly sought the help of others to solve the intolerable problem and has been, in his or her eyes, unrecognized, rejected, or has found the help to be useless or inappropriate.

4. The potentially suicidal person has common basic human needs. He or she wants to exist for someone or something, and wishes life to be marked by rewarding experiences, interesting tasks, and love.

5. The potentially suicidal person has or is experiencing insufficient success in forming relationships, bonds, mutual communication ties with meaningful or helpful others.

6. The suicidally intent person directly or indirectly communicates his death wishes to others, but feels that others have not noted or recognized them. He or she has cried for help and not been heard.

7. The suicidal person seeks death as a final option because no other effective choices appear to exist. To choose to die is not the same as not wishing to live.

---

crisis syndrome, and the probable effects on their gatekeeping behavior such worries may exert.

There is no perfect way to be sure or any magic criteria to help one make a totally valid at-risk decision. At best, one's fears and concerns are a gamble. We work hard in workshops to convince gatekeepers that it always pays to take the gamble and act to get help or intervene. It is well worth any embarrassment involved to hear and be able to believe a youth when they answer your inquiry, "Kill myself? That's a ridiculous idea. I have too much to live for!"

Since saving a life is the fundamental reason for being a gatekeeper, the ultimate criterion is the degree to which a life is threatened. To respond only to those students for whom suicide is a certainty would be to lower the response threshold to where a loss of life is almost certain among those youths whose behavior does not present a data set totally compatible with our expectations about being at risk.

The clinical professional facing such a decision learns to think in terms of **lethality.** The gatekeeper, though lacking the clinician's training and experience, must also learn to use and be comfortable with this criterion.

The only trustworthy source of information regarding this, other than a direct observer, is the person who is at risk. Hafen and Peterson (1983) suggest three guidelines for determining the seriousness of a young person's possible desire to die. These are summarized in these three questions:

1. How does he or she plan to commit suicide?
2. Is there a plan and if so is it well thought out and planned?
3. Has there been a previous attempt?

The first two of these three lines of inquiry are elaborated in Moursand's (1985) list of suggestions which are suggested for being put directly to the potentially suicidal youth if lethality is in question.

1. If you were to kill yourself, what method would you use?
2. Do you have the place or equipment necessary for accomplishing the act using that method?
3. How and when would you or could you do it?

The listener listens to both content and tone of the answers, being careful to note whether or not the plans are realistic, possible to carry out, and potentially fatal. Presented in a straightforward and caring manner, these questions very often elicit a response that provides sufficient information for making at least a preliminary judgment regarding lethality.

Sometimes, judgments of excessive lethality will be in error. This cannot be helped. Activation of the helping system more frequently than proves to be absolutely necessary is far preferable to losing a life through oversight or reluctance to be involved. Tables 3-7 and 3-8 offer help in these decisions by looking at the critical judgment from slightly different or more detailed perspectives. No list is perfect. Any one of these series of questions is far better than none at all.

Support Versus Lifesaving

Not every situation that elicits gatekeepers' concerns for potential lethality has a crisis ending. Prevention is a lifesaving mechanism as much as intervention. The individual's and the school's responsibility is clear. There is a moral responsibility to provide for the best interests of the students. Preventing their death by suicide is no exception.

TABLE 3-7

CRITICAL QUESTIONS ASKED TO DETERMINE LEVEL OF RISK

1. How much do you want to die?
2. How much do you want to live?
3. What has happened that makes life not worthwhile?
4. When you are thinking of suicide, how long do the thoughts stay with you?
5. How often do you have these thoughts?
6. Have you ever attempted or started to attempt suicide before?
7. On a scale of 1 to 10, what is the probability that you will try to kill yourself?
8. Do you have a plan for how you will do it?
9. When and where do you plan on doing it?
10. Is there anyone or anything which could change your mind or stop you?

Adapted from Hafen and Peterson (1983) and McBrien (1983).

TABLE 3-8

DISTRESS SIGNALS AT DIFFERENT LEVELS OF RISK

These set the stage for trouble
1. Acting out, aggressive hostile behavior
2. Alcohol or drug abuse
3. Passive behavior
4. Separation (experienced or feared) from support sources

May indicate loss of control
5. Changes in personal habits of eating, sleeping
6. Changes in personality traits
7. Sudden mood changes
8. Impulsiveness
9. Slacking of interest in school and other activities and accompanying decline in performance
10. Inability to concentrate and do effective problem solving
11. Loss or lack of friends, loneliness

Severe impending problems likely
12. Loss of important person or object in youth's life
13. Feelings of hopelessness
14. Obsession with death or dying
15. Any evidence of suicidal planning, e.g. making a will

Adapted from Giffen and Felsenthal (1983).

With this responsibility goes an equal responsibility for protecting the human rights of the students seen as at-risk. Though the law clearly provides for what amounts to the waiving of the individual's rights to confidentiality when a life threat is present (Wilson, 1981), the school and its representatives should use care to not use excessive zeal when working with a troubled youth or family and to maintain the privacy of the involved individuals as fully as possible.

There is no place in a support system for those whose needs are met by gossip, morbid curiosity, or the desire to invade the private life space of another. Care to provide student gatekeepers with strong staff and professional support in the network will help avoid this. Clearly dealing with the issue in training is also a must, as is a highly visible modeling by staff of professional ethics and concern for the personal welfare of the youth at risk.

If a judgment is made that a young person is at risk, then action must be taken. Intervention, the secondary phase of prevention, becomes the focus of activity. This topic is explored in the next chapter.

CHAPTER FOUR

CRISIS INTERVENTION

"To be or not to be, that is the question."
William Shakespeare

CRISES ARE invariably disruptive. When the normal situation revolves around large amounts of predictable, stable, and planned activities, the disruptive effect of a crisis is magnified and considerably more noticeable. The typical school environment is, of course, in such a situation.

HOW DO PEOPLE RESPOND TO A CRISIS?

Very few things can be as stress producing as the suicide of a family member, close friend or associate. Holmes and Rahe (1967) list the experiencing of someone else's death as ranking very high (first to thirteenth depending upon the relationship) among stress occurrences of sufficient severity as to impair a person's adjustive and adaptive capabilities. Sudden, unexpected death intensifies the difficulty of bereavement.

Even when death does not result, a suicide attempt carries a great effect. When the individual is a young person, the shock is even greater than in other cases. The effect of a young person's suicide or suicide attempt is felt by all concerned but perhaps most strongly by the young themselves and next most strongly by those who work closely with the young. Haim (1974) describes this very well: "The voluntary death of the young person is the locus of the most acute causes of human anxiety. All the projections, defenses, and rejections that operate in relationship

125

to adolescence on the one hand, and death in particular, on the other, converge in the suicidal adolescent." The ability to successfully deal with a crisis situation is made potentially more difficult due to the normal or expected effects of a crisis from suicide upon those affected.

General Reactions to a Crisis

Everyone is affected by a crisis! No individual, regardless of training or preparation, is unaffected; not even when the suicidal behavior is anticipated or expected. But in the best of instances, some individuals' preparation and training help them rise above and even to some extent use the typical crisis effects in order to deal successfully with the situation.

The entire organism, including each of the various sub-systems, is involved in a crisis response. In much the same way, external systems which extend beyond the individual to include family, institutional, community and subcultural systems are also affected. Most of the professionals working in the field of crisis intervention (including crises of health, disaster, war, assault, and suicide) operate on the assumption of a holistic involvement. This means that all of the individual's internal and external life systems must be included in any consideration of crisis response behavior.

Internal or Personal Sub-system Effects

Internal or personal sub-systems includes those sub-systems of the organism which are used in any instance of adjustive or adaptive behavior. These various parts can be categorized in various ways, but for our purposes we'll consider two specific sub-systems: (1) the emotions, and (2) perception and cognition. Though these sub-systems are discussed separately, it should be remembered that the separation is artificial and purely for discussion purposes.

As Janosik (1984) notes, each of these sub-systems experiences or displays distortion in a crisis. In harmony with the holistic principle, each of the sub-systems affects, and is affected by all, of the other sub-systems of the individual and in most cases by the broader external life systems that extend beyond the individual person as well. As a consequence, the distortions of one sub-system tend to affect the operation of and create related distortions in the functions of other sub-systems.

Emotional or Affective Sub-system:
Negative Effects

There are three very common and very important aspects of the typical emotional response to a crisis. These are **anxiety, conflict,** and **frustration.**

Anxiety. Probably the most uniformly experienced effect of experiencing a crisis is anxiety. Anxiety is the general emotional response to any type of stress. It has both positive and negative effects.

As a negative factor, it tends to carry with it a sense of general fear and anticipation of more stress. Sometimes, these feelings of dread become broad and indiscriminately inclusive. Such feelings, called free-floating anxiety, can be very constrictive to problem solving and general coping behavior. The individual knows fear but cannot identify a specific referent for that fear. As a result there is a tendency to play it safe, to venture only into the most predictable and obviously safe behaviors. In the worst instances, such dread becomes an habitual response affecting broad segments of a person's life. In these cases anxiety becomes a personality trait rather than being related to particular and identifiable situations.

Conflict. Conflict is also typically experienced by most of us in crisis situations. The most basic example of it can be seen in the traditional "fight-or-flight" conflict. But there are other types of conflicts, as well. Sometimes, we feel "caught between a rock and a hard place." In a crisis we may feel frightened to become involved but guilty if we refuse.

The ambivalence (literally being caught between two competing or contradicting values) often results in vacillation. Vacillating behavior is neither personally satisfying nor objectively productive. By postponing decision making, we receive neither the gratification that comes with accomplishment nor the satisfaction of successful problem solving. As a consequence, our own lack of effectiveness may in itself provide the basis for more anxiety.

Frustration. Feeling thwarted, blocked off from achieving a goal, is an unpleasant and disturbing emotion. The degree to which each of us can tolerate frustration varies with our own experiential backgrounds. It can and does fluctuate within a particular individual, as well. Repeated stress or large amounts of stress act to lower or inhibit frustration tolerance. Impatience, impulsive and random trial-and-error problem solving rather than goal-oriented behavior is a prime effect of frustration too high to be tolerated.

The Emotional or Affective Sub-system: Positive Effects

This triad of emotional responses to the extreme stress of a crisis should not be considered as uniformly negative. While it is true that all of us can experience reductions in effectiveness due to our emotional responses (and some of us develop ineffective coping habits because of these), this need not be the case. Almost every example of problematic behavior as a result of emotional reaction to stress is really a case of a helpful reaction carried too far.

Let's briefly examine in a general way the triad of reactions mentioned above and note how positive effects may result, effects that can be and are useful in crisis situations. Later, we'll look more specifically at applications involving those who play different roles in a crisis.

Anxiety. Selye's (1976) research has taught us that organisms have a predictable reaction to extreme stress, i.e. a crisis. This "general adaptation syndrome" has three parts: an **alarm stage,** a **resistance stage,** and an **exhaustion stage.** The stages are common to all of us (and apparently many other non-human organisms, as well) and are primarily physiologically triggered. Each serves an important purpose. The alarm stage, the initial reaction to stress, mobilizes the physiology of the body for action through changes in adrenalin production, blood pressure, and other related responses. The resistance stage helps the body adapt to the demands of ongoing stress by keeping energy higher than normal but not as high as in the first immediate "alarm" reaction. It has been described as the "adaptation" part of the body's response to stress. The exhaustion stage signals that the body is approaching the end of usable energy reserves. If properly recognized, it helps avoid the extension of involvement past the point of personal effectiveness and threat of physiological deterioration. Anxiety then helps us mobilize and focus our energy and also provides cues that help us avoid overextending ourselves if we attend to them.

On the positive side, anxiety also provides motivation to act, a reason for seeking behavior instrumental in problem solving. Most psychologists would agree that some stress is a necessary component of effective behavior and that some anxiety, as a result of that stress, is helpful in activating or motivating behavior.

Conflict. The most useful contribution of conflict is to help make us aware of available options. Recognizing the presence of a conflict in our life and being sensitive to the effect it has on our own behavior can be a useful tool in helping us to orient toward making important decisions. If the options have been carefully considered, making a decision is almost always more satisfying and productive in the long run than postponing goal-oriented behavior because of vacillation.

Though resolvement of the ambivalence of choice may not be easy, conflict situations do help with two positive adaptive behaviors. First, in situations where a sense of urgency may direct us toward impulsive responses, conflict, and the confusion over the result of one choice as opposed to another, may slow down our response rate thereby giving rational consideration a chance to occur. Second, knowing that a choice-making situation is not clearly black and white usually encourages us to assemble decision-making data, to get the facts of the situation.

Some of us carry this need to find out all the details and get each relevant detail wrapped up neatly to an extreme, even to the extent of what is commonly called Type A behavior (Matthews & Brunson, 1975). But for the most part, consideration of the several possible outcomes of particular choices is an asset in a crisis situation.

Frustration. Properly attended to, frustration may be the feeling most apt to steer us toward a course of positive adaptation. It is unreasonable to either expect that all frustration can be avoided or that every conflict which produces frustration can be resolved. Effectively coping individuals usually have learned well to recognize the signs of frustration in their own life. Such indicators signal a time to take stock, to evaluate the situation, to consider options. Once an individual learns to accept the experience of frustration as common to everyone and to realize that though we cannot control frustration we can control our emotional response to it, a major step toward healthy adaptation has taken place. The experience of frustration which arises out of a crisis can literally be the genesis for the emergence of a productive aspect of crisis resolution.

Cognitive and Perceptual Sub-system Effects

As with emotions, some stress is useful in mobilizing an effective cognitive response. Perceptual behavior must be considered as a functional part of cognitive behavior, since it is involved in both the obtaining and processing of information. In general, it can be said that the need for problem solving elicits productive cognitive behavior in the human being. But the effects are complex. Up to a point, the level of cognitive productivity increases directly as a function of the motivation to reduce stress (see Fig. 4-1). But the positive effects begin to deteriorate as stress becomes either prolonged or more intensified.

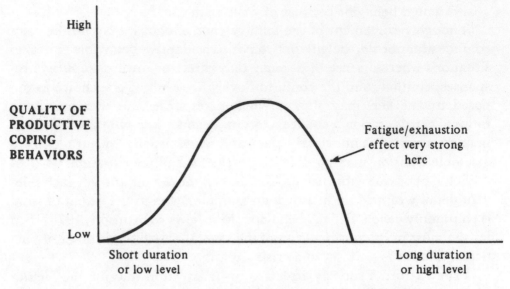

Figure 4-1. No stress at all elicits little motivation, hence little coping behavior. Some stress helps get us going, but too much has a general negative effect upon the quality of our coping behaviors.

Deterioration comes partly as a result of cumulative fatigue (in the case of prolonged stress) and from perceptual and cognitive confusion (in the case of intense stress). At first thought, it might seem that crisis situations will always involve intense rather than prolonged stress. It is true that the precipitous nature of many crises, particularly situational crises, support this assumption. However, in many other instances, particularly in crises arising out of developmental or family dysfunction problems, the crisis is likely to occur as the final step in a long-term series of stress-provoking events.

Consequently, both factors which may contribute to ineffective behavior must be considered.

Steps for Successful Adaptation

What are the characteristics of adaptive cognitive-perceptual behavior? The steps, though physiologically and behaviorally complex, are easily identified. The organism must adequately perform five successive and interdependent tasks.

1. Discriminate, attend to, and process important relevant stimuli in the crisis situation.
2. Process the import of these stimuli through a problem-solving chain which involves use of association, memory and recall, and closure on the meaning of the stimuli in order to establish the available solution options.
3. Consider solution options, evaluate their worth, and select the most viable.
4. Produce the appropriate behaviors involved.
5. Repeat the entire process for the purpose of evaluating the effectiveness of the solution choice and the produced coping behaviors.

Prerequisites for Successfully Performing These Tasks

How does crisis-level stress affect these steps? An individual can perform the steps adequately in the face of crisis — perhaps even be expected to do so at a slightly better level of adaptibility than normal situations might elicit — if the following qualifications are met:

1. The stress intensity level or duration must not be so high as to result in the deteriorating or neglected effects noted above.
2. The stimuli characteristics necessary for identification and discrimination must be available to the individual.
3. The individual must have had sufficient experiential background or preparation as to have established familiarity with a reservoir of response options relevant to the stress-producing stimuli.
4. The individual must conceptualize what effect his or her problem-solving behavior has or will have upon the level of stress being experienced.
5. There must be sufficient energy and motivational reserve available to support the sought-after responses.
6. The responses sought must be part of the individual's response repertoire.
7. The individual must have available the necessary information upon which to judge the efficacy of a produced response.

Sometimes, individuals need help with one of these important prerequisites. Providing this assistance in the face of a crisis is called "intervention."

It should be obvious that primary prevention, long before a crisis is present, can play a paramount role in preparing the individual to successfully handle the various cognitive steps involved in self-reduction of a crisis. In those situations where personal resources prove to be insufficient, thereby calling for "intervention," the application of "outside" or non-personal resources, secondary or crisis intervention may be applied to any one or combination of these prerequisite behaviors.

Adaptive versus non-adaptive cognitive reactions to stress do not fall clearly into a binary, yes-or-no, format. When personal resources approach the danger level of falling short of what is needed, less adaptive behaviors gradually begin to develop or become substituted for those not working adequately. Sometimes, these substitutions are subtle. One of the strongest arguments for establishing an empathetic and sensitive environment in the schools is that such an environment more quickly picks up the approaching need for crisis intervention by noting these. Perceiving that a problem is beginning to develop is a much healthier situation to be in than having to respond in an emergency fashion to a crisis that seems to have appeared suddenly, cataclysmically without warning.

Applying These Principles to Suicide Crises in the Schools

It is a reasonably safe assumption that anyone participating in a suicidal crisis is exposed to an unusual level of stress, whether they be a perpetrator, significant other, intervener, or merely a member of some secondarily affected group.

Consequences of this atypical stress are experienced both emotionally and cognitive-perceptually. Although the psychological processes and principles are the same for everyone, being in a different role (e.g. intervener) substantially affects the specific concerns and problems. It is helpful for the school to be prepared for these differential responses.

A useful way to examine individual responses is to note how effectively the individual is performing the five tasks mentioned above, i.e. inputing stimuli, processing the information received, selecting solutions and applying solutions, and accurately evaluating their own performance. Extreme or long-duration stress makes it difficult to perform these tasks consistently well. Breakdown in coping or adaptive efficiency may be observed in the functions of the sub-systems previously noted. Each sub-system has it's own particular vulnerabilities.

Emotional Areas of Vulnerability

Emotions serve both as "drivers" and as "sustainers" of behavior. How we "feel" about a situation provides us with reinforcing information as to whether or not we wish to maintain our present behaviors or change them in some amount or form. We are apt to "trust" our own emotions above other non-personal data. When there is dissonance between our own feelings and outside indicators, we typically become concerned about the lack of congruity. Under high stress, our concern with and efforts to meaningfully resolve such dissonance may not operate as efficiently as at other times.

Three particular facets of emotional function seem to be especially vulnerable in such high-stress situations. Their relationship to the triad of unhappy feelings experienced by depressed people, the **hopeless-hapless-helpless** syndrome, is easily recognized.

Emotional Stability. There is a "happy medium" for emotional stability. Normally, we are sufficiently flexible as to be responsive to change-indicating dissonance while remaining sufficiently stable as to not be too impulsive or responsive to minor, or insignificant challenges to our feelings.

When emotional functioning begins to deteriorate, the most frequently viewed problems lie in one of two directions: Either we become rigid and fixated in our feelings, unresponsive to any mood-affecting indicators not in harmony with our present feelings, or we become so emotionally labile as to experience unusually large or sudden mood changes. Sometimes, the two are coupled together. An individual may have a polemic swing in mood and then lock-in on the new feelings, resisting all change or swings back toward formerly held, more "normal" mood patterns.

Recognizing Mood Determinants. As stress rises, concern with our own private feelings rises accordingly. One effect is to begin to view our present stressful feelings as being "typical" or "characteristic" of ourselves—"normal for me." Wrapped up in ourselves, we ignore input that might help us more realistically identify causes for our feelings. Either we begin to look solely inwardly for causes or we unrealistically blame outside sources while at the same time granting these forces some sort of invincibility which suggests that perhaps our situation is either unchangeable or perhaps "normal," "deserved" or even to be expected for some obscure reason. Albert Ellis (1977), working from the perspective of Rational-Emotive Therapy, assumes that much of an individual's unhappiness is at least self-controlled if not self-induced due to adherence to irrational beliefs (see Table 4-1).

Emotional Identification. "Misery loves company," goes the old saying. In a sense this is true even under conditions of effective coping. If we are aware that our feelings are similar to those experienced by others, it lends a sense of security. We see others feeling good and we expect similar feelings in ourselves. We see others feeling down but coping with their problems and recovering from bouts with negative feelings, and it reminds us that our negative feelings are not peculiar to us and that it is reasonable to expect things to change for the better somewhere down the line.

Under extreme stress, as our emotional stability begins to exacerbate our problems, we often constrict our emotional identification with others. Feelings of loneliness and helplessness as a result of the assumed isolated individualness of our problems result. Without the social support of identifying with others, feelings of alienation and impenetrable isolation may easily develop. These in turn make the problem worse.

Cognitive-Perceptual Areas of Vulnerability

Cognitive-perceptual sub-systems interact actively with individual emotions. The higher the emotional content of a situation, the greater the influence of emotions upon thinking or cognitive behaviors. The general "focusing" response of the cognitive-perceptual sub-system is advantageous up to a point, since it serves to put less significant issues aside for the moment, concentrating on the problem at hand. But as the level of intensity increases, a threshold is reached where productivity begins to fall — slowly at first, then more rapidly, and finally it may reach a point of nearly total ineffectiveness.

Where, in these necessary adaptive tasks, are the cognitive-perceptual sub-systems particularly vulnerable?

Attention to Meaningful Information. Problem solving requires a searching process which involves the seeking of information, a sorting through of that information, followed by inclusion-exclusion decision making. A delicate balance is necessary between maintaining an "open mind" towards new information and the ignoring or filtering out, or the exclusion, of data that is irrelevant or non-contributory to the process.

Stress at a tolerable level gears us up for this operation by increasing our perceptual sensitivity and cognitive alertness. Too much stress pushes the process too far and our attention becomes narrowed rather than merely focused. Under extreme stress we can fail to note, recognize, or respond to information which may be very relevant to potential solutions. Excluding such new information causes us to be increasingly dependent upon older, more habitual data sets. In very extreme instances pathological cognitive process may be observed, with regressive, child-like and nearly useless, repetitive, habitual, problem-solving behavior being attempted over and over again. Thus, a child, under stress because of being singled-out in front of the class, searches for the correct spelling of a word. Spelling it incorrectly, the child may, in trying a second time, offer the same misspelling as at first.

Trial-and-Error Problem Solving. Unless a problem is an old and familiar one, much of normal problem solving consists of trial-and-error behavior. While it is true that this may be done covertly, that is, the individual "tries out" solutions by thinking them through rather than by actually overtly trying it out, it is still an effective means to exploring solution options.

When we are functioning effectively, we tend to go through a cognitive "sorting-out" process which in effect weighs the pros and cons of potential solutions, considers the consequences of behavior options, and retains or discards potential solutions based on their perceived applicability as measured by past experience, similarities to other situations, and similarly useful data bases.

Under severe stress the process becomes modified. Obtaining a solution becomes so important that goal orientation overrides careful consideration of important intermediate steps. We often over simplify problems, choosing to apply an immediately available but too simplistic solution to a complex problem which requires more careful consideration. We begin to look for any solution rather than for the best one.

Careful trial-and-error with accompanying evaluation of the worth of considered optional solutions may be replaced by nearly random attempts to find answers. Sometimes, the solution seeking becomes repetitive, with a discarded solution being tried over and over again without success. Since we may still be going through a trial-and-error process, unproductive as it may be, it is easy for the highly stressed individual to fail to recognize the lack of effectiveness present, being sensitive only to the amount of effort expended. Doing something, anything, to be active becomes a substitution for continuing to search for the correct solution as far as effective problem solving is concerned.

Self-Monitoring Processes. Much of effective problem solving operates in a type of "servo-mechanism" model, where we continually monitor and modify our own solution-seeking behaviors based upon how well they are working. This process is very closely allied to the receptivity for and attention to new information mentioned above. As stress increases and our attention to outside data declines in both quantity and quality, the effectiveness of our self-monitoring also becomes affected. As we fixate on the severity of our problems and the need for a solution, it becomes much more difficult to patiently perform self-evaluation.

We become more impulsive, tending to judge our effectiveness on action rather than the consequences of that action, and become much more oriented toward immediate stress reduction than long-range problem alleviation.

This vulnerability is heightened when we become less sure of our own capabilities and we begin to feel hapless rather than the master of our own fate. We become increasingly susceptible to unqualifiedly accepting a self-made judgment of our own ineffectiveness as we measure ourselves against a false standard of irrational beliefs about what constitutes acceptable or desirable behavior (see Table 4-1).

TABLE 4-1

IRRATIONAL BELIEFS

---

1. I must be loved and approved by all people I consider important.
2. I must be competent and adequate to handle all situations which may arise.
3. I must be treated fairly and receive what I deserve in all cases.
4. The problems of life must be solved quickly, efficiently, and thoroughly.
5. It is easier to avoid than face certain life difficulties.
6. I must be treated fairly, and to be treated unfairly is unbearable.
7. My past is the all-important determiner of my life and has a permanent effect upon it.
9. Certain people are evil and wicked and should be blamed and therefore punished because of it.

Adapted from Ellis (1977).

Perceiving ourselves as "failures," we are less trusting of our own self-monitoring capabilities. We are more and more apt to reach out for an immediately available solution regardless of its eventual outcomes. Self-monitoring declines to a level of measuring activity (or the lack of it) rather than evaluating outcomes. What feedback is obtained has little usefulness in rationally affecting subsequent behaviors.

MAKING THE TRANSITION FROM PRIMARY TO SECONDARY PREVENTION

In the previous chapter and the first part of this chapter, we have placed considerable emphasis on evaluating the level of stress involved (and therefore the level of risk) for individuals in a suicidal-crisis experience. There is a very pragmatic reason for this evaluation. It is from the significance of this evaluative data that major decisions are made regarding the level or stage of prevention required. If an individual can be observed to display an intact nucleus of coping behaviors, not only is risk less, but the support network can be more concerned with providing either primary prevention (anti-crisis-producing information, environments and activities) or tertiary prevention (reconstructive, rehabilitative, recuperating information, environments and activities).

Secondary prevention assumes that there is a need for outside intervention based upon time pressures, availability of personal resources, or other similarly critical factors. Intervention, though most typically thought of as being directed toward the potential perpetrator, may be necessary for significant others who have or are experiencing tremendous stress, help-givers who find the additional demands of a suicidal situation difficult to be handled alone, and to broader groups who may feel a less direct but still possibly very severe impact.

In the simplest of terms, the decision to move from primary to secondary prevention is based upon the answer to this question: "Is this person at a dangerous stress level because of having to go it alone?" Fortunately, there are some clues to help. These are not absolute answers, but they are functional often enough as to be considered an important source of information helpful in making this decision. It should be kept in mind that the safest rule is "when in doubt, assume the need for help." A mistake in this direction may be embarrassing. The mistake of withholding needed help can be fatal.

Positive and Negative Coping in Suicide-Related Situations

As we have already noted in previous chapters, quickly and accurately determining the lethality of the suicidal situation is an extremely important evaluation. A degree-of-lethality judgment is based primarily upon a coupling of the information about the availability of means with an assessment of the functioning level of the assumed perpetrator's emotional and cognitive-perceptual capabilities. It is obvious that information regarding both of these is essential to assuming the best intervention stance.

When considering the potential suicide perpetrator, lethality is a prime concern. When considering others involved, suicide itself may or may not be a major worry: personal mental health and the negative effects of intense or prolonged stress certainly is.

For those who will be planning, organizing, or managing intervention programs, it is very important to be alert for indications of the coping effectiveness of each of these individuals or groups. Judgments regarding possible hierarchy of treatment, availability of personnel as resources, requirements for networking, necessity for short and long-term follow-up, and similar decision-requiring problems are all dependent upon knowing how well persons are coping with the stress.

Some clues regarding personal effectiveness levels may be useful. These should not be considered as absolute indicators but merely as benchmarks against which to make some measurement of the individual's adaptiveness at the moment. Perhaps even more important than exact levels or styles are any dramatic change in the individual's typical behavior.

In the Person at Risk

Positive Signs:

1. Person's moods match the situation of the moment, with some variance similar to peers as the situation changes.
2. Person seeks out situations and activities which have positive feelings attached.
3. Person discusses moods and problems, showing interest in how others have met and solved their problems.
4. Person seeks helpful information or actual assistance with a displayed willingness to discuss the problem or feelings.

5. A variety of solution-seeking behaviors are explored or even attempted.
6. Person shows awareness of and responsiveness to their own performance, including both positive and negative aspects.

Negative Signs:

1. Dramatic changes in an individual's typical mood pattern or lack of variability in mood regardless of the surrounding situation.
2. Loss of interest in formerly pleasant and rewarding activities.
3. Reclusiveness and the seeking of isolation.
4. Apathy or agitated bursts of activity which seems to have little obvious relationship to the situation (e.g. bursts of anger).
5. More emphasis on the problem than upon solutions, frequently accompanied by signs of less positive activity related to everyday life such as sleeping, eating, recreation.
6. The individual is self-depreciating, expresses guilt, performs quasi-self-punishment behaviors such as giving away personal belongings or denying himself or herself the enjoyment of typically sought-after pleasures.

Among Significant Others

Positive Signs:

1. Increased cohesiveness among family or primary group members.
2. Maintaining of everyday activity level and schedules.
3. Sharing of worry or anger or grief with professional help sources and/or others in similar circumstances.
4. Willingness to accept support and assistance and information.
5. Deliberate attempts to organize and initiate adaptive activities.
6. Demonstration of capability of seeing positive self-attributes in addition to any self-blame or causal concerns.

Negative Signs:

1. Disorganization and deterioration of interpersonal relationships.
2. Breakdown or loss of effectiveness in family or personal routine activities.
3. Withdrawal from normal outside interactions and activities or lack of any sharing of feelings or concerns with others.
4. A reluctance to accept or even overtly recognize the need for support or assistance.

5. Obsessive focusing on problem issues, surroundings, accompanied with repetitive non-productive problem solving or denial.
6. Polemic stances regarding involvement or causal responsibilities ranging from self-abusive guilt on one extreme to a "business as usual," no meaningful involvement, on the other.

In Help-Givers or Interveners

Positive Signs:

1. Ability to carry on with everyday routines and activities.
2. Deliberate actions designed to give relief from stress, e.g. recreational activity or physical exercise.
3. Empathy with those in trouble without undue identification or the assuming of similar concerns about one's own self or situation.
4. Use of other sources of help, e.g. other help-givers, information sources, networking.
5. Orientation towards solution-finding with the demonstration of active consideration of alternate options.
6. Willingness to discuss the personal "cost" to themselves of being involved in a suicidal crisis, and the willingness to give way to others when necessary in order to achieve a personal "time-out" period of stress relief.

Negative Signs:

1. Deterioration in effectiveness of their own professional and personal responsibilities and activities.
2. Fixation on the crisis and crisis-related activities: inability to focus attention on other, non-crisis-related problems.
3. Presence of personal signs of intense stress involvement, e.g. sleeping and eating problems, interpersonal difficulties.
4. Demonstrated feelings of total responsibility, total immersion in the crisis without dependence on assistance from peers.
5. Expressions of fear or despair for the finding of solutions, and anger at failure of activities designed or individuals enlisted to reduce the crisis level to quickly and effectively do so.
6. Inability to recognize one's own declining effectiveness due to emotional and/or physical fatigue.

Among Broadly Impacted Group Members

Positive Signs:

1. Willingness to openly show and discuss feelings.
2. Demonstrated understanding of where, why, and how stress develops and affects everyone.
3. Recognition of the commonality of their feelings about or derived from the crisis situation and actively sharing this with others.
4. Requests for factual information and explanations of the situation and their reactions to it.
5. Spontaneous attempts to reduce stress by either the resumption of pre-stress activities or new activities designed to give relief.
6. Demonstrated ability to recognize the effects of the situation upon themselves and an awareness of their changing reactions (regardless of whether positive or negative).

Negative Signs:

1. Any sustained polemic mood demonstration ranging from mass hysteric responses to stone-faced, "it didn't really happen," or "it doesn't really matter" denial.
2. Fear of the possible generalization of the crisis or confusion or anxiety about either the event(s) or their own reactions.
3. Feelings of being peculiar or different in their response to the crisis and unwillingness to share in any group cathartic or stress-reducing activities.
4. Emotional and/or intellectual isolation from the event as though it had not impinged in any way upon their world.
5. Obsessive fixation on the crisis and its negative effects to the point of more than a temporary interruption of normal routines and activities, e.g. classroom performance, sleeping, eating, playground activities.
6. Fear and self-directed concerns, often exhibited in somatic complaints, nightmares, withdrawal from normal group activities.

The reader is reminded to keep in mind that these are merely "clues" and should not be construed as absolute signs. Healthy individuals may sometimes display some of the negative signs: stressed-out individuals may cover up their deteriorating adaptation remarkably well. Astute sensitivity to these clues will, however, provide useful information in many, many instances. And the list of clues provides a stress-reducing benefit of its own, a helping structure to remind the help-givers that they do not have to carry the burden of making intervention decisions alone.

Principles of Secondary Prevention

Each successive level of prevention has its own characteristic set of assumptions, methods, and individual roles that participants may play (see Table 4-2).

TABLE 4-2

LEVELS OF INTERVENTION

Level	Basic assumption	Methods	Individual roles
Primary	"Knowledge is strength"	Teaching Structured relationships Managed situations Preparation	Learners Developer of skills Acquiring of resources
Secondary	Help is needed to re-establish equilibrium	Support Assessment of strengths and weaknesses of victim Suggestions Use of victim's available resources	Learner Follower Focused model
Tertiary	Problems persist even after crisis resolution	Development activities Care giver Support in taking risks	Resumption of normal living Increased risk

Primary prevention (see Chapter Two) seeks to avoid or change potentially hazardous situations, reduce people's exposure to those situations impossible to change, and to reduce the individual personal vulnerability through the increasing of adaptive or coping skills. Secondary prevention builds upon this foundation. The more effective primary prevention has been, the easier one may expect secondary prevention to be.

Secondary prevention centers around five separate principles or assumptions. All decision making as well as organizational and activity planning is based on these.

Help Is Needed

When the demands upon an individual exceed that person's available resources, a crisis situation occurs. The choice is between failing to meet demands and the consequent deterioration in adaptive behavior versus calling upon some outside resource to supplement individual resources. The presenting or applying of additional resources is intervention.

While it is possible that this may be done without a direct invitation from the person or persons requiring assistance, this need not be so. High-risk suicidal individuals very often send out some form of call for help. Sometimes it is subtle; sometimes it is direct. In either event, it is really an individual calling attention to an insufficiency of resources. It is a plea for intervention.

Assessment of Personal Resources Is Required

Total personal inadequacy should not be assumed merely because there is a call for help or an awareness that someone needs help. In fact, in most instances, an individual probably has struggled more or less successfully with stress for some time before reaching a sufficiently frightening depletion of resources as to elicit a call for help.

Since intervention is only intended to be a short-termed and temporary support, we should always be concerned with the longer termed possibilities. If an individual can receive temporary help while retaining some level of security and trust in their own coping resources, the future is faced with much more confidence.

It is an important principle of intervention, therefore, that as much as possible intervention tactics and activities should involve the use of those resources that an individual does have. Bolstering and strengthening where necessary, complementing with other assistance as needed. To successfully interact in this delicate fashion, it is necessary to assess what an individual's internal and personal environmental resources actually are.

While there is seldom time for lengthy analyses or formalized evaluative procedures, effective crisis intervention workers learn to quickly perform this type of assessment and use the information thereby obtained. The task, though important, need not be all that difficult. Even simple questions such as, "Who is there at home with whom you can talk about problems?" will yield information of this type.

Networks of Resources Are Important

While it is important to use the individual's personal resources as much as possible, a need for supplementary or backup resources is very frequently encountered. Since time and accuracy of application are often prerequisites to successful intervention, networking is critical.

A variety of resources should be available. These should be quickly accessible and provide a number of different types and levels of support. It is important that those most likely in a position to be making a crisis-level contact with outside resources have pre-established role identity and credibility in the perception of those being asked for help. Nothing is more frustrating, and possibly defeating, in a time of crisis emergency than to have to take the time to explain who is calling for help, what their organizational connection may be, why they are calling, etc. Such queries, legitimately and understandably asked, can often be answered in a routine pre-crisis environment networking contact.

Crisis centers, for example, must frequently call upon police and fire personnel for emergency assistance. These centers are careful to establish credibility and close working relationships with these agencies before crises evolve.

A Crisis Is Not Forever

By definition, crises are short-termed. For one thing, the high levels of stress involved cannot be tolerated for long periods of time; for another, tolerance for ambivalence and ambiguity has its limits in even the healthiest of individuals, and the need to reduce this type of dissonance in our lives, to get rid of a crisis, is very strong, indeed. It takes hierarchial preference over many other very strong drives and needs.

As a consequence, secondary prevention, or crisis intervention, must be geared up to move rapidly and produce results relatively quickly. While this may place some unusual demands on crisis interveners, it offers some positive advantages, as well. Those intervening in a crisis have every reason to expect their roles to be comparatively short-lived. Therefore, they may be able to afford a level of intensity and involvement that would not be comfortable or tolerable for longer periods of time.

When crisis time-lines do extend beyond the capabilities of individual interveners, the pre-established network is a major support resource. Sometimes, crisis intensity is so high that the coping ability of interveners is relatively short. Even a few hours of being face to face with a youth experiencing suicidal thoughts can be exhausting. It is then that the network becomes a vital part of intervention. It should include not only "more-of-the-same" intervention resources but also components including professionals trained to deal with very intense and relatively long-lived crises interactions. The "front-line" crisis worker is an emergency-response person. It should not be assumed that the responsibility must be carried alone or for long periods.

Crisis intervention should be considered as temporary support, interim assistance, a bridge between two periods of at least minimally acceptable personal coping. As is noted in later chapters, tertiary prevention activities are designed to pick up and carry longer-termed responsibilities.

Intervention Has Specific Goals

As outlined in Table 4-2, each level of prevention has its own identifiable assumptions and methods. This is equally true for objectives or goals. They are different at each level.

The overall goal of secondary prevention, intervention, is to take charge where necessary to avoid catastrophic effects in a crisis. In a suicidal crisis, these catastrophic results frequently can be death. The catastrophic effect upon a school of a student's suicidal death can be dramatic and far-reaching. In the school already unprepared to meet a crisis, the effect is devastating.

More specifically, there are two functional objectives involved in intervention that, when met, serve to satisfy this overall goal. First, wherever possible, the crisis intervener seeks to shorten the duration of a crisis experience. Whether this is done by problem solving, environmental manipulation or some other means will vary from instance to instance. However, a fundamental goal is to get the individual out of a crisis situation. Second, while a crisis is being endured, the crisis intervener seeks to lessen the impact and negative effects of the crisis on the victim(s) wherever and however possible. "Avoid when you can. Soften the effects where avoiding is impossible," is the guiding maxim.

Application of these principles in a manner that is efficient and effective requires some definition of necessary resources and responsibilities.

Goals, Resources and Responsibilities

Hoff (1984) has noted that there are really two different aspects to a crisis response. One is "crisis management" which consists of the entire process of working through a crisis situation from its initiation to its final resolution. The second is "crisis intervention" which is a more short-termed process, focusing on the immediate needs of the precipitate situation and its victim(s). Certainly, secondary prevention is concerned with both of these, but the implications for organization and personnel are quite different depending upon which of these two goals is being addressed.

Crisis Management

As a general rule, schools are far less involved in crisis management than intervention, particularly in relation to suicide. Though there may be instances where a suicidal crisis has so involved a broad segment of the school population as to present the need for school personnel to see the issue through to final resolvement, this is not usually the case. Crisis management involves ongoing contacts and frequently extended or deep psychotherapy. It sometimes involves training sessions and integrative recuperation activities which extend far beyond the scope of a school's average resources or responsibilities. Such involvement is similar to what Slaikeu (1984) labels as "second-order intervention." He does suggest, however, that the school may become involved in this activity through involvement of school counselors or school psychologists and nurses.

It has been our experience though that when the school becomes an active participant in ongoing crisis management, it is usually as a secondary partner with broader community resources. Treatment plans conceived and initiated by psychiatrists or psychologists may involve school participation or support and as such are very important. However, the school's responsibility is more akin to that of the pharmicist: to fill rather than initiate a defined recuperative prescription.

Some management activities and resources are required of the schools in any intervention stance, however. Readiness is an important product of effective management. This involves an overall sensitivity to the need for crisis response as well as a general emotional and organizational preparedness to fill whatever immediate emergency intervention gap may be needed.

Crises are not always preceded by sudden traumatic events. A crisis is in the eyes of the beholder. When a victim feels that personal resources are overloaded in terms of the demands of the moment, crisis-producing stress is a normal consequence. Effective crisis management foresees the need for ongoing monitoring of the "crisis level" of the school environment and of its inhabitants. Being surprised by the sudden appearance of a crisis magnifies the difficulty of adequate response. If the appearance of a crisis, suddenly or incipiently spawned, is to result in an eventual turn for the better (a desirable outcome for any crisis experience), effective management has an important role to play.

Crisis management, even at the level most often required of the school, involves the capability to play several roles, each of which enhances the probability of success in secondary prevention, as Hoff (1984) outlines. These include:

1. The capability of performing at least some level of psychosocial assessment of the victim(s). In the case of suicide, this includes evaluation of risk.
2. The capability to develop or assist in the development of a plan of crisis response.
3. The capability to implement or assist in the implementation of the developed plan, including having the necessary personal, social, and material resources available.
4. Capability for self-monitoring, self-evaluation of the functional effectiveness of the school's role in the above steps and management's contribution to that effectiveness.

Of course, assuring the presence of these capabilities involves performance of some basic management functions. These include the shaping of organizational attitude and commitment, the training of personnel, and the providing of personnel and material and time resources. There is another very important management function critical both to the initiation and maintaining of crisis-intervention readiness. This is a school and community public relations function. This latter management role says to staff, students and public alike, "We recognize our responsibility and publically affirm our willingness to do our part."

Crisis Intervention

This aspect of secondary prevention work is much more characteristic of the involvement of the typical school system. It consists of meeting the immediate effects of a crisis experience head-on. It is a "minuteman" type of response mode which suggests, above all, a commitment to the assumption that all of the student's life is of concern to those whose primary dedication is to improving the mind and facilitating learning. It is a dramatic example of holistic endorsement of the "sound mind, sound body" philosophy.

Crisis intervention involves three general areas (Pasewark & Albers, 1972).

1. **Establishing or facilitating information flow.** If crisis intervention operates on the assumption that help outside the individual is needed in order to handle a crisis, then it logically follows that a major task and responsibility is to facilitate the flow of information. Several vital data bases are involved. Those involved in crisis intervention serve to a large part as collectors of information included in these bases and as conduits which assure a quick and accurate flow of information from one data base to another.

2. **Assisting victims to adequately perceive reality.** We have already examined some of the effects of high anxiety and stress on adaptive behaviors. As you may recall, narrowing of perception and ineffective and often unrealistic filtering and processing of information is one of the common effects. Much of crisis intervention consists of giving the victim(s) an objective helping hand in sorting out all the relevant details of the crisis experience.

   This includes helping them to accurately perceive the realities of the situation. This is helpful even when realities may be unpleasant, since it better assures a mobilization of effort oriented in an appropriate direction. It also includes an emphasis on the concrete details of the situation along with assistance in accurately examining cause-and-effect relationships and potential outcomes. Conflict resolution options sometimes may be more clearly perceived with outside help.

3. **Assisting victim(s) in dealing with their own emotional feelings and responses.** Handling crisis-related feelings is a two-pronged problem. First of all, such feelings are apt to be more than typically intense and highly focused in terms of their relevance to personal well-being and safety. Most of us have relatively little experience handling emotions of this type and intensity, so we do not tend to be as proficient in doing so. Secondly, due to inefficient information processing and self-monitoring, our own intense emotions begin to feed on themselves in such highly charged

situations. As intensity grows, accuracy, efficiency, and relevance to reality decline.

Most of us suffer from this crisis-related emotional quality deterioration only briefly and recover our normal adaptive level rather quickly as stress declines. But, the presence of a helping hand in the sorting out of reality and a few moments of "emotional time-out" when we don't have to carry the entire emotional load of the situation alone can be very helpful. Many crisis-line workers have had the experience of listening to a high suicide risk decline to a manageable level during the course of a conversation when merely the presence of the less emotional yet empathetic voice has greatly helped the near victim regain control.

The degree to which a particular school will choose to become involved in broadly based crisis management in addition to crisis intervention will depend upon individual appraisal of mission, resources, and needs. But whatever the decision, there is little doubt that school structure, activities, and environment each lend themselves to effective secondary prevention.

CRISIS INTERVENTION WITHIN THE SCHOOL MILIEU

When actually faced with a crisis, we usually do not have the luxury of being able to decide whether or not we are in a situation conducive to intervention. The decision essentially becomes a moral and pragmatic one. Should we become involved and how might we help? Being in a situation that facilitates effective intervention is an advantage that makes the task easier and the decision-connected ambivalence less strong. Fortunately, the school milieu does offer some inherent situational advantages for secondary prevention. Effective intervention simply takes advantage of these already present opportunities.

Teaching Strategies and Crisis Intervention

As noted previously, crisis intervention requires some of the same skills as effective teaching: knowledge of subject matter, knowledge of students, and knowledge of the learning process in some detail, including particularly the effect of anxiety upon individual performance levels.

Much of the student's school room experience consists of learning how to apply information and concepts to practical problems. It embodies the principle that learning is a continual process, always acquiring new information, new ideas. Teachers typically are well-experienced in presenting material in this light. Crisis resolution involves much the same kind of tasks. "(Crisis resolution consists of) . . . working through the crisis event so that it becomes integrated into the fabric of life, leaving the person open instead of closed to the future" (Slaikeu, 1984). Viney (1976) has defined the major tasks of crisis resolution. Among those listed are achieving a cognitive mastery of the situation and learning to make appropriate use of external resources. Again the school can help in both respects.

Patience, sensitivity to individual differences and how these affect one's ability to assimilate new information and solve new problems, practice in translating generic information into personally relevant examples — these are attributes of effective teaching and effective teachers. It is reasonable to assume that educators are far better prepared to learn and apply crisis-intervention tasks than a cross section of the general population. This inherent preparation is too valuable an asset to ignore.

Unique Opportunities for Crisis Intervention

It is generally agreed that the effectiveness of crisis intervention increases directly as a function of its proximity in both time and place to the event (McGee, 1976). Schools frequently experience a unique opportunity for suicide crisis intervention, since their population is so deeply involved with the problem. Statistics easily support the testimony of school personnel that the impact of youth suicide is impinging upon our schools, students and staff, at increasing rates. Within the last year, we have had an urban secondary school principal say, "I have become resolved that suicide is something that we will have to face in our school sooner or later. I fully believe the only questions are when it will happen and will we be ready to help our students." The tendency of young people to generalize their problems and feelings causes the school to become involved with family, vocational, personal and health problems of the individual adolescent almost as a matter of course. The school has a unique opportunity to intervene in youth suicide, simply because it is often in the school environment or in connection with school activities that the problem precipitates. The school often is largely innocent of creating the crisis but is given no choice about dealing with it when it occurs on the school grounds.

There are other reasons to argue for the school having more than its share of unique opportunities. Nelson and Slaikeu (1984) have pointed out that the regular and lengthy contact that a school has with young people puts personnel in a strong position to note and evaluate changes in attitudes and behavior, which may be significant in identifying the presence and reducing the effects of a personal crisis. They also note that the goal of facilitating and expediting normal and healthy growth and development upon which most of the school's activities are based is explicitly compatible with the goals of crisis intervention. Crisis-intervention training for school personnel typically focuses on specific information and techniques: philosophical intents and outcome goals are usually already present, intricately enmeshed with the regular ongoing educational activities of the institution.

As already noted, a significant role in crisis intervention is the obtaining of important information. Data is needed about what is going on, what tasks are facing the crisis victim(s), and what personal resources are available upon which to build or strengthen coping behaviors. A variety of potentially important environmental variables should be examined, weighed and considered for use in ongoing crisis resolution (see Table 4-3). The school is in a strong position to help with this, partly because of its familiarity with the task and partly because so much of the data is more easily accessible in the school situation than elsewhere.

TABLE 4-3

IMPORTANT ENVIRONMENTAL VARIABLES TO IDENTIFY

1. Those things which may be immediate precipitators of suicidal-level stress
2. Those things which help sustain or prevent alleviation of suicidal-level stress once developed
3. Those things which provide support and help the stressful individual tolerate the stress and anxiety of the moment
4. Those things which alleviate, reduce, or eliminate stress
5. Those things which prevent stress or reverse or negate the development of dangerous stress

Finally, an important part of crisis intervention is comprised of network activation. Parents of troubled youth and other community resources must be quickly and appropriately involved. The school often has more effective ties with parents and community resource agencies and individuals than any other community institution.

Matching Capabilities to Needs

When a crisis arises, it is not a simple case of everyone going their individual ways as usual. Neither the incident nor people's strong emotional response to it can be ignored.

We have dealt with situations where the high school students' favorite teacher was a suicide in the midst of the school year, where a student-body president was saved from a suicidal death by only the most fortunate of accidental interventions, where a substantial portion of a college dormitory literally witnessed the on-campus suicide of a classmate, where a staff member has left the schoolroom desk for lunch and never returned, a suicide. We have tried to find a way to explain to elementary school pupils why one of their classmates would choose to die by his own hand through hanging.

Something more than a casual response is required. Because the presence of a crisis status in itself suggests the pressure of intensity and the need for immediate action, it is important that whatever responses are made do contribute to crisis reduction as a minimum and optimally to crisis resolution, as well.

A variety of response stances are available to the school. Almost any of these will be helpful toward meeting these goals, though each may offer different types and levels of intervention. It is important that school personnel take the time to consider their own school's particular needs and response capabilities as part of the advance planning and preparation for crisis intervention. These considerations should be broadly based across the school and community population, because whole-hearted endorsement and involvement is as important to success as are specific skills or techniques.

Essentially, such considerations consist of noting the needs that arise in the various sub-tasks of crisis intervention and ascertaining which of these will be accepted as part of the school's responsibility. Subsequent networking decisions depend heavily upon such definition, since none of the critical tasks can safely be ignored. Someone must take responsibility for each task. If the school excludes itself from a categorical responsibility or capability, then care must be taken to establish contact with persons or agencies who can and will meet such needs.

What is the range of such tasks? Here are some of the major important functions in crisis intervention. Consideration of these and perhaps
others as well can be a starting point for establishing roles and responsibilities.

1. The need to respond promptly with immediate psychological first
   aid at the presentation of an acute suicidal crisis (Moursand,
   1985).
2. Recognition and evaluation of incrementing levels of risk suggesting an impending crisis.
3. Providing personal, empathetic support of a temporary nature.
4. Determining what has been done, what can be done now, and
   what alternatives exist for new behavior or redefinition of the
   problem (Slaikeu, 1984).
5. Providing data for and collecting or maintaining a data base. This
   includes data about overt behaviors, emotional patterns, health re-
   cords, interpersonal behavior, cognitive development, aptitude
   and accomplishment or performance efforts and activities (see
   Slaikeu, 1984, for a thorough discussion of how these separate bits
   of data may be compiled into a meaningful personality profile for
   use in crisis work).
6. Establishing and maintaining formal or informal networks of support groups.
7. Identifying ineffective and/or helping build more effective coping
   skills (see Table 4-4 for a summarization of effective coping behaviors that may be of concern to the school).
8. Development and training of a core of trained personnel on-call for
   crisis-intervention assignments (within or perhaps even extending
   outside the school).
9. Establishing and coordinating the application of a networking system throughout the community.

The list is not meant to be exhaustive, but these are some of the areas
where the school may wish to make a contribution. They are certainly
areas of major concern in crisis intervention and ones that should not be
overlooked when developing a unified plan for thorough crisis intervention. Each of these is a service function worth developing in some detail.
To enlarge upon every one of them goes beyond the province of this
book. However, Chapter Seven provides some guidance to materials
and sources for ideas and assistance to assist school personnel in making
and implementing all of these need-capability decisions. The authors

TABLE 4-4

CHARACTERISTICS OF EFFECTIVE COPING

---

1. Actively exploring reality issues and searching for information
2. Freely expressing positive and negative feelings and tolerating frustration
3. Actively invoking help from others
4. Reducing complex problems to manageable bits and then working the smaller problems through one at a time
5. Being aware of fatigue and tendencies toward disorganization
6. Pacing one's self and maintaining control wherever possible
7. Successfully managing feelings by being self-accepting, flexible if necessary, and working on mastery
8. Self-trust and a positive self-concept
9. Applying a general optimism about eventual outcomes

Adapted from Caplan (1964).

have assumed, however, that there is one area of suicide crisis intervention in which every school should be involved and for which every school must prepare. This is the area mentioned first in the previous list: **psychological first aid.**

PSYCHOLOGICAL FIRST AID IN THE SCHOOL ENVIRONMENT

The rationale for applying **psychological first aid** is more than the invoking of a temporary "bandage" intervention. Being at high-risk because of an unfortuitous combination of high stress and lowered coping capabilities does not mean that the individual involved is devoid of resources. Total "psychological life support" is warranted far less often than the inexperienced intervener might suspect. Often, a modicum of support, promptly and wisely applied, will suffice to either reduce the crisis to manageable dimensions or serve to bolster the person past the point of potential disaster. It is a myth that "once suicidal, always suicidal." Deficiency in the skills or actions needed for coping with extreme stress are in many cases temporary, and once the crisis is past, normal or near-normal coping levels may become rather rapidly restored. As Shneidman (1985) has so accurately stated, "The main clinical rule is: Reduce the level of suffering, often just a little bit, and the individual will choose to live."

Even in those cases with deeper and longer-lasting problems, immediate intervention activities may serve very well to relieve enough pressure as to allow the individual, even though they are not yet free of problems, to proceed more effectively on a problem-solving course. As Caplan (1964) reminds us, crises represent a breakdown of what were probably formerly functional coping behaviors, rendered, in many cases, only temporarily inadequate. Restoration of personal coping capabilities is the objective of psychological first aid.

The concept of **psychological first aid,** as part of an overall model for effecting crisis intervention, has probably been best presented by Slaikeu and his colleagues (Slaikeu, 1977, 1979, 1983, 1984; Slaikeu, Lester, & Tulkin, 1973; Slaikeu & Willis, 1978). The reader is referred to these works for thorough presentations of the model, particularly to *Crisis Intervention: A Handbook for Practice and Research* (Slaikeu, 1984). An introductory outline, patterned after but not exactly the same as Slaikeu's, is presented here to help in the initial conceptualization and planning of intervention programs in the schools.

The major premise of the Slaikeu model is that there are two discriminable levels of crisis intervention. The first of these is that psychological first aid is an initial series of actions designed to adapt broader problem-solving approaches (e.g. Lester & Brockopp, 1973) to the pressing demands of a crisis situation. The second level is involved with longer-termed "crisis therapy" designed to resolve crisis problems, more or less permanently lower risk levels, and establish what really become primary-prevention behavioral and emotional habits. The two levels are sometimes referred to as "first-order" and "second-order" intervention.

First-order intervention adapts to suicide crises very well. As noted by Shneidman in the quote cited above, temporary intervention is often very useful in lowering suicidal risk (sometimes even with long-lasting effects) by helping the individual restore adequate levels of coping behaviors.

Principles of Psychological First Aid

The major objective of this intervention strategy is to reestablish immediate coping in the victim(s). The triad of tactics employed to accomplish this objective involve:

1. Providing support so that the burden is not borne alone
2. Reducing the lethality of the situation to save a life

3. Providing contact or "linkage" between the victim and resources outside the victim(s).

Slaikeu (1984) has defined five basic steps that are involved in the application of these tactics. Each of these may be readily applied in school environments by typical school personnel with a very reasonable expectation of success.

Step One: Making Psychological Contact

The intent here is to open up and help maintain a two-way communication flow. This facilitates understanding; provides emotional, even physical support; and creates an empathetic "therapeutic atmosphere of acceptance" (Johnson, 1985) which encourages and aids reestablishment of personal problem-solving and coping behaviors.

The intervener's activities include invitations to the victim to share feelings and perceptions, careful listening, and a Rogerian-like (Rogers, 1951) reflection of acceptance and empathetic understanding. Essentially, the intervener is reestablishing one-to-one contact between the victim and a supportive, interested, and involved outside world. This is an immediate positive and encouraging answer to any self-perceived perceptions of isolation, alienation, or feelings of being alone. It says, "There are those who not only **can** help but who **will** help."

TABLE 4-5

GUIDELINES FOR INVOLVED PARENTS

---

1. Be patient with stressed-out youth. Their behaviors may be especially aggressive or immature during these times.
2. Take all threats and gestures seriously. Even if the behavior is "attention-seeking," it is a "call for help" occurring in a critical manner.
3. Your major responsibility is fourfold:
    - Demonstrate your love
    - Demonstrate your acceptance
    - Demonstrate your tolerance
    - Find and solicit whatever outside help is needed.
4. Communicate: keep talking; share even if it is painful. Isolation at these times can be life-threatening.
5. Offer tangible assistance and direction with no strings attached. This is a time for helping, not for negotiating long-range trade-offs.

Parents and other individuals involved as significant others should be encouraged to display and demonstrate these same attitudes as much as the school personnel involved. Table 4-5 is a list of initial-crisis-contact tips for parents as used by the authors in working with school and parent prevention groups. These positive attributes are inherent in the suggestions listed there.

The inhibitions students may hold in regards to actively participating as interveners (or recipients of help) in a suicide-intervention program are at least in part alleviated with an understanding and awareness of how the intervention utilizes these non-threatening approaches. Peck et al. (1985) has listed some of the expressed student concerns noted in the highly successful San Mateo program. These included:

1. Dilemmas of conflicting loyalties: "Who can I safely tell without being disloyal to a friend?"
2. Concerns over privacy and "official" use of crisis-related information: "Will this be held against the student?"
3. Concerns over loss of independence: "Does this mean the student loses control over their own destiny?"
4. Concerns about the involvement of others: "How is this going to affect parents? Who will be told?"

Appropriately applied, this initial personal-contact approach carries with it an aura of open and honest acceptance which really helps relieve many of these important fears and concerns.

The attitudes and activities of the initial intervener at the moment of crisis carry further implications. They set the stage for longer-termed follow-up therapy in a way that greatly improves the probability of success for subsequent help-givers. The interactions used by crisis counselors in the second-order, or what is sometimes called second-process, crisis approach can be seen to be extensions of these same attitudes (see Table 4-6).

Step Two: Exploring the Dimensions of the Crisis

The assembling of data about a victim and his or her environment during acute crisis intervention should be limited to searching only for that information immediately relevant to achieving the goals of psychological first aid. Briefly reiterated, these goals are to help share the

TABLE 4-6

SECOND PROCESS COUNSELING WORK IN CRISES

1. Counselor is a concerned helper.
2. Victim is encouraged to express and discuss feelings.
3. Counselor empathizes with expressed feelings.
4. Counselor gains information about the crisis situation.
5. Counselor works with victim to formulate a defining statement about the crisis problem.
6. Counselor and victim together work out and agree upon the strategies to be used in crisis resolvement and prevention of re-occurrence.
7. Implementation and evaluative review of stress factors involved are jointly undertaken by counselor and victim.
8. Victim crisis emancipation and decision independence gradually is phased in.

Adapted from Rusk (1971).

burden, reduce lethality, and establish linkage with outside support. Slaikeu (1984) suggests focusing on but three time frames, the "immediate past, present, and immediate future." Baldwin (1979) has also stressed the importance of defining some of these critical issues in the initial phases of working through a crisis.

Translated into queries, these areas are concerned with identifying precipitating events, obtaining information about the nature and extent of the now-present crisis situation along with the current availability of personal resources, and the need to know what the near future holds in terms of further crisis and/or need for more extensive help in the development of better coping resources. The nature and range of these queries will vary with the type of crisis involved. More incipiently developed developmental crises may present a different pattern of data for all three time periods than a more unexpected situational crisis that comes suddenly, unexpectedly, and often with greater surprise to significant others.

If the interveners are well-prepared, the investigative or inquiring aspect of intervention is more easily accomplished; well-prepared help-givers are apt to be better apprised of typical (and at times even the highly individualistic) problem areas for youth in their school, quickly available resources for additional observational information, and the scope and availability of immediate- and longer-range crisis assistance available in the community.

The search for exploring the dimensions of a crisis should not involve a disproportionate amount of either energy or time. Psychological first aid involves a relatively short period of elapsed time, and the emphasis is on forming a temporary defense against the assault of extreme stress in order to carry the victim through until broader-based reinforcements are involved. In the ideal situation, crisis workers quickly learn what information is vital, what information is helpful but not critical, and what data is relevant but not immediately helpful. A hierarchy of inquiry behaviors is quickly established, with time not being wasted on obtaining that which is neither critical or helpful.

Even in the abstract and intangible area of emotional feelings, it is helpful to the help-giver to be sensitive to the types of information about affect that are actually significant, not merely interesting. Unfortunately, little definitive research has been done in this area, but current investigations are beginning to present some very helpful information.

Leenaars and Balance (1986), have attempted to differentiate between "genuine" suicidal involvements and "psuedo-suicidal" or "para-suicidal" actions which resemble suicide behaviors but probably have different motivational bases and certainly different relevance for crisis intervention. Their research has indicated that "genuine" suicide notes are characterized by some distinctive themes or content (see Table 4-7). Their research may eventually give us more insight into the "suicidal" personality type or types.

TABLE 4-7

SIGNIFICANT STATEMENTS IN GENUINE SUICIDE NOTES

1. Feelings and attitudes of ambivalence
2. Crucial role of including active withdrawal of support of significant others
3. Evidence of ill health
4. Feelings of hopelessness, confusion, pessimism about being able to have good interpersonal relationships
5. Constricted logic
6. Very strong emotions
7. Reporting of some calamitous prior relationship
8. A sense of rejection

From Leenaars and Balance (1986).

Step Three: Exploring Options
for Action

When problems are present, solutions are needed. Solutions, in this context, are used in the very short-term, immediate present sense. It does not mean the same as it would in crisis therapy or the long-term establishment of effective coping mechanisms or the undertaking of environmental manipulation or change.

Sheehy (1976) has outlined some changes in one's covert perceptions that evolve as a result of significant "marker" events. Included are perceptions about one's inner self in relationship to others, the balance between feelings of security and danger, a sensitivity to the passing of time and the temporal importance of events and feelings, and an inner sense of vitality versus a type of apathy or lethargy or stagnation.

Workers must decide whether to take a facilitative stance, complementing the victim's coping efforts but leaving primary responsibility up to the victim, or a directive stance, where responsibility is shared by the victim, the crisis intervener, and sometimes other help-givers, as well. An indication of the proportion of responsibility which can be assumed by the victim as compared to that temporarily assumed by outside resources should be garnered from the information gathered in Step Two. Sheehy does emphasize that when crisis-coping or crisis-recovery responsibility is to be assumed by the victim, given the potentiality for dangerous consequences in the event of failure, it is very important to deal with the present, the "NOW" rather than the "BEFORE" or the "AFTER" behaviors or expectations. Again, the three objectives of psychological first aid provide the outline for decision making.

In electing options for action, the second objective, saving a life through reduction of lethality, is of prime concern. Both the other two areas of activity, i.e. support and resource linkage, are subjugated to and dependent upon this prime lifesaving emphasis.

Moursand (1985) has noted a whole range of action options available when facing a suicide crisis. Included are:

1. Hospitalization — which may be either forced or unforced
2. Referral for psychiatric treatment
3. Referral for psychiatric evaluation
4. Activation of support systems — including primary person-to-person support, secondary group and situational support, formally organized support measures, and informally organized or operating support contacts

5. Opportunity for stress reduction through catharsis and close personal empathy contacts
6. Deliberate stress-bridging "contracts"

School counselors can often be especially helpful in this aspect of psychological first aid because their training and preparation (as well as role definition in some school organizations) enables them to be involved in two separate but critical ways. They bring specific technical skills to the crisis situation. These skills often facilitate the evaluation of lethality, exploration of the victim's available resources, and expedite linkage with appropriate outside resources. In addition, counselors have usually had special training and experience in demonstrating empathy, genuineness, warmth and similar interpersonal attributes which are sorely needed by stress-troubled individuals (Fowler & McGee, 1973).

Step Four: Assisting in Taking Concrete Action

Some aspects of making action decisions in a crisis present unusual demands on the help-giver. It is well to help those readying to play this role to prepare for them. Among these aspects are:

1. **Dealing with the special ethical problems of life-threatening crises.** The traditional definitions of client confidentiality changes under life threat, and different criteria must be heeded for moral, pragmatic, and legal reasons. As Moursand (1985) indicates, for example, the mobilizing of support systems may break the confidentiality of the individual. Consequently, care should be taken about making the typical and traditional promises of confidentiality when counseling a suicidal individual, and one should be prepared to make difficult decisions regarding the sharing of personal information which would be kept confidential under other circumstances.

2. **One must be prepared for unusual time demands when the maintaining of personal and ongoing contact is critical.** It is not unusual for telephone crisis workers to find themselves involved in a telephone call of several hours' duration when it is apparent that the personal contact is the major lifesaving support of the moment.

3. **Those who would give psychological first aid must know how to make contact for and carry through on psychiatric and medical referrals.** This involves such practical knowledge as knowing where to find telephone numbers, with whom to speak at broadly

functioning agencies such as a hospital, how to obtain quick and functional emergency response from police and paramedics, how to smoothly transfer responsibility to a professional crisis-work agency. And, as a very important aspect of this function, the crisis worker must know how to encourage the suicidal individual to comply with suggestions for seeking outside help. Sometimes, this involves such personal involvement as going hand-in-hand with the high-risk individual to a help-giving facility.

4. **Personal "contracting" is sometimes required.** To establish this bulwark against yielding to stress, the worker must know how to accomplish a "contract not to be self-destructive"; when to do so and when not to attempt it; how to formulate a contract; and how to transfer responsibility for the "healthy" signee's role to others. Suicide crisis centers can provide examples of "contracts" and give help in understanding and accomplishing the decisions and other responsibilities involved. Most crisis-work texts give examples, as well (see Table 4-8).

TABLE 4-8

A SAMPLE SUICIDE PREVENTION CONTRACT

I, _____ , agree not to kill myself, attempt to kill myself, or cause any harm to myself during the period from _____ to _____ , the time of my next appointment.

I agree to get enough sleep and to eat well until that time.

I agree to get rid of things I could obviously use to kill myself such as guns, weapons of other kinds, poisons, potentially harmful medicines, My life is worth more than any material possession.

I agree that if I am having a bad time of it and I feel that I might be tempted to break any of these promises, I will call my counselor _____ at _____ or will immediately call the Suicide Crisis Center at # _____ .

I agree that these conditions are important, worth doing, and are a contract I am willing to make with my counselor. It is my firm intention as a point of honor to keep this contract.

Signed: _____ Date: _____

Witnessed by counselor: _____

Adapted from Getz et al. (1983).

5. **Finally, crisis workers need to be prepared for the heavy personal emotional cost that such work carries.** This important contribution to others carries tremendous rewards. It is awesomely satisfying to know that you have been at least partially responsible for saving another's life. It is at least equally demoralizing to have tried and failed. There is a special sadness and frustration at having been unsuccessfully involved in a suicidal crisis situation. This sadness goes beyond even the terrible impact that suicide has on everyone intimately involved. Working in this area heightens one's own sensitivity to a conceptual and emotional involvement with highly charged topics — death, immortality, suicide, family loss, frustrated hopes. No one can remain an "island" apart from the rest of humanity and work in this area. The help-giver should be prepared to meet both success and failure and to recognize his or her own need for help when the stress of giving becomes too high.

There is an inherent time crunch to crisis work which affects both victim and helper. Moursand (1985) noted four distinct phases:

1. Rise of tension level due to external causes
2. Increasing tension which is accompanied by an equally increasing sense of ineffectiveness
3. Pressure to find solutions in a hurry even if extraordinary solutions are invoked
4. And, if tension continues to rise, eventual feelings of disorganization in coping behaviors, a sense of hopelessness, and an emotional response of frustration and hopelessness.

This increasing pressure, as experienced by the crisis worker, is often the most immediate precipitator of coping problems for those workers.

Most workers feel that being in a position to work with the action-options which may maintain life and bring hope to a desperately frightened and discouraged individual brings rewards far outweighing the costs. Nevertheless, there is cost involved, and workers need a good dose of primary prevention themselves in order to be adequately prepared to pay this cost.

Step Five: Linking with Network Resources

When professional crisis workers are involved in psychological first aid, the final step of the process, according to Slaikeu's (1984) model, is to set up and implement a following-up process that monitors progress, effectiveness of treatment plans, and the involvement of various enlisted resources.

To the degree that school personnel may be involved at the same level of commitment and sophistication, Slaikeu's fifth step is most appropriate. For those in the school whose interaction with a suicidal crisis is likely to be less focused and professionally oriented, we have substituted this final step, instead. This is not to suggest that school personnel should simply refer a troubled student to other sources and then forget about the youth. On the contrary, we have stressed the importance of the school offering and maintaining a longitudinal support and assistance program for high-risk students. However, most of us involved in crisis-response teams in the schools will find that the action which marks the final phase of psychological first aid is that of linking up with resources and programs that assure a continued successful interaction with the youth. This is accompanied by a sometimes subtle but nevertheless definite shift in type, nature, and extent of primary responsibility from the school to other agencies. These outside help sources may or may not subsequently formally interact with the school in a treatment plan.

Primary prevention preparation is, of course, a major asset in facilitating this final step. In the face of a high-risk situation it is extremely stressful, and often unnecessarily time consuming, to have to make initial explorations and first-time contacts when faced with an actual crisis.

Assuming a network organization plan is in operation, several tasks face the purveyor of psychological first aid.

1. Decisions on the type, amount, and immediacy of outside support needed. Levels of crisis intervention vary as Jacobsen et al. (1968) have indicated. These range from plain environmental manipulation which may or may not involve networking per se; to general supportive behavior including cathartic listening; to generic approaches which include special short-term work by those trained to handle special crisis-related problems, e.g. parental training classes; to referrals for individually planned crisis intervention and treatment plans typically carried out by those with extensive training.

2. Even in those aspects of crisis resolution carried out under the auspices of the school, some thought about timing and type of referral is necessary. Matter and Matter (1984) have suggested that counselors may wish to invoke specifically targeted instances of primary

prevention for those youth whose status seems to indicate the potentiality for developing high risk or whose past bouts with stress have involved such critical levels, already. The schools may be involved in this type of work, since it may be concerned with topics compatible to the school environment as communication skills, problem-solving skills, vocational choice, and parenting skills.

3. When possible high lethality is encountered, the school is involved by necessity, if even for only a relatively short interim period between crisis recognition and the establishment of resource linkage. Shneidman (1985) has outlined that the management of the highly lethal patient involves monitoring, consultation, some especially sensitive attention to transference, and the involvement of significant others.

4. There are also very pragmatic operational concerns. These include record-keeping and permission clearances congruent with the organizational precedent and legal definitions of the school community and state. Temporary coverage for the normal responsibilities of the help-giver must be arranged. Adequate and appropriate feedback information to other staff, and often to fellow students as well, must be considered and arranged as decided upon. Parental involvement must be arranged ranging from the need for immediate notification to laying the foundation for productive ongoing relationships with the school staff and other students.

Small as these individual details seem, managing them is part of the role definition of the intervener and an important aspect of the resource linkage procedure.

MAKING THE TRANSITION FROM INTERVENTION TO REHABILITATION

Certainly, once the immediate crisis is ended, linkage is established and the myriad of follow-up details are in hand, there is need for more than a deep sigh of relief and a simple moment of reflection.

The post-crisis effects of a suicidal experience are like the rippling of waves from a stone tossed on a quiet pond. They spread across long distances, encountering and affecting many people, some of whom may be far removed from any obvious relationship with the event. These effects have subtle but definite effects upon the business of everyday living and learning. Any school system that has expended the time and energy to become involved in primary prevention, and then crisis intervention, must surely be ready to accept the responsibility for being actively involved in rehabilitative and recuperative activities, post-vention, follow-up, the activities commonly involved in what is called **tertiary prevention.**

An immediate need is for providing some ongoing support to those of the staff who have recently expended great emotional energy by being involved in crisis intervention. These people have every right to expect the school to respond to their acceptance of this important duty with an equally committed responsibility for giving them time and means to return their lives and emotional status back to a reasonable level of normality. Some of the workshop outlines and resource materials in Chapter Seven deal specifically with these topics.

Two other segments of the school population will present needs to which the school should respond. These are those who have been left behind by a successfully completed suicide. In those cases where crisis intervention has been successful for one reason or another, there will be those who are in the process of recovering from a suicidal high-risk state and who are in the process of putting their lives together again.

The following chapters will provide guidance for the school in helping those who present special needs.

CHAPTER FIVE

WORKING WITH THE STUDENT WHO HAS ATTEMPTED SUICIDE

"Although the world is full of suffering, it is also full of the overcoming of it."

Helen Keller

FOR MANY PEOPLE, working with an individual who has attempted suicide is almost equally as frightening as facing the threat of an impending suicide, itself. Most of us encounter strong feelings of ambivalence in this and similar situations. The ambivalence is typically comprised of being unable to ignore the impact of the situation and the moral compulsion to be of service and a desire to help, which conflicts with feelings of personal insecurity, lack of relevant social competencies and having inadequate helping skills. The feeling is similar to meeting with the family of a departed friend soon after their loss. We want to be of help, but it is not a situation eagerly sought or easily adjusted to in most instances.

Retreat, flight, and even denial are common responses to such ambivalence and are often encountered in post-suicide-attempt situations. Because there is this strong ambivalence and strong emotional motivation to avoid a particularly demanding situation, schools need to categorically plan this part of their suicide-intervention program with some special attention to both individual and organizational concerns.

MAJOR CONCERNS

For most situations, such concerns can be summarized under four general headings:

167

1. Concern over the role: "What should be done and said?"
2. Concern over maintaining regular, normal school functions: "How do we handle this special problem without disrupting our essential educational mission?"
3. Concern over people's reactions: "How is this going to affect other students, teachers, staff? How is the individual who tried to kill themself going to react?"
4. Concern over possible repetition of the experience: "Will this person 'do it' again?"

Each of these concerns needs to be addressed. Fortunately, there are some helpful answers and some useful guidelines to follow.

What Should Be Done and Said?

The responsibility to "do something," to be involved, is one that cannot be easily avoided by the school if any semblance of moral integrity is to be maintained. School personnel will be perceived as sources of potential help whether or not such a stance is deliberately assumed. Teaching staff, for example, are frequently sought out as confidants by troubled students and play an important role in such therapeutic relationships (McKenry, Tishler, & Christman, 1980). The role of confidant is one assumed by those seeking such support and is not necessarily dependent upon teachers or staff seeking such interactions.

Strengths and Assets the School Has to Offer

The school environment itself offers strong support and some special recuperative assets for the recovering victim of suicidal behavior. As Husain and Vandiver (1984) have noted, there are at least two major functions of this type for the school and each of these provides very important assistance at a critical recovery time. The school, perhaps more than almost any social institution, is in the position to offer relief from social isolation due to a lack of effective interpersonal relationships. Since the school environment in general is one of learning and acquisition of new skills, the relief offered can be more than a temporary respite. It can also initiate and help the individual acquire and perfect new socialization behaviors which become prophylactic as well as recuperative.

The school and its staff can also serve as an understanding and concerned "bridge" with more deeply involved professional help. By lending an aura of acceptance and encouragement for the individual who is seeking out and obtaining professional help, the very process of working on problems is given social approval and credence, each of which is especially important to the young person who is especially sensitive to any exposed position that makes him or her seem "different."

The school has the capability to offer a broad variety of resources to the individual who is in the process of rebuilding a productive life. These include:

1. Manipulation of the environment so as to modify stress factors the individual may face
2. A predictable daily routine and schedule which in itself tends to "normalize" the process of living
3. Both broadly based and highly personalized social support systems
4. Varying pace in daily activities and demands matched to the individual's needs and capabilities
5. Emotional reassurance through association with others who display reassuring and positive attitudes, emotions, and concepts
6. Decision-making experiences that can be structured in a win-win format
7. Learning experiences about new options and skills relevant to positive mental health and effective decision making
8. Opportunities for safely practicing skills not yet fully acquired

The list could be expanded further, but it is obvious even from this brief survey of the positive contributions a school can make that the school has rich resources which may be rather easily and naturally applied to the process of becoming well and whole again.

Interfacing with Outside Treatment Plans

It is necessary to recognize that important to successful recovery as the school's position is, the school does not and should operate in the guise of a major purveyor of psychotherapy. The school's position is one of complementing professional treatment plans, ancillary support and facilitator of positive growth processes. It is not a treatment center and its personnel are not therapists.

Two major objectives should be foremost in planning and implementing the school's contribution to recovery: First, the school should very carefully avoid conflicting or competing with professional treatment plans. Second, the school should make every effort to provide an environment and experiences that by their inherent nature actively support and facilitate any professionally generated treatment plan as well as the individual's own private attempts at re-growth.

Avoiding Interference. Psychotherapy and resulting treatment plans can become very involved. There may be some instances where the individual's treatment plan will be formally shared with the school by the individual or agency directing treatment. In such cases, successful interaction is more easily initiated, since guidelines for the school's role will likely be included. In most instances, however, treatment plans, at least in detail, will not be formally or extensively shared with school personnel. Any specific information obtained by the school is likely to be in more broad and general terms and to emanate from the individual (or his or her family) being treated. The information may or may not be specifically useful in planning the school's role.

In terms of general planning and preparation, it is likely to be more helpful for the school to think in terms of creating an environment and providing experiences generally in harmony with broad goals typical of most types and levels of psychotherapy for high-risk suicidal individuals. This relieves the school of having to be too concerned with the more specific aspects of an individual's psychotherapy, unless specifically detailed by and requested of the school by those managing the professional treatment.

Typical Psychotherapeutic Goals and Objectives. Treatment plans and goals for psychotherapy for suicidal individuals can be complex. Shneidman (1985), for example, lists ten examples of practical treatment objectives that might be reasonably applied to suicidal individuals. He includes treatment designed to:

1. Help reduce the pain and suffering involved
2. Fill frustrated needs
3. Find viable solutions to existing problems
4. Provide relief from stress
5. Provide positive emotional support
6. Correct attitudes
7. Increase positive behavioral options
8. Increment interpersonal support
9. Decrement lethal suicide behaviors
10. Invoke pre-crisis positive coping patterns.

Given such a variety of therapeutic goal options, it would be difficult indeed for the average school system to gear up to assist with every goal or possible combination of goals. Instead, it is far easier to become familiar with broader and more generic counseling or psychotherapeutic goals for suicide attempters and to establish a daily experienced environment consonant with and supportive of these. Very rarely, if ever, will these conflict with individualized treatment plans. The finer nuances of individually planned treatment objectives in most instances represent special refinements and emphases of the broader goals. The school's general preparation will be distinctly helpful and supportive of these and can be carried on without fear of interfering with other plans or processes.

Toolan (1978) suggests that therapeutic involvement should extend beyond the professional therapist as a matter of course. The positively contributing roles the family can play is emphasized, for example, including a sense of caring about the troubled individual and an implicit endorsement of a link with a more satisfying future. The school can function in much the same way.

It should be remembered that therapy and recuperation efforts are directed at long-term habits, sets, behavioral patterns and negative causes, as well as at the immediate problem of the moment. Since the school is routinely involved in helping people to acquire the skills of effective living in a variety of ways, the process of being an actively contributing backup to psychotherapy presents no special problems.

Moursand (1985) indicates that there are many instances where the subject's own emotional habits as evidenced in anxiety, anger, guilt, self-esteem problems, or feelings of helplessness require the therapist to at least temporarily provide some sort of surrogate or backup decision-making and support group. Since it is important that the subject eventually be a functioning part of such a surrogate group in order to facilitate eventual autonomy and functional independence, it is helpful if the transition from total support to shared functioning to individual independence can be easily and rather naturally accomplished. Since this progressive approximation of individual risk-taking and independence fits the everyday procedure of the typical school, the school is often elected to formally or informally play this important role.

The goals of formal, professional therapy with an individual who is suicidal are many and varied as a number of authors have outlined (see Table 5-1).

TABLE 5-1

POSSIBLE THERAPEUTIC GOALS FOR THE POST-SUICIDAL YOUTH

1. Providing a safe environment for dealing with unbearable feelings
2. Fostering of autonomous feelings of self-mastery
3. Rejecting misplaced feelings of self-attribution and guilt
4. Identification of cognitive and emotional patterns which produce or maintain stress rather than alleviate it
5. Coming to grips with the ambivalence about dying and the recognition of reasons for living giving rise to this ambivalence
6. Successfully managing feelings or subjective components of cognitive problem-solving habits
7. Rebuilding a sense of hope and open options
8. Improving self-image
9. Finding and maintaining satisfying social resources
10. Building a satisfying yet realistic life plan
11. Recognizing reality and learning to deal with frustrations and unmeetable demands
12. Acquiring skills to resolve genuine situational problems
13. Learning to adequately express feelings
14. Developing impulse control, patience, and faith in one's own ability to seek out a meaningful compromise when in conflict situations
15. Learning to recognize hazardous or difficult situations

From Gill (1982), Hoff (1984), Lazarus (1980), and Otto (1972).

In a concise summary statement, Shneidman (1979) has reminded us that the therapist in actuality seeks to replace one set of negative, nonproductive feelings with another set that are productive, useful and rewarding. Feelings of helplessness, aloneness and emptiness are replaced by a sense of mastery, social relatedness, and inner security if therapy is successful. The school is in a position to make significant contributions toward these ends.

Maintaining Normal School Functions

All this is not to suggest that the frequent goodness of fit of therapy with normal school functions indicates that working with post-attempters is "business as usual." Certainly, this is not the case, and were school personnel to assume this stance it might well precipitate more problems. The troubled individual could easily interpret such nonchalance as meaning, "They don't care," or "I'm weak and undeserving, not really understood." Such an experience might well validate the danger-ous hapless-hopeless-helpless syndrome. But, neither is it necessary for a school to drastically revise and reshape its normal operating pattern to accomodate the positive roles and objectives outlined above.

A very real need of these individuals, who in the act of returning to school are taking a significant step toward lasting recovery, is for a stable, predictable and normal environment. Being aware of the need for a special kind of sensitivity and acceptance does not mean major alterations to the everyday flow of school activities and experiences. Neither does it mean shielding the recovering individual from the normal stresses and strains that every student regularly encounters. Experience with these stresses in a normal environment offers the best opportunity for successful coping of the same type as practiced by one's peers. Thus, the individual has the opportunity to reappraise his own ability to handle problems, "be like others," and to resume a non-distinguished pattern of day-to-day adjustment to whatever problems may come along.

The post-attempt recovery period is not a crisis situation. Both the victim and those who must intervene respond differently under the pressure of a crisis. Crisis situations are atypical, unusual situations calling for atypical and unusual responses. The recovery process should be quite the antithesis of a crisis. Best results are obtained in situations and environments that are reasonably routine in the every-day sense of the word and which carry both an implied and overt tone of normalcy.

It is far more important that those who work with recovering youthful attempters have a genuine interest in young people in general and are sensitive to the **normal** problems of **normal** youth than that they possess or apply some type of special knowledge or techniques about suicide. School personnel, perhaps more than any other readily available resource in the typical community, are in a po-sition to fill this prescription. A broadly based aura of understanding and sensitivity, coupled with ongoing accessibility and acceptance, will alleviate most concerns specific to the need to specially handle this student. The school that has already striven to develop an ongo-ing primary prevention program has already taken most of the posi-tive steps necessary to be able to meaningfully help the post-attempter. Some of the specific interactions and functions that may be helpful are outlined later in this chapter.

Is Recidivism a Risk?

Individual's who have seriously considered or possibly even attempted suicide do not carry some special distinguishing brand or observable mark. Suicide knows no definable cross section of the population as its special target. Estimates of the number of normal people (normal in the sense of not being psychotic or evidencing any particular psychiatric anomaly) who have considered suicide as an answer to their problems vary greatly but in each case usually run far higher than one might think. A very recent survey (Fritz, 1986) indicates that in a broad cross section of college students, ranging in age from 17 to over 50, the percentage who report having at least once seriously considered the option of suicide as a solution to their problems may run as high as 50 percent. Certainly, this group, representing a very wide spectrum of vocational interests and life-styles of all ages and both sexes, does not have any readily observable characteristics in common that would cause them to be labeled as "post-high-risk suicide."

The extreme nature and devastating results of suicidal behavior have added to the mystique, myths and general taboo characteristics with which society has endowed it. The fact of the matter is that for the very large majority of recovering suicidal individuals, especially including those who are youthful, the range of problems and general adjustment behaviors are far from atypical. In most cases, the failure to successfully handle stress is more a matter of quantitative differences than qualitative. Consequently, those recovering from a serious experience with this extreme form of coping behavior need not be considered as especially different from others who recover in much the same way from similar problems where their responses have been less serious and less extreme.

It is a clearly established myth that "Once a suicide risk, always a suicide risk!" Large numbers of people do recover from the experience and go on to live happy and productive lives. Given proper attention at the critical junctures of their problem experience, they may be even healthier after their bout with suicide than before. Having attempted suicide once does place an individual in a category of higher risk than the general population. But the number of single-instance suicidal ventures, particularly in non-psychotic youth, outweighs the number of repeaters.

These positive outlooks are stressed, not because there is no risk, but because the risk is far lower than uninformed people generally suppose and because the fear of another attempt often ranks high among the concerns of those who face the prospect of facing and interacting with the recovering suicide. Some individuals do indeed repeat their attempts to end their own life. There is, however, strong evidence that these cases of recidivism seldom occur under circumstances where all other indications are for a successful recovery. It will be helpful for school personnel to be cognizant of the facts of success and failure in treating youthful suicide and to be aware of and sensitive to the signs of both recovering health and deteriorating coping mechanisms.

Indicators of Successful/Unsuccessful Recovery

Suicide does not rise from a vacuum without cause or precipitating stressors. Suicide is an extreme attempt at adaptation in response to perceived stress and concomitant demands for coping. There is evidence (McIntire & Angle, 1980) that recidivism among adolescents is essentially related to the "failure to change his or her circumstances or the inability to respond to changes in the environment."

Obviously, the environmental context in which one lives is an important variable. As a student returns to the school environment, there are numerous readily observable indicators of whether or not the individual is making progress toward a healthy and stable life. If the school has been previously involved in the situation by virtue of primary and secondary prevention activities, it should already be aware of behavior patterns that existed prior to the attempt. By and large, if things are proceeding well, one should expect to see either changes in the student's adjustment problems or changes in the emotional and cognitive response to their demands. Changes in response modes are probably more typically observed than changes in problems. The problems that give rise to suicidal behavior in youth are often no different in nature than those that most youth experience and in many instances are, in themselves, largely unavoidable.

Willingness to tolerate frustration is a positive sign. Reasonable "risk taking" in challenging situations generally indicates a more positive level of self-esteem and less fear of or inability to tolerate failure. Where the troubled student may have acted out or withdrew to a lonely isolated existence, the recovering student should show less or decreasing amounts of such behavior.

The indicators of rising stress and coping inadequacies noted in previous chapters can be applied to post-attempt students in exactly the same way that they might be applied to the student body at large. One should not expect indicators of mental health, or lack of it, to be different for the recovering adolescent. The school which assumes a responsibility for regularly monitoring the mental health of its student body should expect to perform well in this specialized instance, too. There are certain situations or sets of circumstances that are well documented as being related to significantly increased stress and as a result are positively correlated with suicide risk, too. The presence of any of these in the life of a youth should present concern. The youth who has already experienced sufficient adjustment problems of the magnitude as to elicit suicidal behaviors may be considered to be especially vulnerable to these particular problems. The vulnerability comes not from being different in any discernible way but from the probability of having fewer emotional resources available at the moment and less of a history of positive coping from which to draw some inferred strength to meet the heavy challenges involved. Such special circumstances include:

1. Any involvement with substance abuse
2. Serious physical health problems
3 .Traumatic loss of a significant other
4. Dysfunctional family relationships

In our experience with volunteers manning telephone crisis lines and counselors doing primary screening interviews relevant to estimating the level of suicide crisis present, we have found it helpful to suggest learning a brief checklist. Users are directed to examine and evaluate several critical variables in the life of an individual whose progress in alleviating a crisis is in question. These are:

1. Is the individual's life situation at home, work, school, etc. the same now as it was when the crisis erupted?
2. Is the individual's general attitude and outlook on life the same or are there observable changes?
3. Is the individual involved with new or different solution options than were being attempted at the time that the crisis occurred?
4. Are there new support systems in place?
5. Is the person linked to professional help?

It may be difficult to precisely ascertain answers to the basic questions on the checklist, but it does provide a structure for covering a number of important variables and seems to offer increased confidence and security to those who use it. In general, of course, one is simply asking,

"Are things in this person's life the same or are they changing?" Unless the changes are negative and catastrophic, changes are usually considered as positive signs since they represent new horizons and options, acting as substitute responses for suicide which enables the person to choose to live instead of die.

How to Respond When a Repeated Crisis Looms

Despite everyone's best efforts, there are occasions when an attempter's recovery does not proceed well and renewed high-risk status occurs. Probably, the worst aspect of such a scenario is that everyone's worst fears are realized, and all the various concerns, anxieties, and fears are renewed with vigor. Those who have been intimately involved with the individual may find themselves facing a real test of their own self-confidence, experiencing all the insecurities and feelings of personal inadequacy which frequently accompany a grief situation.

In some instances, the relapse may come as a surprise. If such is the case, it is probably best for the school to consider that it is not reasonably rational to expect to correctly monitor everyone's emotional state. When the behavior repeats precipitously, coming as a surprise to all, it is more than likely true that a mistake was made in evaluating risk level at the time of re-entering the youth in the school situation. Guilt, the most common response (though often closely followed by anger), is an understandable but probably not genuinely deserved reaction by those impacted by the victim's relapse.

The fundamental principle we strive to place in the minds of school personnel with whom we work is that they are not "lifesavers" shouldering total responsibility for a troubled youth's life. Instead, the best (and the most effective role) the school can hope to reasonably play is to be alert "gatekeepers," striving to be ready to open the gate to more reasonable and viable options than suicide. The school is a source of support; it is not the major line of defense against suicide.

If the school has been well-prepared in the three preventative phases, it is more likely that the individual's developing problems will be noticed sooner or described more succinctly than in the youth's previously developing crisis. If such is the case, there are fairly well-defined steps to take and roles to play. By and large, they are identical with those outlined previously in the chapters dealing with identifying risk and intervening. Hafen and Peterson (1983) have outlined a ten-point plan of action to use with adolescents with apparent serious risk. It is good advice. We use it with some minor modifications (see Table 5-2).

TABLE 5-2

SOME DO'S AND DON'TS TO GUIDE STUDENTS IN INTERACTING WITH RETURNING PEERS WHO HAVE ATTEMPTED SUICIDE

Don't try to be a rescuer.	Do be a friend.
Don't work at "cheering up."	Do be willing to show your own good feelings at having the person back.
Don't try to build a rational argument against suicide.	Do be willing to share experiences.
Don't feel like you have to "do something to help."	Do be willing to interact.
Don't try to find out "why?"	Do be a listener.

Adapted from Hafen and Peterson (1983).

Though a relapse is, of course, a major crisis for the troubled individual, it probably does not differ significantly in treatment approach than would an original suicide attempt. The individual concerned is at higher risk, and self-destructive action becomes easier to consider since the taboo ground has already once been crossed. But, despite the obvious dangers involved and the frustration of having to start over along what sometimes is an arduous and lengthy recovery path, probably the greatest problems, as far as the school is concerned, lie in dealing with those other than the suicidal individual. The person experiencing the crisis, once their crisis status is ascertained, is most likely quickly to be put in touch with professional help, which will then assume most if not essentially all of the treatment responsibilities.

In the event of a crisis being repeated—a previous attempter again attempting suicide—the treatment and all but the most initial crisis-intervention responses will shift to professional networked resources. But the school still must deal with students and staff who may be experiencing the emotional shock and fallout of reliving a frightening and discouraging event. The problem, though often widespread and sometimes heavy in its effect, is not made any more complex particularly by virtue of the relapse. People's reactions are most apt to be reprises of their original responses; in some instances more severe because of the shock, and in others less severe because of having already learned that a crisis is something they have already proven capable of handling.

There are no really different or special techniques for handling the repeated experience. All those support responses that were of help initially can usually be successfully re-applied. Once the shock phase has passed, individuals are likely to be surprisingly resilient. When the shock effect seems to be particularly severe, some of the approaches used in handling grief reactions (see Chapter Six, "Helping Suicide Survivors in the School Setting") will be useful.

How Will Those Involved Be Affected?

Those who maybe affected by the return to school of a suicide attempter fall into two categories (excluding the returnee): (1) those who may be affected only in indirect ways and (2) those who for any one of several reasons are likely to be directly or intimately affected. Though the process of reintegration into the school community typically goes more smoothly than worried personnel are likely to anticipate, some attention to the interaction effects for each of these should be considered.

Those Indirectly Affected. The problems faced by this group may be less apparent and harder to define, especially in terms of who is and who is not affected. For this group, the issues to be dealt with are broader and more generic and less involved with the personalities than the generalities of suicide, crisis, and post-crisis experience. Several sets of guidelines are provided as a result of major catastrophic crises that have affected school children, including the *Yom Kippur War* experience (Neill, 1977) and witnessing a classroom homicide (Danto, 1978; Keith & Ellis, 1978). Much of the work dealing with grief of survivors is relevant here, too.

In the case of the interaction of this broader group with a returning attempter, the problems are probably very similar. General questions of what may to adults be seen as blatant naivete are of concern. Younger children may want to know if suicide is "catching." Parents may have similar concerns as they ask whether or not it is healthy for "normal" children to share the same educational space with a special child. Neill (1977) has suggested that the most workable approach is to involve those concerned in all three aspects of the three-stage prevention model through teaching, crisis intervention when necessary, and the rehabilitation process.

Danto (1978) offers several very helpful suggestions that may be easily applied to the post-suicide situation. He notes that children are likely to be extra concerned about the concept of death, and some "death education" may be very helpful. Helping students to separate reality from myth in terms of what suicide is and isn't, and to distinguish fact from fiction regarding the locally significant event, is another positive step that school personnel probably should take. Care should be used, however, as to not overdramatize the situation.

Students may be concerned with broad social issues involved, such as the possible far-reaching consequences of violent behavior, personal and community responsibility for helping others, principles of mental health, and availability of sources for help. Each of these provides an opportunity for a meaningful contribution by the school, useful in both the immediate situation and in the longer-range mental health education of the students.

In most instances, there is no reason to directly involve this broad group with any prescriptive personal interaction with the returning attempter. The major contribution that can be made to the rehabilitative welfare of the returnee is to promote any attitudes and activities that in general improve the mental health status of the school environment. Much can be done toward this end, with beneficial spin-offs for the whole school community.

Those Directly Affected. Two major issues are encountered with this group. One, they may very well need some form of recuperative experience themselves as they face the reality of a near-death in their group. Two, this group is most likely to experience direct interaction with the returning attempter and may be assigned or feel that they have some direct responsibility for helping with the rehabilitative process. In order to be effective in the latter, the former issue must be successfully handled.

The emotions of a crisis may be relived to some extent, as the presence of the attempter serves as a reminder of what has transpired before. Though this is, in the vernacular of the times, a "heavy" experience, it can easily be a very positive and constructive one at the same time. It may facilitate getting feelings of insecurity and worry out in the open. It may help build a sense of reciprocal social responsibility which has the dual effect of building self-confidence in one's own level of contribution to society while at the same time providing security in the awareness of the availability of support from others.

The most common question directed at school personnel will probably be, "What should I do and say?" The answer is not difficult. By and large the importance of being normal, not acting in any special different way, should be stressed. Normalcy, predictability, acceptance and consistency are all valuable aids to recovery for the returning student. Those who will have close contact with the student can help best by being themselves. More specific answers should deal more with feelings and attitudes than specific behaviors. If students can be assisted in handling their own worries, fears, and attitudinal concerns, the behaviors which follow can largely be allowed to transpire naturally without special attention.

Students may insist upon some specific do's and don'ts to alleviate their anxiety. A fancy list is not necessary (see Table 5-3 for a sample set).

TABLE 5-3

GUIDELINES TO FACILITATE SOCIAL AWARENESS AND THE
SUCCESSFUL OPERATION OF A SOCIAL-SUPPORT NETWORK

1. Learn to actively listen to others with genuine concern
2. Encourage others to openly express their feelings by practicing this yourself
3. When you're worried or concerned, share this with someone, especially someone close like your parents or best friend
4. Try to correctly weigh the importance of problems and recognize that most problems are relatively short-lived
5. Try to learn how others cope with their problems and borrow any good ideas you encounter. Share your ideas with your friends
6. Know where to find really good help when you feel you need it. Try to acquire this information before the need is desperate
7. Practicing communicating to others about your own ideas and feelings, particularly those which may be difficult to clearly explain
8. Learn to recognize that everyone has problems, no one solves all their problems, and that to fail as well as to succeed is normal and to be expected

Adapted from Hoff (1984).

If these students show a significant amount of concern about their own ability to cope, a worry which may be emphasized by the presence of the attempter, they might be reminded of primary intervention strategies which help assure mutual social awareness and the creation of a supporting network. We use a set of guidelines (see Table 5-4) similar to the intervention strategies outlined by Hoff (1984). We often suggest to classroom teachers that these may be easily integrated with other social science or health topics. Students involved in these should find support and receive some relief from their own stress-performance anxieties. It should not be difficult for schools to build similar guidelines that seem to work well with their own student body. Even the process of working out a set of guidelines can be helpful.

TABLE 5-4

HOW TO RESPOND WHEN AN ATTEMPTER'S RISK LEVEL
APPEARS TO BE RISING AGAIN

1. Always be willing and ready to listen
2. Think in terms of the seriousness of stress and stress reactions
3. Orient on the intensity as well as the nature of the emotional effects that can be observed
4. Always take a troubled youth's comments about suicide and suicide-related problems seriously
5. Be prepared to ask directly about the level of risk: "Are you again considering suicide?"
6. Follow through on your concerns: don't be mislead by apparent spontaneous recoveries from disturbing behaviors. If the problem has been serious enough to worry you once, it still should be investigated
7. Be affirmative and supportive even in the face of high concern
8. Take tangible and overt action
9. Ask promptly for help and consultation with your networked experts. If the youth is under treatment, notify their professional contact
10. Involve broad support as quickly as possible, including family and other significant others

From Hafen and Peterson (1983).

ROLES FOR SCHOOL PERSONNEL

Suicide, despite its extreme and apparently bizarre characteristics, is not an isolated event appearing in the midst of the stream of life like some foreign object sticking out of the current's flow. The suicidal act is instead the "end of a chain" of events as Shneidman (1985) has very clearly reminded us. Recovery and rehabilitation should also be considered as part of that same chain with decided connections to what has transpired before and contributing a necessary continuity between yesterday's and today's events and the promise and hope (rather than the threat or fear) of tomorrow.

Perhaps, the major overall asset the school brings to the recovering student is this sense of continuity and consistency. It offers a known environment that is predictable and trustworthy with few surprises, is stable and dependable, and yet at the same time possesses the characteristics of growth, progress and new experience. So, in a major sense, the most important role the school can play is that of presenting an environment that is safe and accepting, structured to present challenges in acceptable amounts and forms, and designed to accommodate a variety of people with many individual differences.

The school also offers another major asset. Though what it may bring to the returning attempter may be no more than what might be obtained through other cultural groups and institutions, structured as it is to provide a learning experience to the uninformed and a growth opportunity to the not yet matured, the school is in perhaps the best position to take the time to clearly offer these special experiences and do it efficiently. Efficiency is often a very important variable in the decision-making process of the suicidal person.

A number of years ago a friend of ours, seriously contemplating suicide as a problem-solving option, clarified his thinking for us with these words: "There are times when the tomorrows are not worth the todays." For this individual, suicide was being considered as a viable option, not because there were no other options. Instead, the cost of the other options appeared to be too high. Too much effort, incommensurate with the rewards, appeared to be involved. Such an approach is entirely congruent with the concept that suicide, as the possible last link in the chain, occurs only after less costly options appear to have been exhausted. From such a perspective, suicide does have adjustment potential, though it may not offer adaptive possibilities. Many theorists in the field choose to examine and define suicide as merely an extreme example of costly adjustment, dramatic, and especially important because of its irreversibility but probably not much different than other "last-chance" attempts at adjustment in the face of catastrophic-end events. Miller (1978) describes how the adjustment process is related to the efficiency or conservation of energy principle: "A system which survives generally decides to employ the least costly adjustment to a threat or strain produced by stress first, and increasingly more costly ones later."

Shneidman (1985), formulating a "new definition" of suicide, has stressed the relationship of suicide as an adjustive act to the living system explanation of adjustment in general. The ambivalence about dying, and the very typical willingness to call for help once a possible helping source is recognized, would suggest that the suicidal person is not only seeking adjustment but the least costly adjustment available. Suicide is elected because no less costly option appears available. When less costly or more efficient options become part of the at-risk individual's perceptual field, they are apt to be selected instead of suicide. Calls for help are seeking easier solutions. When these calls are answered, the less costly options are frequently selected and the "at-risk" level is lowered considerably even if the precipitating problems remain yet to be solved.

Healthy school environments can play a very important function in the recuperative process by presenting problem-solving and support options that are readily available, efficient, less costly, effective and safe in terms of accommodating less-than-perfect responses. In the larger sense, this is the role any support system plays. It works because it is there. Suicide becomes a viable option when nothing more efficient is present.

The school is in one of the best possible positions to play this important role in what was previously described as **tertiary prevention,** the basis upon which long-lasting rehabilitation and persisting mental health is constructed. Further suicidal behavior is prevented through becoming familiar with and adopting less costly, more efficient and better working adaptive functions. There are at least four different ways in which the schools can contribute to this process.

Providing A "Holding" Environment

As Menninger (1938) has discussed, the death-related concepts involved in a suicide attempt are atypical to normal problem-solving experiences. The victim must, for example, deal with the concepts of having nearly died, having nearly been killed, and having nearly committed the act of killing. It is not difficult to understand, then, why recuperation from the experiencing of stress so severe as to cause one to consider suicide is a complex process. Several intertwined but independently important facets are involved.

The attempter returning to school must deal with the following issues:

1. Returning to a somewhat demanding and stress-producing situation
2. Facing individuals who are now aware of one's own vulnerability and apparent inadequacies
3. Generalizing the therapeutic concepts introduced in the safer environment of the counseling room to the world of reality
4. Monitoring one's own recuperative progress to avoid relapse
5. Facing and solving or satisfactorily avoiding the old problems that were involved with the prior destructive stress
6. Facing the unknown and perhaps unpredictable stresses of new experiences and everyday living.

To expect one to abruptly face all these issues, totally immersed in them as suddenly as one might leap into a pool of icy water, is often asking too much. In many instances, treatment plans will involve a phasing-in of this fresh risk-taking activity. The slowly increasing successive approximations of normal everyday problem facing and problem solving may take the form of the individual being directed to work on certain aspects and ignore others, or the problem issues may be conceptualized as broad general concerns, with the individual working on solving modular pieces as decided in the treatment interaction. In either case, it is very helpful for the individual striving to regain total personal equilibrium to have the advantage of being in a situation which certainly has aspects of unaltered reality, making demands for growth and satisfactory coping behaviors, but which at the same time offers somewhat more security, perhaps more patience and acceptance, and a more conducive environment for careful growth at an idiosyncratic pace.

A "holding" environment offers experiences shaped more to individual needs than does the world at large. It provides more experiences relevant to the developing of skills, changing self-concepts, and the acquisition of the skills of successful living. It is typically a warmer, more sensitive, and more individually concerned environment than experienced elsewhere. Such a mission is completely congruent with the typical functions of today's schools. Re-application of these capabilities to the needs of the returning youthful suicide attempter does not represent substantially new constraints or demands for the school. It is relatively easy for knowledgeable school personnel to provide such a learning context without damage to the school's primary teaching mission.

Why Is a Holding Environment
Necessary?

Youngsters involved with suicide are not the only ones who can profit
from a holding environment. Coping behaviors develop from maturational experiences. When these experiences have been missing or non-
contributory to the growing process, various problems can develop.
Suicide is only one of the problem reactions. Typically, three different
types of youth find it especially difficult to find an environment and role
that fits their needs, capabilities, self-concept and sense of integrity
(Meeks, 1971). These include those whose experiences have been so unusual that they have come to expect a role that is in itself unrealistic and
perhaps unfulfillable, those whose experiences have been impaired or
lacking in important shaping components so that the youth has developed needs which are internally inconsistent or in conflict with each
other, and those whose experiences have been relatively normal but
whose perceptions of the contemporary world are so confused or inaccurate as to cause them dismay or even panic.

For the post-suicidal youth to unsuccessfully progress through this
maze of problems, a holding environment may be critical. The youth
must learn to accurately perceive reality (as it is related both to the world
"out there" and to one's self) and to acquire the skill of constructive self-
scrutiny, a literal self-monitoring of one's own progress. For this to occur
in the individual who has recently experienced perhaps the greatest of all
self-doubts, the lack of confidence in being able to live, the challenge is
frightening. A holding environment allows this self-scrutiny to occur
without the need for absolute self-judgments and immediate reparative
or reactive actions. In the holding environment there is opportunity for
trial runs at decision making, more time for making firm decisions and
an atmosphere of emphasizing the processes of working at progressive
adjustment rather than upon final and total outcomes. Impulsive,
stress-driven, self-depreciatory actions become less necessary.

If an individual is returning to normal living, facing the real world is
the ultimate reality. To successfully accomplish this return, the typical
treatment plan will deal with any one of several components of problem-
solving, sometimes briefly, sometimes extensively (see Table 5-5). The
school is often in a position to actively help with several of these and
thereby automatically provides a holding environment conducive to
solid recovery.

TABLE 5-5

SOME TYPICAL COMPONENTS OF A PROBLEM-SOLVING-ORIENTED
TREATMENT PLAN

Task One: Working on general approaches to problem-solving including:
  Identification of problems to be solved
  Establishment of goals
  Clarification of steps to meeting the goals
  Choice of tasks and order of tasks to be accomplished
  Review of ways to observe and evaluate progress

Task Two: Modifying of attitudes towards:
  Self
  Others
  Situations
  Aspirations and accomplishments

Task Three: Facilitation of communication including:
  Sending messages to others
  Interpreting messages received from others
  Monitoring messages between others
  Providing information to elicit and expedite help and support from others

Adapted from Hawton and Catalan (1982).

Making a Holding Environment Work

One must be careful not to overemphasize the concept of a "holding" environment, making it to be more than it really is by stressing the idea to the point of reification. Many schools already have what might well be labeled as holding environments by virtue of their warm and friendly atmosphere, well-performing student personnel services, and involved staff. Such schools will need to do little differently. In the process of working specifically with recovering suicide-attempt cases, some general guidelines may be helpful.

Stages of Recovery. As the individual once more phases back into the world which prior to the culmination of his or her crisis was a combination of rewards and costs, the process closely resembles the recovery stages experienced by those recovering from grief (Rosenfeld & Prupas, 1984). The holding environment provides support of several different types—types which change as the individual re-acquires coping strengths and skills of adjustment. If the school can provide some support in each of these stages, it will have applied a working holding environment in the process of doing so.

Initially, upon first returning, the individual needs considerable buffering. This should be applied tactfully and carefully avoiding creating the impression of lack of faith or confidence in the recovering individual. Instead, the goal should be to signal genuine acceptance of the individual regardless of strengths and weaknesses, a non-evaluative acceptance. What giving takes place should be of a type that does not indicate an expectation for reciprocity. The clinician calls this type of giving "non-demanding interaction" or "unconditional acceptance." The individual should not be discouraged from giving in return: a desire to do so is normal and healthy. However, no expectations of something being given in return should be indicated at this time. This creates the badly needed initial atmosphere of safety and interactions which do not depend upon positive evaluation to remain.

Generally, this one-sided acceptance is short-lived. It is not usually needed for very long and probably is not helpful, perhaps even harmful, if continued unabated for very long. Most individuals will broaden the interactions into reciprocal give-and-take situations on their own. As time elapses and the individual continues to grow, a type of weaning takes place. The individual begins to need and seek some private space, some social distance. Tolerance and acceptance by others are still important, but there is less need for social concordance and total acceptance. The recovering individual gains in ego strength and self-confidence with each passing success and is able and usually willing to face a world of competitive ideas and friendly disagreements. During this stage, support and help become somewhat less personal in a direct one-to-one fashion and impinge less on the private life-space of the individual. Support and help should become more a function of a general atmosphere that affects and is universally available to everyone. The recovering individual will gain self-respect and confidence during this time if allowed to contribute to the welfare of others, to give as well as take.

The final phase consists primarily of facing reality and striking out as far as personal problems are concerned. The healthy school environment that seeks to practice **primary** prevention will strive for an atmosphere which allows such individuality yet offers general support systems for anyone regardless of the type or level of stress being encountered. The individual is essentially "flying on his own wings" in this final recuperative stage and needs little more than a generally friendly,

interested, and supportive environment. Specific support teams or activities or structured environments are not usually needed. From this
stage the individual moves easily and imperceptibly into routine coping
functions, reacting as anyone else might to demands, extraordinary or
not. A sensitive and caring environment helps as it would anyone, but a
holding environment per se is no longer needed.

Getting Close to the Adolescent. Many adults find it frustrating if
they try to get close to adolescents. The adolescent does not find it all
that easy to be intimate with others or to share deep personal feelings
(especially to adults). Recovering adolescent suicide attempters are no
better or worse in this regard than other youth.

If there is a secret to sharing intimate moments with an adolescent, it
is probably not to strive for them but to let them happen naturally if and
when they will. As Meeks (1971) has advised us, adolescents like to take
what amounts to "trial dips" into relationships. They don and discard relationships and problem-solving stances (including those that involve
personal alliances) frequently and often without apparent rhyme, reason, or warning. They are not known for permanent commitments, irreversible loyalties, or long-lasting allegiances.

From the viewpoint of the adult, one of the most difficult aspects of
maintaining a holding environment is having the ego strength and patience to tolerate and accept this on-again, off-again relationship pattern
of the adolescent while retaining a more or less constant and open, accepting stance yourself. However, it is exactly that which helps create a
holding environment.

Errors of Assumed Responsibility. Few adults take the responsibilities of creating and applying a holding environment less seriously than
necessary. In fact, most errors lie in the opposite direction. These happen sufficiently often as to warrant a few words of warning.

First, bluntly stated, care should be exercised no one involved assumes any ultimate responsibility for the returning attempter's life. Such
an assumption is dangerous and irrational for several reasons. It is probably a burden that cannot be consistently carried. As Shneidman (1979)
has emphasized, the one person who holds total and ultimate responsibility for an individual's life is that person. To take on that awesome responsibility for another is neither reasonable or helpful. Even when
done with the best of intentions, it typically results in a "rescuing" pose
which at its best foster's unhealthy dependency and at its worst increments feelings of helplessness.

Second, errors of attribution frequently are found in both suicidal people and people seriously impacted by a suicide or suicide attempt. Most commonly, individuals err in the direction of assuming too much causal influence, guilt or responsibility. This is a serious problem that must frequently be dealt with between the victim and the therapist. Unfortunately, it also is commonly encountered with others involved in the situation.

School personnel should not assume that they have primary causal roles in creating suicide risk. The occurrence of such is very rare and when present is usually obvious and blatant, not subtle to the point of needing to be inferred or assumed. Additionally, those active in creating and maintaining a holding environment are at best only creating a facilitative environment, typically not a context that directly impacts and focuses upon the recovering individual's main problems. Consequently, the holding environment is typically not primarily responsible for either the progress or relapse of the recovering student. It is very easy for individuals seriously involved in the holding environment task to make the same types of errors of attribution as does the suicidal individual who says, "I must be unworthy, at fault, or I wouldn't feel so guilty."

The temptation to assume this type of responsibility is great. It is neither realistic or healthy. The advice we usually give those interested in being supportive is simple. We tell them, "Do the best you can and then let the individual concerned handle it from there." We are indeed our brother's and sister's keeper, but we cannot live their lives for them, nor make all their decisions. If they need that type of constant-vigil support, they should be in a special place with full-time attention.

Effecting a Support System

It would seem to be a truism to state that the returning adolescent attempter needs and can benefit from an active support system. It is of course very obviously true, but perhaps the most important point to convey to those who accept responsibility to help in such situations is that the support system, essentially a broadly based amalgamation of friends, plays a very involved and important role in recovery.

People of any age can be incorporated into the support functions that friendship groups provide, but peers meet these needs of the adolescent perhaps more easily and with less effort for the troubled youth than do adults. The school is in an enviable position in this regard, since it has many peer-group individuals available and in a position to play these roles with a minimum of pragmatic problems and less artificiality than might be true in other surroundings.

Active and Passive Support from Friendship Groups

Everyone needs friends, but the need is central to the adolescent (Meeks, 1971). Friendship plays both active and passive roles for the typical adolescent, and the importance of these roles is emphasized for the youth recovering from a crisis of any type. When the crisis has evolved into suicidal behavior, the youth is particularly vulnerable to unmet needs in this area due largely to the sense of loneliness, isolation, and alienation typical of suicidal thought.

In an active sense, friends provide the acceptance and narcissistic support that the adolescent craves to supplant his or her own lack of positive self-evaluation and minimized self-confidence. Friends provide a type of group ego strength which is available for tapping as the individual adolescent feels the need. That there is strength in numbers is personified for the adolescent. The friendship group also actively fosters growth by forcing the individual into group membership-related social responsibilities and realities. A certain amount of reciprocity of active behavior is required if the adolescent is to receive maximum benefits from the group. Yet, such demands are often subtly stated and less evaluative in a public standard sense than are responsibilities associated with broader-aged and less personal groups.

In a more passive sense, the group provides a substitute or surrogate parental function as it allows or even encourages the adolescent to assume independence, to loosen the traditional ties with parental figures. An interesting paradox is encountered. The adolescent peer-friendship group can typically be found to be encouraging both independence and allegiance at the same time. It is as though the group were saying, "Strike out on your own, be your own person!" While at the same time, a contradictory message is also conveyed: "Do not ignore us or the necessity you have for remaining part of us, loyal to our concepts, endorsing of our behaviors."

It is easier for the adolescent to practice independence with the friendship group than with parents, since authority roles are softer, less enshrined in cultural tradition, and the group is less clearly punitive when individual-serving rather than group-serving choices are made.

The adolescent risks and experiences less guilt and less fear of permanent rejection by peers for unacceptable behavior. The peer group expects some conformity but also seems to equally accept the tentativeness of the bonding and the occasional foray into individualism.

The friendship group also serves as a source of identification for the adolescent, who very often finds this important commodity in short supply within himself or herself. Difficult to define or clearly describe for adolescents as much as for adults, a sense of ego extension is incorporated within this cohesive, yet highly flexible and constantly evolving group, which subtly helps an individual "find themself."

Guidelines for Developing the Supportive Environment

Essentially, the task is one of establishing an operative social networking process. The fundamental basis for building such rehabilitative (tertiary prevention) functions lies in the principles outlined in Chapter Two on primary prevention. Individuals involved must feel that there is a genuineness to people's concerns that extends beyond the boundaries of any contemporary event or situation.

In other words, support for the returning attempter grows out of an atmosphere previously adopted by the group, which clearly asserts, "The health and welfare of our group is dependent upon the health and welfare of our individual members." Too often, the opposite is assumed: "We are faced with a special problem. We can create a sense of real group identification through reaching out to help."

While it may not be impossible to successfully adopt the latter stance, it is certainly far more difficult, slower to react to precipitate individual needs, and shorter-lived in its overall contributions to the school's mental health environment.

In addition to the general principles of primary prevention, some additional helpful suggestions can be provided. Hoff (1984) has developed a list of characteristics for establishing and operating an effective crisis-management plan. These certainly apply to the rehabilitative stage as much as anywhere else. Hoff suggests:

1. That any active plan be developed in collaboration with the victim. This emphasizes the importance of reciprocal group identification and argues for a system which operates regularly in "normal" times to avoid embarrasing public focus.

2. That the plan be problem-oriented. Functions should be solution-finding oriented, active as well as passive.
3. All aspects of the plan should be developed with attention to being appropriate to the functional level and dependency needs of those involved. The developmental status and needs of the adolescent or child must be taken into consideration if a support system is to work.
4. The plan must not be artificial or arbitrarily imposed upon a differently functioning environmental milieu. It must be consistent with the culture style and needs of those involved.
5. It must be inclusive of significant others and broader social-support networks which may also be operating to meet the individual's needs.

Polak (1971) has also stressed the importance of using broadly based social network strategies in working with returning victims of personal crisis situations. Doing so not only broadens and deepens the resources available and strengthens a sense of wide support, but it also models a community-wide sense of identification which can last far beyond the chronological limits of the school experience. Some (Hansell, 1976; Hoff, 1984) would suggest that broad social network strategies are essential to success and that, even then, may not be sufficient unless the recuperating individual takes an active participating role.

The Returnee's Interaction and Response

Since the returning victim is to be an active participant, some consideration of what to expect from this specially troubled youth should be considered. The returning attempter is involved in a very sensitive conflict. There is an age-inherent need for freedom and autonomy coupled with the realistic awareness that in the recent past self-adopted total autonomy has resulted in near self-destruction.

All adolescents are hypersensitive to any manipulative control (Meeks, 1971). Their sense of autonomy is tenuous, susceptible to change, vulnerable to challenge, and self-frightening due to the uncomfortable exposure and loneliness it necessarily incorporates. All of these feelings are exemplified in the youth who has attempted suicide. Any supportive system must allow for what may at times appear to be mutually exclusive behaviors: those which allow the individual to be a separate, independent individual, and those which allow the individual to be submersed and protected in the safe anonymity of the group.

It is unwise to force the issue in either direction. Those who would construct and maintain a supportive environment must be willing to be patient and tolerate a nearly constant ambivalent response from those they would help. All involved should be aware that such behaviors are normal to adolescence and therefore normal to the returning suicide attempter. There is no reason to expect that the problem is especially more severe with the returnee. It does occur in a more dramatic context encompassed with worries and concerns more intense than may be true in other instances. The willingness to tolerate and sustain support in the face of these behaviors and the anxieties they may invoke is the hallmark of a good supportive environment.

Meeks (1971) has presented two very important guiding principles (written for therapists but true of all who participate in the recuperative support process): First, those who would help should "take responsibility for the adolescent's behavior only when it is essential for the youth's welfare." And, second, that those whose personalities and needs include a need to control or dominate others are poorly suited to helping in these types of situations. Since such feelings of need to dominate most frequently arise out of other feelings of insecurity and uneasiness, good preparation designed to reduce anxiety, inform and train will minimize the probability of such non-contributory responses to the returning attempter's needs.

In a positive sense, adults in the supportive environment can be very helpful by allowing the youth to use them as sounding boards, safe persons upon whom to project trial images of concern, even anger and negative self-images, with the youth knowing that those who perceive these less-than-pleasant emanations understand and are not threatened. The most likely danger in such circumstances, if adults are prepared to handle the conflicts involved, is that the recuperating victim may elevate the adult to an unrealistically idealized, or even as Meeks (1971) describes it, a "venerated" status. The supportive adult can lessen the likelihood of this problem developing by encouraging autonomy, refusing to luxuriate in the pleasant bask of being idealized, and encouraging more and more independent social risk taking by the youth. Comfortable as this surrogate nest is, the recovering victim must eventually fly on their own or be trapped in further dependency which may be as destructive as the alienation they have recently experienced.

It should be kept in mind that there are many motives for suicide; it is not a simplistically explained event. For every motivational pattern there can be expected a different set of rehabilitation motives, feelings, and behaviors. Murray (1967) has noted some major categories of suicidal motivation:

1. Pitiful forlornness, a sense of grief and distress
2. Anger and extrapunitiveness
3. Guilt and remorse, intrapunitiveness
4. Withdrawal and escape
5. Eggression or desertion, purposeful aggressive withdrawal for the purpose of breaking contact with a situation or persons.

Whether one's motivation for self-destruction has stemmed from one of these or other reasons, the process of re-adapting to the world of coping can be expected to vary accordingly.

Those in a supportive environment only peripherally involved with a formal treatment plan may never come to know the motivational background for the self-destructive act. Therefore, the most effective stance is to operate without preconceived expectations that one must know the motive in order to respond appropriately or that different stances are required for different motivational patterns. Such may be true in intensive psychotherapy. It is not true for supportive groups. Warmth, acceptance, allowance for personal space and self-selected pace for becoming involved in reciprocal social interactions will contribute strongly to all other recovery efforts.

The Significant-Other Network

Strange as it may seem, suicide is, in most instances, a social phenomenon. The suicidal individual almost invariably is responding to tensions that involve internalized relationships between people (Fowler & McGee, 1973). Even when the primary stressor is something like an incurable medical problem, a major portion of the stress field usually consists of concerns about decreasing abilities to meet social interaction goals. The victim's vulnerability has some genesis in interpersonal relationships. Consequently, most therapists feel that the acquisition of better coping skills and the substitution of more productive adaptive options than self-destruction can and should be acquired in similar relationships.

While casual everyday social interactions can provide a healthy culture in which to develop and practice these needed skills, those who interact closely and intimately with the individual play more critical roles.

These are, of course, those we label as **significant others.** Significant-other roles are played by a variety of people in many different social positions. Immediate family are, of course, very apt to be cast in such roles, but the school environment offers many opportunities for significant-other relationships to develop, as well. Teachers, student personnel staff, oftentimes members of the peripheral support staff such as cafeteria or janitorial personnel, friends, classmates, and student leaders may each play a significant other role for other individuals in the school.

The school has two primary concerns in regards to these special people: (1) to identify them wherever possible so as to provide them with support as they are looked to for special help by the attempter, and (2) to provide them with somewhat more latitude within the school structure than might normally be routinely so. A teacher playing the significant-other role for a returning attempter may need some extra time for the process. A student in the same role may need more permissiveness in scheduling or class deadlines because he or she may need to shape their life to two persons: themself and the one they are helping.

Such extraordinary leeway is not typically needed for long. Development of extended dependency upon significant others is to be avoided. Special demands are apt to be operant only during a relatively short period of time as transition back to normal living is accomplished.

Roles and Functions

The returning attempter needs significant others to perform two very important functions. First, they must play a specialized support role. These individuals have already achieved a special status in the eyes of the attempter. They are, in some fashion, special people whose presence or actions or responses carry special importance. They are "others" who are **significant** in their effect upon a particular individual.

Consequently, every single facet of support interaction, as noted previously in this chapter, applies with extra emphasis to the significant other. Their support (or the lack of it) is more quickly perceived, more deeply experienced, and has longer lasting effects. If positive relationships are experienced with significant others, defensiveness and social stress-induced impulsive behavior is less apt to develop.

Second, significant others provide important pedagogical functions. They are especially effective as role models. They can demonstrate and personify effective adaptive behaviors. They are living criterion models against which the attempter may compare and measure personal atempts to grow and develop in their adaptive skills. Though they do not always really have any more understanding of the individual for whom they have special significance, they are usually so perceived. Therefore, any feedback, shaping responses, directions, suggestions, or even direct guidance may have more impact than from other sources.

These two functions permit the significant other to provide some very effective contributions to the recovery process. The recovering suicidal individual needs significant others as listeners, as sources of dependable responses (people they can depend upon), as willing help-givers, as companions of a type who serve as "anti-lonely" and "anti-alienation" protection, as receptors for self-revealing insights, as interpreters of personal failures and successes, and as bridges between the vulnerable self and the dispassionate "outside world."

Motto (1985) has noted four discernible aspects of the overall treatment process. These are facets that involve the formal patient-therapist relationship and everyday interactions with a society into which the individual is beginning to become once again immersed. They most certainly are functions in which the significant other can and should play important roles. These are:

1. Establishing an initial dependency-gratifying relationship that is non-threatening
2. Providing opportunity for emotional growth
3. Establishing opportunity for self-sufficiency without fear of abandonment
4. Developing a diminishing dependency and increasing autonomy.

These are all very positive consequences that may be gained from healthy significant-other relationships.

Many feel that crisis times present some rather special opportunities for working through problem behaviors with long histories, problems that may have been so habitual as to be accepted as normal, going unnoticed until precipitated into focus via the crisis. There is not much unequivocal research data supporting this thesis but widespread acceptance, nevertheless, and much anecdotal evidence which would seem to lend credibility to the concept.

To the degree that it may be true, it would seem equally reasonable to suppose that "significant others," by virtue of their special "significance" to the troubled individual, may be in a strong position to be of real help in the learning or re-learning process.

Life-Transition Theory

Much of the involvement of significant others in the recuperative process of a suicidal youth is built upon the assumptions inherent in life-transition theory (Brammer & Abrego, 1981). This theory supports the idea that facing a life crisis can be a learning as well as a traumatizing event. It is assumed that since a crisis clearly interrupts old behavior patterns, substituting crisis responses (which may not be healthy either) for them, it is a likely time to consider substituting new patterns for old. It is further supposed that since a crisis often draws attention to real or perceived self-inadequacies, it frequently results in critical self-examination and appraisal, as well.

Hansell (1976) stresses the social factors involved in both crisis resolution and development and reiterates the elaboration of situational analysis and resolution of problems via crisis resolution as originally emphasized by Caplan (1964). "Constructive resolution" is the term applied to describe the rebuilding process which theoretically can result in a new situation and status that is better and less stress- or problem-producing than the former.

Very closely akin to the "self-actualizing" theorems of Maslow (1970), this view of crisis (and crisis recovery) sees the crisis as an actualizing opportunity which actually invites the human being, as a growth-oriented organism, to seek to respond positively to people in crisis. In practice, some have difficulty equating such an assumption with the apparent disinclination of people to "become involved" in crisis situations, particularly when the victim may be a stranger. However, almost everyone agrees that the more identification there is between observer and victim, the greater the likelihood of observer involvement.

Building upon this observation, it would seem to follow that victims may expect their own perceived significant others to become involved. And it would further follow that those who see themselves as significant do seem to become involved more readily, with less latency of response and perhaps with more effectiveness. Our own practical field experience in crisis and post-crisis recovery situations seems to support such an assumption.

Schools might be very well-advised then to help those perceived as significant others to perceive themselves in that role, too. The entire concept of primary prevention might legitimately be described as creating a more broadly based resource of reciprocally perceived significant others which become available as needed for support, guidance, and direct aid.

The Subtle Value of Close Support

It may very well be that significant others have a more pervasive influence in part because they are seen as being primarily involved in terms of a broader relationship and only secondarily focused on the presentation of support as a major role. We do know that "denial" is a frequent defense mechanism for those in crisis. Being in the presence of close friends, understanding individuals who share some sort of longer-termed intimacy, lessens the need for such defensiveness. We have all known instances where individuals in crisis have maintained an overt "stiff upper lip," showing the depth of their anguish only when confronted with someone close to them.

The active presence of a positively contributing significant other offers several opportunities for healthy responses. The individual is given an implied permission to experience, display, and begin to deal with intense personal feelings. Support may be presumed to be at-hand without explanation or delimiting qualification demands: worthiness need not be proved. A working link between the past, present and future is personified by their presence. Relative normalcy or adequate coping, even in the face of cataclysmic disaster, is demonstrated. It is interesting to note that in such situations those who play these significant roles seem to experience feelings of release and growth, as well. Their self-reflection and adaptative habits undergo self-analysis, and they often report the experience to be exhausting and uplifting at the same time.

We feel that even less-than-healthy significant others may be constructively involved, since they too can then be re-shaped and newly shaped functional allegiances may be formed speaking well for a healthy tomorrow. Husain and Vandiver (1984) have clearly suggested that in the crisis-recovery situation it may be necessary to involve the entire primary group in some sort of treatment experience. Actively and deliberately involving significant others may facilitate this broader recovery phenomenon.

Cautions Regarding Close Support

There is more than one type of support. Support may take the form of security, acceptance and warmth as provided by the counselor (and others, too). It may occur in the form of reassurance which is garnered through the experience of change from high to low stress. It may involve help with specific tasks and decisions. It may even take the form of direct frontal action as in the event of active crisis intervention. With this in mind, it should be emphasized that significant others may function successfully in any of these. However, it should not be expected that each should function in all. The limitation to what one may reasonably expect of a single individual, regardless of their influence, is real. The "significance" that a particular person may have for the returning attempter may vary considerably. Consequently, the broader the application of significant-other support, the better. Duplication of effort is of little concern. Failure to have anyone to respond in a particular area of need may be of considerable import for those who must struggle to recover.

There are also limitations to support, itself. Brammer and Shostrom (1982) point out that these limitations should be noted and that they may occur within either the giver or the receiver of help. For example, support creates a form of dependency relationship. This can result in anger and guilt over either taking too much or over someone demanding too much of you. Dependency is in itself a paradoxical aspect of recovering and therefore harbors ambivalence. It reminds one of the security of being cared for while at the same time it is easily counterproductive to one's striving to be safe through the knowledge of one's own ability to adequately cope. Too much support can be read as sympathy, insincerity, pity; too little as rejection, devaluation, loss of hope. Both the process of giving and receiving of close support in the process of recovering from a crisis involve emotional expenditures which are in a way like minature crises in themselves. They are demanding of energy, underlining our awareness of our problems, and are tolerable only if temporary and at levels for which we are prepared to cope. Sometimes, both the helper and the receiver of help will require further assistance. There is a tendency for the attempter to disown his or her own inner life and this is reinforced by a parallel tendency to act (Meeks, 1971). Action may be preferred to patience or even semi-passive responses. Thus it is easy to reject help and help giving in response to the frustration inherent in this difficult task. Significant others may be especially vulnerable in this respect, since they may have more at stake, more demanded of them, and have less chance to experience "time-out" recuperation of energy and motivation. Such reactions influence other behaviors. Job and classroom performance may temporarily suffer, and the school should be aware of this and be prepared to make appropriate adjustments.

Despite all these reservations, however, giving support is a richly rewarding experience. And, the receiving of support may be an essential prerequisite for going on living. Significant others are involved in both sides of the equation.

Learning to Live

Even the most understanding of friends and an environment that is warm, understanding, and accepting will not provide all that is needed to accomplish a successful recovery from suicidal behavior modes. The individual must rebuild coping skills, develop internal resources, and literally learn to live. Without such personal development most of the other facilitative aspects of the environment may be wasted.

This "learning to live" objective is essentially a learning task. It involves all of the important aspects of learning, acquisition of facts, generalization and discrimination skills, functional memory and recall, application, and the ability to self-monitor one's own progress. Since the school exists to help with exactly these processes in regards to academic subjects, it is in a strong position to help in these broader objectives, as well. The subject matter may be different, but the processes are identical.

School personnel and structure can be very helpful by providing an environment conducive to learning and supportive of the individual in the tentative process of building and learning to use new skills. A safe environment in which to practice, patience with partial accomplishment, help with difficult pieces of new experience, and support through regular association with others who are also learning are very useful to the returning attempter and bolster individual efforts to learn.

Important Areas of Focus

These individual efforts may center about one or more of the variety of areas where deficit behaviors in the past have either added stress or failed to provide the mechanisms for reducing stress induced by other sources. Getz et al. (1983) notes at least ten different areas where a returning individual may need improvement in order to resume normal adaptive functioning. He includes:

1. Confidence in one's own intellectual abilities
2. Accurate reality testing
3. Ability to attend to or concentrate on critical stimuli
4. Memory
5. Conceptual judgment
6. Tolerance of strong feelings
7. Effective impulse control
8. Quality relationships
9. Adequate self-esteem and self-confidence
10. Insight into personal problem areas.

In each of these, the general role of "learning" is obvious and the school's probability of being of help is apparent.

Miller (1978), writing in regards to the function of a living system, says, "When a barrier stands between a system under strain and a goal which can relieve that strain, the system ordinarily uses the adjustment process of removing the barrier, circumventing it, or otherwise mastering it." It is only in the event that these positively oriented procedures do not work, he adds, that the organisms typically resort to the more aggressive and extreme approaches of attack, displacement, primitive nonadaptive reactions, or escape.

Suicide, as an adjustive response, fits the latter group. The organism will invariably opt for the less energy-expensive and more adaptive option of mastery of problems if the option is perceived as being available. One of the very important pedagogical functions of the school is to help the individual learn how to search for, perceive and recognize, and then apply optional problem-solving techniques. During the learning phase of these important skills, the focus need not necessarily be upon the personal problems of the individual. The school has no reason, or even right, to be a surrogate or complementary therapist. It can, without fear of impingement upon the personal life space of the returning attempter, be of major assistance in the process of learning how to do these important steps which lead to "learning how to live."

The goal, as Meeks (1971) reminds us, is for the youth to increase self-understanding and inner psychological strength and flexibility. These should be the focus of the school's response, not the removal or suppressing of any certain annoying or worrisome personal behavior or trait.

Primary Objectives for the School

Probably, the most difficult aspect of the school's involvement is to convince the adolescent that the inquisitive process of learning self-analysis (as far as the school is concerned) is related to learning the skills rather than to focus on specific personal problems. It may be difficult at times to work on asking relevant self-progress-monitoring questions such as, "Why did you do that?" or "Is that approach really going to help?" Tact and professional teaching skills are necessary to keep from impinging on delicate areas and depressing rather than incrementing learning.

The ultimate goal is a form of autonomy where the individual youth, though a functional part of the group, begins to take self-responsibility, where appropriate, accompanied by a sufficiently high level of self-confidence as to suggest that such autonomy is not a correlate to alienation or aloneness. Meeks (1971) says that one of the most positive signs is when the youth starts "manning one of the oars," helping with the process himself or herself. The school offers some very real advantages as a place to make progress toward this goal.

The therapist would remind us that it is important for the adolescent to realize that there are self-based controls and causes for behavior. Whether these are explained and perceived as psychodynamic narcissistic needs or the irrational beliefs and emotions of a rational-emotive approach, problems arise when this important concept of some autonomous self-control is not learned or applied by the troubled individual. Self-control arises from a belief in at least some self-determination and election of options. Freedom to select options can be experienced only in a context which includes an affirmation of the individual's ability to acquire personal skills which enhance choice and effective response to unavoidable constraints.

It is in this mode of thought that the school can make its most positive contribution. If the youth learns that few situations are absolute and that even when an unmodifiable situation is faced, more than one action response is typically available, then adaptation becomes a response to the reality of self, not an impulsive attempt to satisfy or escape from demands for absolute performance, or perfect adjustment. The school can help the returning attempter acquire a malleability in the face of conflict and stress which provides the necessary strength to avoid ever having to face the final permanent answer of suicide to what is in most cases only a temporary problem.

CHAPTER SIX

HELPING SUICIDE SURVIVORS IN THE SCHOOL SETTING

"There is no greater sorrow than to recall a time of happiness in misery."

Dante

THE NUMBER OF individuals who may be legitimately labeled as "victims" of suicide is staggering. These "survivors" far outnumber the attempters. Andress and Corey (1973) estimate that on the average at least six persons, in addition to the perpetrator, are personally affected by each suicide. This figure is consistent with the authors' experience in the general community population. It certainly is consistent with what we have experienced in facilitating structured survivors' groups. At the same time, it appears to be probably a far too optimistic estimate when referring to a suicide which has more or less directly impinged upon the lives of the students, teachers and staff of a school.

A Community-Wide Effect

Not infrequently, the whole community may stop and ask, "Why did this have to happen? How vulnerable is each of us?" A large city in the Pacific Northwest recently experienced such widespread reactions when a popular and well-known public school teacher was found dead of exposure, a suicide which was both dramatic and far-reaching in its effects. The immediate school where the teacher had taught became temporarily immobilized. Students were devastated, not only those who had personal classroom contact, but others as well. Teachers and administrators found it exceedingly difficult to carry on as though school operations

were proceeding normally. Wisely, regular classroom activities were sus-
pended for a few days while school officials, bolstered by a large team
from the local Suicide Crisis Center, offered a series of rehabilitating
workshops and talk sessions for staff and students alike. Less extensive
but more intense grief therapy involving teachers and students especially close to the primary victim continued for a number of months. In
this case, as school and community reacted sharply to the crisis, the
school and community was ready to respond and the secondary victims
of a tragic experience received help and support which was severely
needed.

Unique Opportunities for Helping

The school environment provides its own share of adjustment problems for survivor-victims of suicide. Fortunately, at the same time, it can
also present unequaled opportunities in which to provide support for
those who have lost someone through suicide. While a completed suicide
is a true tragedy and brings with it unquantifiable cost and suffering, it
can also initiate a broad-based healing process. This process can result
in more than just recovery for the grieving and often frightened victims
or survivors. It can also produce an atmosphere of greater mental health
throughout the student body and staff, an atmosphere with lasting long-
range positive effects which extend to mental health issues far broader
than suicide.

In terms of the specific issue of suicide, a more committed and
meaningfully involved school population brings increased sensitivity
and a willingness to react to precipitating crisis situations. Because of
this, further suicide attempts and loss of life may be greatly decreased or
even totally averted. Each staff member is an important strand in a net
of support for the suicidal, as well as for those both directly and indirectly affected by a suicide experience.

Student populations are unique groups in terms of their cohesiveness. The school environment exerts an inordinate amount of influence
upon the individuals and groups of which it is comprised. The regular
daily contact, and the accepted assumption that the school is a place in
which to find dependable information, to acquire knowledge and to
share experiences designed to both shape and acquire new behaviors
heightens the school's influence. When individuals within such an influential environment experience anxiety-producing events, the effect is

widespread, reinforced by mutual group experiences and reactions, and can be, at times, virtually cataclysmic.

SPECIAL CONSIDERATIONS FOR THE SCHOOL

Being aware of this uniqueness, one must focus upon several important considerations always involved in the rehabilitation, mending and healing period that follows a crisis experience. Special attention must be given to both the positive and negative effects of peer pressure, to the effects of identification with peers (especially when the attempter may be a peer), and the degree to which faculty, staff, and students are sufficiently familiar with and sensitive to the subtle nuances as well as the obvious aspects of their own behavior and that of others.

The School's Unique Perspective

Fortunately, in the contemporary modern school, concerned teachers and staff may be more knowledgeable about some of the important details of important life-situation factors than even members of the family. Certainly, this is often true of the student's peer group. How often we hear parents say, "If only he (or she) had shared with us what was shared with his (or her) friends."

The authors were recently involved in such an unhappy situation. A 17-year-old, popular high school girl took her own life while her parents were on a weekend vacation a short distance out of town. Her parents were heartbroken, heavy with grief which was complicated by their guilt over not having recognized their daughter's dire straits. In sad retrospect, the family members all agreed that the teenager's problems had not appeared to be as difficult or extreme as they proved to be. "If we'd only known of the pain she felt . . ." was their lament, offered even as they were beginning to learn to deal with the futility of assistance coming offered too late.

The situation was made still more pathetic when it was later discovered that schoolmates of the suicide victim had heard statements such as, "What I do won't matter anyway . . ." and noticed decreasing interest in grades, boyfriends and social events. But these teenage peers, close as they were to the victim, were lacking experiences or training that might have helped sensitize them to the critical importance of such remarks and behavior. It is sad to note that a call for help had been made, heard, but not recognized. In careful retrospect it was clearly established that no one could reasonably be blamed for the final tragic progression of events that culminated in this young girl's death. The symptoms had been obscure and the young girl had been very psychologically disturbed. Still, the wide-reaching effects of the death were shared by many.

It may be even more tragic, and it certainly is more reprehensible, when a young person dies in a crisis situation marked by the failure of family or friends or peers or school personnel either to recognize their responsibility to prepare to give needed assistance in advance of an emergency crisis situation or to respond with appropriate help when requested. School personnel are typically quick to respond when the needs or problems of a particular student are clearly presented. Many times, school personnel perform surrogate parental functions far beyond the formal definitions of their job for children who are struggling with the strongly disruptive effects of a dysfunctional family member. They often act as temporary buffers in times of non-school crises and may even be the only real source of support that a young person has in instances of temporary stress.

Everyone agrees, however, that the best and most long-lasting support probably comes from the positive contributions made by a healthy and supportive family. Because of this, school personnel are most likely to think of their contribution to the mental health of the individual student to be in the form of supporting other sources, e.g. the family, the physician, the clergy.

We think it is important to call attention to another contribution available to the school, a contribution very often overlooked by school personnel and certainly not typically stressed in the training of teachers or school administrators. Teachers, counselors, administration, staff, and students are often afforded opportunities not available to parents in even the healthiest and most functional homes. They are observers of a portion of the young person's life seldom seen by parents or any of the other traditional support resources. They witness at first hand the learning experiences of the growing child and they have the opportunity to perceive more peer interactions than probably any other person or persons in the student's life. Sometimes, they observe the projected results of home and non-school experiences as they surface in the school, but there are also times when they are in a position unavailable to anyone else.

DISTINCTIVE ROLES, DISTINCTIVE OPPORTUNITIES

Increased opportunity and responsibility for the school comes not from an indictment of the effectiveness of the family. They come instead by virtue of several factors resulting from the distinctive role and position of the school and its staff, factors often beyond the control and influence and certainly not necessarily the fault of parents or as a function of the family's health and well-being. Being aware of the circumstances that give rise to these roles, with their potential for increased effectiveness, is important for school personnel who would serve their young peers well in time of crisis recovery.

School-Based Experience as a Causal Factor

These unique opportunities are most obvious when the need to respond rises out of an experience directly shared by the school population, e.g. the suicide of a student or teacher. An example from our own case files illustrates both the point and a noteworthy response by a school system.

A busload of elementary students of an urban school district were on their way to school and witnessed a fatal automobile accident. Students and driver together witnessed firsthand the death of a passenger thrown from a car next to their bus. The impact was profound. Police, approaching the bus a few minutes later for the purpose of gathering information, found driver and students huddled together in tears, with the driver attempting to console his small charges though he was weeping himself.

The students (and the driver) were taken to the school gym while parents were contacted. School personnel quickly moved into the gap, physically holding and cuddling the children, talking with others about topics ranging from their own shock and grief reactions to basic issues related to death and dying. As parents, a school physician, and neighbors arrived at the school, they were invited to participate in a grief recovery process which was already well underway. This school offered far more than the three R's to its students. It's genuinely warm and appropriate response forged close bonds between school and neighborhood that will not easily be loosened or quickly forgotten. Later, more structured follow-up discussions were held in the classrooms, in PTA meetings and even in school-wide assemblies where speakers such as a local paramedic presented practical and useful information.

While it is certainly to be expected that the children's families would have been equally supportive had this accident occurred in their presence, the fact is that the school had no choice but to act when the crisis occurred while students were at least nominally in the charge of the school. The school clearly helped victims become recovering survivors.

Another example: Who among us will ever forget the space shuttle disaster and the look of dismay on the faces of the school children who watched from their classrooms, safe from physical harm but fully exposed to the emotional shock waves that affected school children across the nation?

One of the authors' sons returned home from preschool classes announcing to his father, "The space shuttle crashed. I saw it on TV at school." This was followed by the pronouncement, "There were mommies and daddies inside and they died." This child's teacher had had no choice but to deal with the immediate situation. An explanation and reassurance were necessary and obviously were given, for the child went on to explain, "But our teacher told us that there were other people at home who loved the children and would take care of them."

The same message would have been a vital asset for literally thousands of school personnel across the country as they dealt with the focused impact of a crisis situation which could be neither avoided or ignored.

Other Contributing Factors

There are other aspects of the school situation that contribute to the distinctive roles and opportunities experienced by the school. Awareness of these are of intrinsic help to the school's aspirations to function most effectively. Without exception, the most effective and consistent responses come from schools that are prepared. Advance training and preparation for dealing with the crisis of grief and fear increases the probability that such healing interactions will occur. These are:

1. Large blocks of time regularly and consistently spent with students, time that can be effectively utilized in the healing process.
2. The availability of information about how children react and behave in an environment often more exposed and vulnerable than that of the home.

3. The luxury of the opportunity to objectively analyze from an outside perspective both problems and responses to problems.
4. The presence of many individuals with specialized training in human behavior, the implicit trust of those with whom they interact, and, potentially, the position and ability to effectively recognize and manage crises.

Each of these is worthy of special attention.

Extended Contact Opportunities

From the beginning of a child's education to completion of high school or college, the school and associated persons and activities may have a greater influence on students' behavior than any other single factor. The amount of time and influence of the school constantly grows: from kindergarden or preschool where children spend only a fraction of their waking hours, to secondary and post-secondary settings where students may spend almost all of their days and evenings in school-related activities which serve as nearly constant role models.

It is obvious that a positive set of experiences will significantly color a young person's future in many aspects of their maturation and development. When the experiences they encounter may be modeling how to effectively respond to the sudden loss of a friend or loved one, the need for especially productive experiences is critical. In our experience we have observed nothing that can be offered to the crisis victim ad lib, on the spur of the moment, which yields results as directly effective as do those responses that stem from careful preparation and training. There is nothing as effective as pre-crisis preparation.

Many suicide crisis centers offer ongoing programs of information and preparation for teachers and students. The Anchorage, Alaska Center, for example, holds a series of "Prevention and Intervention" workshops in schools. Sometimes, these are in response to growing concern of school administrators over repeated instances of suicide attempts among students. Others are undertaken as a result of the forward thinking of school personnel and parent groups who endorse the philosophy that "an ounce of prevention is worth a pound of cure." Certainly, in terms of the context of improving students' capabilities to deal with crisis, there can be no argument. In the above programs, efforts of the Center's personnel are augmented by other social service professionals, psychologists and counselors from the university, and many, many specially trained volunteers working as a team with the school. The Anchorage Center has further cemented the team effort by including school, university and business personnel on its board of directors and involving them in the building of long-range delivery of service programs.

Similar efforts can be found in many sites. The Cherry Creek (now S.P.A.R.E.) program in Colorado and the extensive workshops of the San Mateo, California schools are fine examples of specific training and preparation for meeting the special needs of students before the need arises. The Crisis Center, with which the authors are most closely associated, does considerable work in educational settings as evidenced by several series of presentation/intervention sessions in schools where a suicide was attempted or completed. Following several attempts by students to take their lives, administrators at a local junior high school requested a team of crisis interventionists to meet with students. Post-suicide attempt rehabilitation was the goal but was considered in the greater context of improving the students' school experiences and, thereby, many aspects of their lives.

Specialized Data Bases

Knowledge about students may be garnered from a number of sources. Information derived from the pupil's academic classroom performance can be used as a baseline against which negative or, hopefully, positive changes may be measured. A decline in classroom performance may indicate that a young person is experiencing difficulty or, in the case of the suicide survivor, that the healing process is not proceeding well. Likewise, an improvement in quality or quantity of work can signify that the clouds are lifting. Sensitivity to a student's recovery and renewed interaction with the everyday demands of the academic program conveys a message to the survivor and the survivor's peers, as well. The message is one of sincere interest, an evaluation of personal worth, and the implicit guarantee of available support and help.

School performance and activities less easily evaluated by objective grade-type criteria will provide equally helpful data in making similar judgments of the survivor's "progress."

Though both the demands and the product differ from the 3 R's type activity, the creativity and personally initiated spontaneity required in arts classes, for example, offers situations that can yield rich insight into an individual's capability of coping with his or her world. The quantity or "ease" of productivity may suggest the capability of the individual to focus on issues less critical to everyday living, to put worries and concerns aside for less acute issues. The content of the product of such work, essays, stories, or poetic compositions may be very enlightening. Note, for example, the poignant personal feelings expressed in the *Excerpts From a Survivor's Poem.*

EXCERPTS FROM A SURVIVOR'S POEM*

A LAST LOOK

When I was four years old
I used to wonder what
your voice would sound like once
you started talking.

Seventeen years we were
brothers in one room
my voice, and your voice.
Then you killed yourself
Dad went crazy, died
My grief was stopped
with rage that you could do
such a thing to me.

And there was also fear.
No male in my family
lived but me; I was
twenty-one. Perhaps
my sex could be a poison.
I dug at myself to find
and defang that cobra
if it were in me. . . .

I don't know how I came
to bend my back as if
I'd slung your adolescent
body on my shoulders
headed for some Boy's Town
of my mind, carrying
you through my life
unable or unwilling
to look at you or let
you drop, whining that
you wouldn't share the load. . . .

Today, in fantasy
I raise your body up
just to hold
and say goodbye to.

---

*From Rosenfeld and Prupas (1984).

Maybe I also want
to warm you still, be hugged
by you, but you quickly
decay and I must drop
you back into the earth.

Poor little guy who killed
himself, who is becoming
earth at last, I miss
you and remember you,
I mourn you too, but I
am near the end of mourning.
                              end

Artwork may be of equal interest. It may reflect the nature and extent of the student's current concerns. Therapists frequently use the drawings of clients to help understand the dynamics of feelings and behavior being experienced. The three drawings by survivors included here help illustrate this (see Figs. 6-1, 6-2, & 6-3). Though not done in the school room, such material very often will emerge in situations which are not overtly related to any professional or formal therapy arrangements.

Figure 6-1. Survivor's Drawing No. 1

In the first drawing (Fig. 6-1), an adult survivor, illustrating his feelings as part of a survivor-group treatment experience, illustrates the painful ebb and flow of feelings experienced by the survivor as grief is slowly worked out and life struggles to regain its normal status. Elaborating on this drawing, the "artist" writes:

I am a rock on the beach just at the water's edge. Behind me is the forest and the sun — peace and tranquility. In front of me is the ocean, turbulent and cold. The ocean is my pain and my confusion. Sometimes it covers me like the ocean covers a rock. Sometimes I can see the forest; I am myself again.

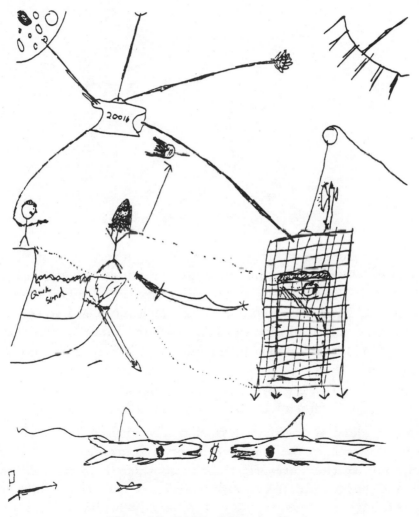

Figure 6-2. Survivor's Drawing No. 2

Figure 6-3. Survivor's Drawing No. 3

The second drawing (Fig. 6-2) was done by a very confused and up-set teenager whose mother had recently committed suicide. No artist's explanation is necessary to perceive the mixture of hurt, anger, fear, and other feelings with which this individual is struggling to cope.

Describing the third drawing (Fig. 6-3) the survivor artist, noting feelings of inadequacy and helplessness stemming from the suicide loss of a loved one, writes:

> I am a tree. I have always shaded the people I love but now a part of me has died. I've lost a limb and no one can enjoy my cool shade.

Similar material, perhaps less clinically focused but certainly of descriptive worth to the sensitive observer, may be available in the schoolroom. Teachers are urged not to consider themselves clinicians, nor should they attempt to use such material as a clinician would projec-tive techniques. However, youth will frequently display feelings through drawing or writing when at the same time they might feel very reluctant to speak of them openly. Observed strong feelings and heavy emotions are worthy of at least some attention and further explanation.

Physical activity levels and performance may also provide useful indicators of adjustment levels. Physical education classes or the pupil's involvement in competitive or playground athletics can indicate a lower or higher energy level perhaps characteristic of the individual's overall energy level. Teachers are in an optimal position to observe changes and trends in a student's behavior. Such information provides another piece to be carefully used in solving the puzzle of providing an optimum "recovery environment" for those who need to successfully "survive."

An Outside Perspective

But other pieces may be found, as well. These can come from friends, parents, and teachers. The victim also may provide helpful information. Sometimes, being able to talk about feelings in a situation away from the loci of those feelings permits more freedom. Those less closely associated may offer a model of calmness and "healthiness" which is cathartic and healing to the survivor. As in dealing with the person "at-risk" of suicide, it is most helpful to talk about the problem, to openly face the worries, to share anxieties rather than to gloss over, ignore or assume that despite the traumatic experiences of the past, business "goes on as usual."

The maturing child grows increasingly independent of parents and other family members. Other individuals, not necessarily part of the family, become the objects of close bonding, identification, and emulation. Relationships with others achieve even greater significance as the child approaches adulthood. The developmental tasks of adolescence personify this. When a child enters the adolescent years, friends and acquaintances, rather than parents, become the most frequently utilized sources of information about life and living. Encountering problems does not necessarily change the trend. Contemporary research underlines this fact.

In a recent survey (Ross, 1985), high school students were asked to note those with whom they would be most likely to confide about problems. Choices included parents, other adults, teachers, school counselors, school nurses, and doctors. "A friend" was the most popular choice, selected by over 90 percent of those questioned. Informal inquiries by the researcher supported the conclusion that the students interviewed felt that there were only certain problems they could share with parents, teachers, etc. The range was limited. But "friends," in the opinion of these students, could be trusted with "anything." In a sense, these friends offered an objective, non-crisis environment in which feelings could be vented and information more safely shared. School situations oftentimes can provide a similarly safe and helpful milieu.

Personnel with Specialized Training

In the school setting, many of the primary confidants of students in trouble are lacking in specific knowledge of appropriate response modes to crises. While school counselors and school nurses are most likely of all school personnel to be experienced in addressing suicide-related problems, they too may not have the kind of specific information needed to deal with suicide-related crises. Without specialized training in crisis intervention and a focus on suicide, even counselors and nurses are apt to be ignorant of many of the options available under such circumstances. They may also be lacking some of the skills necessary to most effectively promote successful healing and rehabilitation. On the other hand, these same personnel to whom others turn to in time of crisis can be very easily trained and assisted to supplement their already available skills and techniques with those special aspects which will make their contributions to crisis management and resolvement particularly effective. Finding and utilizing persons with special skills and abilities, or training those who are both able and willing to learn, is imperative whether they be staff members, parent volunteers or members of the community who are willing to invest themselves in the successful development of the community's children.

NETWORKING

Let us not forget that survivors, by definition of their experience and emotional status, are at higher risk than others. The same principles that hold for primary suicide prevention are relevant for application in survivor work, as well. Effective suicide-survivor programs make use of the established concepts of crisis intervention in their work with this important population of suicide victims. The guidelines for effective intervention (see Chap. Four) are as useful with survivors as expected attempters.

When individuals and agencies with special skills can be joined together, no matter how informally, the result is a very useful consortium
of support and help which is known as a "network." In all but the most
ideal of situations, dependence upon resources that transcend those of
any single source or agency is not only useful but often vital.

It is tremendously helpful to have a wide range of resources upon
which to call. This becomes most evident in emergency or crisis situations where directly effective help must be obtained quickly. Since it is
frequently the case in suicide-related problems that the matter is one of
life and death (often with an immediacy time factor involved), it becomes especially important that the informal communication lines between the various components of the network work quickly, easily, and
well. Networks give assistance in the form of active help and services;
they also provide a rich source of information about both the help available and also, in many cases, about the individual involved. It is important, however, that the use of the network and the data provided through
such associations be carefully examined for accuracy and reliability.

Validating Network Data and Functions

Though a wide data base is useful, perhaps even essential to the efficient formulation of a positive recovery environment for the survivor,
some precautions should be noted. Facts should be carefully separated
from rumor. Hypotheses or judgments consensually cross-validated
should be distinguished from isolated opinions and assumptions. Data is
only data and should not be substituted for the "real" aspects of life. The
validity and reliability of even soft data such as this should be carefully
considered. Networking probably provides the best protection from
either inadequate or over extended generalizations. Some form of cross-
referencing or cross-validating of assembled information is necessary.
All sources should be utilized.

Parents possess knowledge and impressions of their children based
on a child's lifetime of experience. The perspectives of parents often
come from a slowly building fund of rich information which has accu-
mulated from years of observation, inevitably offering more opportunity
for acquiring insights than that which is available in a few semesters.
Much of the information collected by the school can and should be cross-
referenced with parents.

There are other ways to validate the assembled information. These
include: networking with other agencies (and individuals), use of

community sources, and the use of school sources. Networking with agencies and individuals outside the school allows for the broad perspective of a number of professional areas and viewpoints. The impact of an attempted or completed suicide touches all aspects of the survivor's life. If, for instance, the effects of the loss disrupt familial interactions, a professional specializing in interventions with families can probably best judge the extent of the problem and recommend the most viable treatment options. Knowledge and experience-based suggestions can be implemented by school officials to round out an effective rehabilitation plan for the student.

Extending the Network

Full use of community sources can provide confirmation for hypotheses by extending the behavior sample beyond school and home. Potential sources of information can be found in a wide range of places. Staff members of such organizations as boy's and girl's clubs, scouts, recreational and athletic organizations, hobby and skill groups, and church organizations may, in different instances, provide meaningful and helpful information and insights. If the student is or has been employed, concerned employers and supervisors are often helpful and many times very willing to be of assistance. In each instance, however, care must be taken not to violate the individual student's right of confidentiality. But, in many cases, the presence of the problem is widely known and of concern to broad segments of the population so contact may be made without confidentiality problems.

School sources of information should include personnel and resources beyond those "directly and presently" involved in the care of the survivor victims. This can include professionals, such as psychometrists, who have access to the student's projective and diagnostic information, physicians, or even dentists who may have had occasion to get to know the survivor well. All possible sources of information should be considered when determining the severity of a grieving student's distress.

Problems Inherent in Extended
Networks

When numerous sources of information are being utilized, the potential exists for inconsistency of data. Different conclusions could conceivably be drawn from different aspects of the information assimilated.

When the variance of available data is low, that is, much of the data supports a single conclusion, the immediate course of action to initiate treatment may be relatively easy to determine. When conclusions must by necessity be based on high variance data, very careful consideration must be given to information suggesting the worst of all possible scenarios and all the nuances of variances involved. One should not be impulsive or a "doomsayer," but failure to respond aggressively in the face of suggested impending crisis reactions can, and sometimes does, result in avoidable disasters. Shneidman (1985) suggests that an extremely high percentage of suicidal reactions can be successfully predicted. What appears to be the critical variable is the assembling of critical data and putting it in the hands of those who are best able to interpret it. Through regular staff meetings, coordinated by a key staff person, information vital to the recognition of the student in crisis can be assembled. Coordination can follow, with the appropriate help-givers and services being activated.

The Value of an Extended Network

What finally emerges is a network of information sources, each with a valuable contribution to make to the process of understanding survivors who are struggling to recover from their own crises, crises precipitated by the suicide of a significant other. Every person in a suicide survivor's environment has a potential role in a "support net," buttressing the victim's coping mechanisms as necessary, facilitating hastened rehabilitation. Coordination of responses through education beforehand not only makes for the most efficient response to a completed suicide, but it should also lessen the immediate suffering of survivors and facilitate their long-range rehabilitation. Shneidman (1986) emphasizes the importance of considering the entire environmental "press" of the individual caught up in the suicidal process. This important concept, embodied in the **personology** of Henry Murray (1967), reminds us of the important social interactions of suicidal behaviors. Use of a society-wide network in rehabilitation is a logical response to an event that has so many social factors in its etiology. But even in the absence of preparation, significantly helpful response patterns can be developed in the school. Every school needs to be ready to have someone step into a position of coordination of the support network.

The support network ideally should be coordinated by a staff member with training in the area of mental health. This will often be the school counselor or nurse. On the basis of information supplied by a variety of concerned individuals, the struggles of a survivor can be identified even when not overtly obvious in terms of the formal system. Once recognized, an appropriate response can then be orchestrated. Many different individuals, playing diverse roles, applying some reasonably simple principles, are potentially involved. Identification of these individuals, descriptions of the roles, and presentation and explanation of these principles follows in the remainder of this chapter.

Support and Help-Giving Roles

While the role a staff member or student plays in the school support network may vary, all potential interveners may be seen as offering either support or some clearly defined intervention technique or some combination of the two. Both of these aspects of problem resolution are vital. Relatively successful behavior-change organizations, such as Alcoholics Anonymous or various weight-control groups, achieve their success, in part, due to the integration of support and help-giving functions, often performed by clinically unsophisticated volunteer participants.

Support for a suicide survivor includes such uncomplex actions as simply taking the time to talk to him or her when things appear to be not going well. In order for the survivor to feel comfortable, personal rapport must be built. If the victim is a student, it is often helpful for the support-giver to engage in common, enjoyable activities that are enjoyable and part of the stable everyday life. In such instances, an informal pickup basketball game on a playground court may be far more therapeutic than it appears. The student or staff member offering support may join the grieving student at lunch or in other everyday activities. The survivor may not reach for the hand extended to him/her immediately, but the knowledge that someone is there, concerned, and above all available, is priceless.

"Help-giving" is seen as a specific action or group of specific techniques that enable the suicide survivor to accommodate the loss and continue on productively with the business of living.

Specialized and complex clinical intervention techniques are clearly best handled by trained personnel, who may often not be available among typical school personnel. While school counselors are ideally situated and frequently trained to offer more direct and involved clinical interventions, almost any member of the school staff can be trained on the job to effectively apply the principles of crisis intervention and primary support and help-giving. Techniques, such as rapport-building, problem identification, selection of potential solutions, and the developing of an action plan, are fairly straightforward, easily learned and applied, and yet can provide a significant portion of assistance required by those enmeshed in the grief that often follows a suicide death.

ROLES FOR DIFFERENT SCHOOL PERSONNEL

Each member of the school staff provides a vital strand to the web of support for those who have experienced a crisis. Each has a unique and individually distinctive role to play in creating an atmosphere where healing can most easily take place. In every vocation, each individual provides a distinctive perspective not otherwise available. These separate roles, impinging in different ways and in different aspects of the survivor's life, help the survivor to feel totally surrounded by caring people. Competent intervention by appropriate professionals reassures those in crisis that the support network is providing not only well-intentioned but knowledgeable and effective help. The roles are as varied as the job definitions of those who play them.

The Teacher

The traditional classroom teacher directly observes the individual student in one-to-one situations more often than any other single staff person in the school. The classroom instructor is in the ideal position to note and assess changes in mood, attitude, behavior, and appearance.

The regular, consistent tracking of students in crisis can be easily integrated with normal classroom routine and need not be an unusual or extra burden. Relatively little time and effort is required to assess and record what may prove to be critical information about a troubled student. Since these types of students represent a very small subset of the school population, the task is neither large nor onerous. One or two brief inquiries or even covert observations are often sufficient to provide the necessary information, which can then be recorded in a very brief and informal way, much as one might note special recitation skills or record attendance.

In addition to the traditional classroom, educators consistently interact with students in a variety of other settings. Among these are the athletic field, atypical classrooms specializing in vocational or technical instruction, art labs, and various laboratories. Sensitive staff in these settings can make a very useful contribution.

The coach, for example, is frequently an instructor who is emulated and sought out by his or her charges. By the nature of the activity involved and the more open, often individualized nature of athletic activities, coaches (and team trainers and managers, too) may be approached more often as significant others or even near-peers by students than are other school personnel. The student's desire for a closer-than-average relationship suggests the possibility of more easy sharing of personal information and a less defensive presentation of feelings and self-disclosure information.

The shop teacher is in a similar position. Working in a less formal environment and with a structuring of activities that requires individual performance and instructor-pupil contact, there is opportunity for personal interaction and observation of varied types and instances of the student's socialization with peers, responses to individual and group demands, and reactions to stress factors of various types.

Business methods and home economics teachers may find themselves in roles that approach surrogate-parent relationships. Classroom activities become miniaturized laboratories of home and work situations, stages for communicating interests, aspirations (or loss of them) for the future. Students' actions and reactions may be both less constricted and more revealing than in the more traditional schoolroom environment.

An encouraging word from the librarian lets a student know that someone is there who cares. Suggestion of a book for the student's perusal or genuine interest in what the student is reading strengthens the internal school network. A sincere interest in a troubled student's hobby, sports or vocational interests, and a willingness to aid this student conveys the message that the library is a place to go not only to expand knowledge but for respite when the outside world is frightening or overwhelming. In a more professional sense, the librarian may also serve as the resident expert on literature related to a variety of mental health issues, i.e. handling stress, developing communication skills, even such specific topics as post-suicidal crises and how to survive them. Providing helpful material and information is a distinctively useful contribution to staff and students alike.

With an appropriate "set" for information gathering and active involvement in the student-support network, these educators represent a major resource to the school's internal support and rehabilitation network.

The Administrator

The administrative style personified in a given school's operations is a major determinant of the degree to which individual personnel will freely commit themselves to an in-school network for the support of students. The school principal's commitment to the support-network concept is imperative, determining the atmosphere in which such a system operates, or perhaps even whether or not this type of rehabilitation is possible at all. A superintendent of schools has the same influence on a school district. The school principal has at his or her disposal an extremely powerful reinforcer: personal attention. In the authors' experience, there seems to be no greater thrill for a student, especially younger students, than to have the principal personally acknowledge them in a warm and friendly way, talk to them in the hall or sit with them at lunch, recognizing them as individuals.

But, in addition to lending official sanction and support to other staff and personal attention to students, the administrator plays some other important roles. Perhaps, the most significant of these is an internal and external role model.

Internally, the chief school administrator sets the tone and mood for the entire school. Staff and teachers will both consciously and unconsciously model on the performance of the principal. The principal's own behavior makes strong suggestions about what will and will not be looked upon with favor, and staff are quick to note these cues.

Externally, the principal represents the entire school, to much of the community. It is the principal, or the principal's representative, that the parent, the businessman, the fireman, the policeman, the service club views most directly. It is through the principal that much of the community becomes acquainted with the school. For the school that is led by a principal who highly values good mental health for students and the rest of the community, networking becomes easy. For the school administered by a principal who leaves such concerns up to others, there are many extra hurdles to vault to accomplish the same ends.

TABLE 6-1

FUNCTIONS AND GOALS FOR DIFFERENT PERSONNEL

Position	Goals	Functions
Administration	Maintain and supervise active support system	Provide needed flexibility for staff and student, demonstrate active support of school involvement
Classroom teachers	Monitor student recovery Input information into school support network	Note academic performance, general behaviors, interaction with peers.
Atypical-classroom teachers (art, etc.)	Supplement observation available in regular classroom	Provide opportunity for expression of feelings, emotions, creative expression
Physical activity teachers	Supplement observation available in other classroom situations	Provide opportunity for physical interaction with others, competitive activities, handling frustration
Library staff	Information resources, temporary respite from group involvement	Acquire suitable materials relevant to students' problem areas, provide place for quiet individual work
Student personal staff	Bridge to outside network components, focused support to student. Guide rest of staff in providing support	Monitor rest of internal support network, keep supportive contact with student, maintain liaison with family and outside network
Support staff	Non-academic situation observation, augment supportive milieu	Note eating habits, social interactions, provide warm personal contact

Support Staff

Cafeteria staff are in an excellent position to guage whether a troubled young person is successfully coping. Eating is one of the primary recreational activities of adolescent males and, to a lesser degree, females. Any divergence from normal eating patterns suggests a break in the trend of normal behaviors and may signal a developing problem. A food-service employee can deliver that little extra tender loving care by giving a depressed-appearing student an extra kind word or morsel of food.

Non-teaching staff members, such as those who may work in the bookstore or snack bar, or volunteer assistants connected with extracurricular activities may also provide meaningful input regarding the emotional well-being of students. While these individuals may not typically be full-time key members of a student-support system, their ability to help through a friendly word, support, encouragement, or a moment or two of individual attention should not be overlooked. Each positive interaction with the environment that the suicide survivor experiences increases the probability of an eventual successful re-integration into a healthy ongoing life frame.

Custodial staff are often respected and admired by students. They have the advantage of being adults among the students, but enjoy a less-threatening status since they are not teachers. In a junior high school where we have worked, one of the custodial staff is known by all to be a special friend and confidant of the young people. He's given wide latitude by administration to offer support and give the personal warmth which the students seem to seek of him. The school staff knows that it is "George," of all the adults in the building, who most generally hears first of a student's problems or accomplishments. This custodian is also encouraged to be a participant in staff in-service workshops dealing with management of troubled students. He is already recognized as part of the school's informal support network. With some additional information and training, he might become a major contributor to students' mental health and the ability of that particular school to provide survivors with a rehabilitative atmosphere. This is an example of the use of a staff member's personal abilities which extend beyond formal job definitions in surprising directions. No potentially valuable contributor should be overlooked.

Student Personnel Staff

All of the staff members discussed above interact with the student in what amounts to paraprofessional capacities. That is, their support networking is over and above their traditionally defined roles.

Student personnel workers (such as school nurses, psychologists, speech therapists) have an identified "health function" which suggests that their role may be more focused on these support tasks than others. If the range of contributions available from these personnel is freely utilized by the school, staff and students alike will identify these individuals as those in a special position to provide help. Students will often turn to these "specialists" in time of personal crisis, whether it is physical, emotional or some mixture of both. Other school personnel become used to making "help-seeking" referrals to these people so that when a referral is made in time of severe problems or potential crisis, it does not carry any special shock characteristics or the taboo of the student being in "real" trouble.

In some school districts, the school psychologist may not be readily available to the individual student in each school. In some districts, school psychologists work out of central offices or serve schools on a rotating-assignment basis. In such situations a primary contact network of on-site student personnel people needs to be established so that the student's need for contact with the psychologist can be facilitated and, when necessary, expedited. The psychologist's special training is often helpful in both an immediate and consulting mode.

The school nurse will play a similar role in many school communities and, like the psychologist, may be especially useful in providing a ready access route to outside help sources such as psychiatrists, physicians, and help-giving agencies in the non-school community.

Of all the school staff, the school counselor may, by definition, have the most crucial role to play. The counselor has highly specialized tasks to perform. The responsibilities range from internal staff-support functions to active liaison roles when helping the school to interact effectively with outside social-service agencies or professional therapists. The counselor's role with school personnel can be characterized as focusing on instructional and coordination responsibilities. Because of specialized training and knowledge relevant to the mental health field, school personnel and students may be apt to ask more of the counselor than can reasonably be expected. School counselors are not therapists per se, and though they may be the bridge between school and the therapist, the roles and responsibilities do differ and such differences should be made clear to all concerned.

Differing Roles of the School Counselor and the Professional Therapist

The school counselor indeed has primary responsibility for the emotional survival of students in his or her charge; this is a charge not unlike that of the professional therapist. But the two roles are **not** the same and must not be confused.

The school counselor applies a wide variety of skills and special techniques to meet this responsibility. These range from the monitoring of students at-risk and channeling appropriate support resources, to conducting crisis therapy. The role of the school counselor should not, however, be confused with that of the professional therapist. There are significant differences. The objective of the school counselor, to facilitate student adjustment to the school environment, is very similar to those applied in any situation utilizing a crisis-intervention model.

The therapeutic approach most often utilized by the school counselor consists primarily of two aspects:

1. Helping the school develop an environment conducive to good adjustment as it facilitates the learning experience.
2. Responding to immediate concerns rather than initiating a process of personality change aimed at addressing deeper or longer-term problems.

In the span of a single session, a student and school counselor may progress from rapport building to problem identification to problem solving. Ongoing therapy is not an objective of the student-counselor relationship and is more appropriately delivered by a professional therapist willing to network with school personnel.

School Counselors and Psychotherapy

The school counselor is neither trained for nor hired to perform deep and long-lasting therapy. Survivors of suicide do indeed frequently need long-lasting and complex therapy. Survivors may continue to grieve for several years (Cain & Fast, 1972) and associated problems may be both far-reaching, in terms of impact on the victim's life, and deep-seated. A therapeutic relationship between a survivor and a professional therapist is designed to be responsive to the victim's complex and often far-reaching needs. Such a procedure demands both specialized training and time commitments which are not congruent with the school counselor's preparation and job description.

The counselor-student interaction is not, however, any less important. It does offer a type of support and recovery facilitation important to the survivor and difficult if not impossible for a professional therapist to provide. This includes the manipulation of school environments, everyday contact and sensitivity to a student or staff survivor's recovery interactions, and the necessary contacts to expedite the return to normalcy in the school environment.

Consequently, the developing of a counseling relationship between a professional therapist and a survivor does not negate either the responsibilities of or opportunities available to the school counselor. One relationship does not replace the other. They are complementary.

The counselor's interactions may be the critical ingredient that allows the student survivor victim to function on a daily basis. Each day is a potential crisis for those struggling to survive a suicide and may present new difficulties in coping. The counselor is in a position to be in daily contact with the student and to recognize the first signs of any downward spiral. The need for an active, on-site, regular program of recovery cannot be overstated. There are ample tasks for both the school counselor and the professional therapist.

The Counselor as Coordinator and Implementer

The school counselor plays a distinctive role in the school. He or she plays an important role as the centerpiece of a coordinated system responsive to the needs of troubled students. Whereas administrators are in a position of easing the initiation of such a program, the counselor is often responsible for actual formulation and implementation of the rehabilitative program. This is no incidental role but rather one with significant professional implications.

The primary responsibilities of the school counselor are these:

1. To bring to the situation a background of professional knowledge about human behavior and adjustment.
2. To apply professional skills in the evaluation of behavior and the manipulation of interactive environments conducive to good adjustment.
3. To model sensitivity and responsiveness to the needs of others through relationships with students and staff.
4. To provide a coordination role, when appropriate, to crisis prevention, intervention, rehabilitation and management.

5. To serve as a guide to sources of more specific information to meet individual problems and concerns.
6. To help coordinate and effect a bridge between the school and community resources in the area of good mental health.

TABLE 6-2

THE SCHOOL COUNSELOR'S CONTRIBUTIONS
AND RESPONSIBILITIES

Background and Training assets	In-house roles	Networking roles
1. Knowledge about behavior 2. Skills for shaping good adjustment 3. Evaluation skills 4. Environmental management and manipulation	1. Modeling of sensitivity 2. Responsiveness to needs of others 3. Effective relationships with staff and students 4. Coordinate crisis prevention, intervention and management within the school	1. Guide to information sources 2. Coordinate bridge between school and community resources

THE IMPACT OF BEING A SURVIVOR

Loss of someone we care about is a traumatic experience. We come to expect that our world, and the people in it, will remain constant. Even when the world about us or personal circumstances are in turmoil, we hope for and usually anticipate some measure of support and approval from close friends and family. The loss of a parent, child, sibling, or friend through death initiates a change in our lives that is both profound and irreversible. We are faced with not only the loss of a significant portion of our own personal support system but also must confront the reality of our own mortality and potential ultimate vulnerability. "If only he (she) were still here . . . or I was with him (her) . . ." is the frequent cry of those left behind.

There is no questioning the intensity of the experience. At such a time, one's whole body, entire existence, seems to be drowned in the unforgettable horror of the event. Everyone reacts with shock as evidenced in cognitive, emotional and even basic somatic functions. However, different people respond in different ways. One of the important tasks facing those who would work with survivors is to be able to recognize these different responses, realizing that different as they are, they often stem from similar experiences.

Bargaining and Self-Degradation Reactions

Many grief-stricken individuals bargain with God to return their loved ones at any cost (Kubler-Ross, 1969), hoping to be able to offer some personal offering or sacrifice in trade for a reversal of reality. However, only with the acceptance of the reality of loss, and the finality of the event, does the survivor begin the healing process.

Reactions to a death by suicide may be even more profound and disturbing than those resulting from deaths attributable to other causes. In part, this is due to the stigma surrounding a death by suicide, a stigma which magnifies the significance of the loss of support and amplifies the feeling of loneliness encountered by the survivor. Calhoun, Shelby and Faylstick (1980) found that parents of suicidal children were often viewed with dislike by other adults. As a result of such rejection, sometimes subtle and sometimes painfully evident, individuals will sometimes begin to accept a degraded self-concept, coming to see themselves as unworthy, inferior persons who somehow have deserved the calamity that fate has thrust upon them.

Guilt Reactions

When others demonstrate rejection coupled with intimations of even a possible assignment of causality to the survivor, the results can be even more devastating. The survivor will sometimes incorporate the feeling of direct guilt in addition to the feeling of unworthiness. This has frequently been observed in the authors' clinical experience.

In one instance, we were dealing with the parents and family of a young man who had recently took his own life. He was from a traditional Oriental family. Normal cultural mores strongly emphasized the primary importance of all family members receiving the approval of the parents. Respect for the parents and the evaluation of parental approval was high and genuine. In the process of events, the young man became involved with an older woman of another race. His own awareness of his violation of assumed parental trust developed into a guilt-precipitated estrangement. Eventually, as the situation became known in detail by the family, his self-perceived estrangement developed into a very real ostracism. Following several months of apparently unsuccessful efforts to re-establish favor in the eyes of his family, particularly his parents, the young man conceded defeat and elected to take his life.

It would be easy to draw quick and simple conclusions regarding the possible causal or precipitating effects the family's position may have contributed to the suicide decision in this circumstance. Similarly, it would at first glance be difficult to argue with the reality of the family justifiably feeling some personal guilt. Similar feelings are prompted by the circumstances of a large proportion of suicide attempts and successful completions. Directing attribution towards one's self is a common response. However, its commonality does not necessarily support its rationality.

In the case in question, an extended and closer examination of the primary victim's life history yielded validated information negating most if not virtually all of the family's responsibility. The facts of the case were that the victim was found to have a long history of depression and inability to cope with day-to-day stresses of almost any type—certainly not limited to either family contexts or interactions. While his school record was more than adequate, he constantly threatened and apparently seriously considered dropping out. Such drastic action was averted only through intensive counseling by the university staff and an active support network of friends and professors, quietly and unobtrusively abetted by the family. Notes and diaries found after his death indicated that suicide had been a serious consideration of his for several years, postponed only by the regular supportive interaction of family and friends. Even his suicide note alluded to emotional pain spanning experiences over the years that did not appear to even remotely involve the family. The final apparent "loss of face" may indeed have been a precipitating factor. No clinician would call it the "cause" or hold the family responsible.

We note this case to emphasize an important point. The decision to commit suicide is a personal one. It is a major error to consider suicidal people as exemplifying some group suicidal stereotype. Situations which appear to pressure the suicidal individual into the final fateful decision are not necessarily viewed in the same manner by he who elects to kill himself as by others, nor are they necessarily ascribed the same stress factors that others might assign. Stress, like beauty, is in the eyes of the beholder.

Intellectualizing Reactions

Many times in our lives we are confronted with crises for which we are not prepared. A large portion of these include emotional trauma in addition to the direct effects of the problem itself. Most people are better able to "think through" a problem than to accept it emotionally. To squarely face and accept the emotions would be to admit and display vulnerability at a level of frankness that is difficult for many of us. As a consequence, we very often develop the habit of resorting to interpretations and explanations that focus almost entirely on the cognitive or thinking aspects of the problem. This allows us a semblance of "dealing with" the problem while protecting us from the potentially more painful and less easily resolved emotional side. This process, frequently encountered in counseling and therapy, is called **intellectualization.**

One of the most significant factors in the recovery process following a personal experience with suicide is the release of feelings of responsibility for the perpetrator's death. Often, survivor victims may intellectually accept the death of a friend or relative as not resulting from their actions. The problem they may encounter is in assimilating that fact on an emotional as well as intellectual level. This task is made all the more difficult, if not impossible, in those instances where one of the motivations of the suicide perpetrator appears to be revenge directed towards the survivor.

One of the authors counseled with a woman whose daughter killed herself after a series of intrafamily confrontations. Following almost complete re-integration by the survivors, the immediate family received a suicide note that had been sent to a distant relative by the suicide victim. In the communication, the parents were named as the cause of their daughter's problem. The family was devastated and the recovery process was set back many months. Despite the unusual precipitant, this family's experience typifies the fluctuating emotional reaction to a personally relevant suicide experience.

In some instances those left behind may finally, after weeks or months, work out their grief and feel as if their lives are once more in order. The agony of loss becomes relegated to another time and place. In other cases, certain circumstances, which are often only incidentally encountered, will leave the survivor(s) feeling as if the loss had just occurred. Even the best adjusted "significant other" may occasionally experience the momentary shock and disorientation which initially characterized their early period of mourning.

Denial Reactions

When we experience a loss of something very valuable, our first reaction is apt to be one of disbelief. "Can this really be so?" we appear to be asking. Even such a simple thing as the loss of a wallet will result in this kind of behavior, with a repeated check of the trouser pocket to be sure it is really gone.

When we have not been prepared for a change, time may be required for the acceptance of its reality. It may take still longer for a thorough integration of that loss to occur throughout the rest of our life. When the change is precipitated by the loss of someone very close to us, the process of acceptance and re-investment in other activities and relationships is even more difficult.

A professional colleague recently lost his mother due to natural causes. In the course of his professional practice, he came in contact with numerous others who had recently suffered similar losses. Despite his professional training and experience, accommodation to his own loss when confronted with these similar experiences of others proved very difficult. "I can't believe this has happened to me," he found himself commenting a number of times. It occurred to him that it had "always been others" who had experienced such a loss. His helpful advice and guidance to them did not work as well when self-applied.

It is obvious that even in the best of situations and with far more than minimal preparation, loss of a loved one to death, especially a sudden death, presents an adaptive problem of potentially enormous proportions. The reality of death and its finality is difficult to quickly assimilate under optimal conditions. To deny the reality of death, thereby postponing the difficult adjustive process, is a very typical and normal reaction.

Those who have experienced the loss of a loved one through suicide may suffer a greater initial shock reaction than do persons who lose someone to death by other causes. The authors have counseled with parents who totally deny the circumstances of the suicidal death. Not only is the act of suicide given no credence, but the reality that the dead child will not be present and participating in ongoing family activities is not even given consideration. There is both clinical pathology and poignant emotion displayed in their comments. It is heart wrenching to observe the desperate clutching for futile hope evidenced in the explanation, "He's just out camping. He'll be home soon."

Depression as a Reaction

Depression is an almost universal reaction to the death of a loved one or to the serious consideration of one's own impending demise (Kubler-Ross, 1969). With suicide survivors, depression tends to set in at about the same time as the acceptance of the occurrence of the suicide event, itself. Rogers (1951) explains depression as occurring from a person's aspirations for themselves being something different from experienced reality. The survivor manifests depression as the loss of the perpetrator is accommodated. Consistent with Roger's theoretical framework, the cause of post-suicide depression may be seen as the dissonance between the wish for the return of the deceased and the realization that such is impossible.

From consultations with colleagues who deal extensively with suicide survivors, it appears that the presence of guilt accompanying depression occurs in a large majority of those suicide survivors whose "down" moods approach a clinical depression. This is consistent with Worden (1982), who states that pathological grief reactions differ from "normal" grief, in that those unusually affected experience self-deprecating feelings and loss of self-esteem. In our experience, this occurs in the suicide survivor in the presence of guilt apparently related to the failure to recognize the perpetrator's condition as being that of one seriously considering suicide or from a perceived ineffectiveness of adequacy in intervening when perceptions of impending suicide were present.

Anger Reactions

Anger is a common response. It is sometimes sufficiently severe as to be self-debilitating. It varies from being directed inwardly at one's self to being a type of guilt-ridden anger at the perpetrator for having "created such a problem." The prime effects of anger are addressed in detail later in this chapter.

SPECIAL FACTORS TO CONSIDER

The emotional trauma brought on by a suicide has a differential effect on persons and groups, depending on the factors involved and the interaction of some important variables. Many of these are not as yet clearly defined or measured in the research literature, and this task is the goal of many current suicide researchers. In the meantime, those of us who work in the field still must face the reality of some of these factors, even if their exact function remains to be precisely defined.

One which almost universally appears to differentially affect survivors is their interpersonal "closeness" to the suicide victim. Those with the strongest emotional ties, such as family members, friends, colleagues, etc., are seen as being in the main target group for experiencing severe emotional impact in a suicidal death. These effects, known as "primary group effects," have heavy impact on the schools when the suicide has been the parent, sibling or close personal friend of students, faculty or both. If the event has occurred geographically within the school complex, the physical propinquity may cause the primary group effects to spread farther than might be otherwise expected.

Those more emotionally removed from the suicidal person are often affected in very different ways. These reactions, labeled as "extended group effects" in the literature, are important to consider here because school personnel and peer students frequently fall into this category, and their problems, though different from those close to the victim, are still very real and often have strong impact on even this more removed group.

The Effects of Suicide on Primary Group Survivors

Not everyone is equally affected by a suicide. Those most immediately or strongly impacted are usually labeled as "primary" survivors. In some instances, it is difficult to decide who is and who is not a "primary survivor," but paying special attention to those whom we are sure fit this category is important.

Identifying the "Primary" Survivor

Primary group effects are seen in individuals who obviously fit the category of survivor-victims. These people are often (though not always) easily seen as being emotionally close to the perpetrator. Included would be parents, children, siblings, friends, and even playmates. In the school environment, others should be included or at least considered. These include close friends, lockermates, frequently classmates, teachers, coaches, counselors, and administrators. While not all of those listed above may appear to have shared the close personal relationship which friends and family experienced with the attempter or perpetrator, each may feel a sense of personal involvement and therefore the potential for assuming some immediate responsibility for the victim. One should consider the possibility that any one of these may be thinking, "What could I have done to stop it?" or "Maybe they would still be alive if I had only . . . ."

Teachers, administrators, and other service-oriented school professionals have positions which as a matter of course direct them toward assuming personal responsibility. It is easy to see how dedicated and sincere school personnel, though not a member of the nuclear family involved in the suicide, can easily be included within the primary group. For this type of school personnel to perceive their defined duties to include some type of moral responsibility for the traumatic event of a suicide is not a major step.

In addition, career choice in itself may tend to increment the incidence of this occurring. Those who choose teaching or similar professions often have a special commitment, a sense of dedication, to helping children and generally enriching children's experiences. This is easily coupled with assumed responsibility for the actions and behaviors of children entrusted to one's care. The children's failures are shared as are their joys and sorrows. When the child chooses suicide, the affected adult may feel some responsibility for the choice itself or, more subtly, for the decision-making process that eventuated in such a tragic result.

Elizabeth Kubler-Ross (1969) lists the five stages of grieving following the loss of a loved one as being: (1) denial and isolation, (2) anger, (3) bargaining, (4) depression, and (5) acceptance. Each of these is indeed experienced by the suicide survivor, but a more in-depth explanation is necessary to provide an understanding of the intensity and breadth of the impact of suicide upon survivors. It is also important to note the high variance of actions in different people and the typical difference in reactions between those personally associated with the perpetrator as compared with those whose relationship may have been significant in terms of the effect of the tragedy but could not be considered a close intimate relationship.

The impact of a self-caused death on individuals primarily affected involve a number of very important behavioral and emotional reactions. These are summarized in Table 6-3.

TABLE 6-3

SURVIVORS' EMOTIONAL AND BEHAVIORAL REACTIONS TO SUICIDE

Emotional reactions	Behavioral reactions
Shock	Tears, inactivity, confusion, inability to be goal-directed, excessive verbalization, panic
Sadness and depression	Long-lasting or repeated crying or talking about the event, sleep and eating disruption, lowered interest in regular activities, lethargy
Guilt	Worry, self-reproach, atoning actions, refusal of pleasurable activities or offered relief from stress, either withdrawal or excessive non-goal-oriented actions
Resentment and anger	Accusations toward victim or others, refusal to interact with other grievers, abrupt refusal to discuss event or victim (sometimes mixed with guilt behaviors)
Loneliness	Expressions of boredom, excessive dwelling on the past, dissatisfaction with pleasurable events or offers, isolation, shyness
Denial	Steadfast maintaining of everyday "normal" functions, refusal to display emotions, impatience with grievers, ignoring of all things relating to victim or event

Shock. As previously noted, the initial reaction to the news that a loved one has taken their life is one of shock. The message can be so devastating as to make the situation and surrounding circumstances seem unreal. In such an event, denial of the death may occur. The experiencing of a shock of this dimension and the resulting emotional reaction can be seen in this example.

A participant in one of our survivor groups, the father of a teenage daughter who several years previously had committed suicide, told us that the initial reaction to the news of his daughter's death transported him back to an experience in his childhood. He clearly recalled having received a package of fireworks for which he had been saving for almost a year. He acutely relived the excitement that grew as he lit the first explosive. He felt he actually watched once more as the fuse burned down, then went out, prompting him to pick up the incendiary for a closer examination. As he closed his hand, the firecracker exploded. The feeling of excitement and happiness was swept away in an instant, replaced by a numbness that spread over his entire body, replaced with a throbbing pain as sensation in his hand and fingers returned. Still, he only had a vague awareness of what had actually happened to him. "It was some hours," he reported to us, "before I really could think through the actual experience. I just kept remembering seeing the firecracker wrapped in it's red paper, sudden light, and then numbness and finally pain." His longer-term reaction to his daughter's suicide recapitulated the firecracker accident. At first, in the instant recall, and later as his grief worked itself out, he went through interrupted joy, numbness, pain and difficulty in recalling details of the event.

With the death of his daughter, the numbness persisted for months, the pain continued for several years. Only through time has this gentleman been able to put his life in order. The pain of the experience may never be extinguished but appears to lessen with the passage of time. Interestingly, recall of specific events connected with the tragedy have become clearer rather than faded, and his ability to cope with this has improved. It is as though he has managed to face reality and in so doing has mastered it.

Debilitating Sadness. Following (or sometimes simultaneously with) the initial-shock reaction, a variety of other emotions rend the survivor-victim. Probably, the most pervasive of these is an engulfing but not necessarily well-defined feeling of sadness. Other feelings seem to feed off this diffuse sense of sadness. Clients in the authors' survivor groups frequently explain that they always return to a dysphoric feeling as though it were meant to be their status quo.

Resentment and Anger. Oftentimes, an individual considering suicide, through some sort of hint or disclosure of the suicidal intentions, places significant others in a position where they must essentially independently elect to act or not. If action is taken, the friend or loved one must necessarily assume some role in the selection of method or form or type of intervention: essentially, offer up some sort of value judgment about what may be most helpful. This is a burden of tremendous, almost unimaginable responsibility and not easy for anyone, regardless of their personal mental health, to assume. The prospective survivor quite literally may feel as though the troubled child or adult has given them a life-or-death responsibility.

Reactions are varied both in type and their effect on the survivor. A very common response to this burden is of resentment. "How could they do this to me?" is the common complaint as fear and sorrow and worry and anger become blended together. Such confused reactions may be intensified in the school environment when the potential helper is a friend or staff person who feels neither adequately prepared nor legitimately selected to deal with this most serious of crises.

Those who have survived a suicide experience discover similar feelings of resentment, sometimes even rage rising amidst their sorrow. The completed act of suicide forever changes the life of those left behind. Some survivors in the later stages of adjustment to a suicidal death are infuriated that their lives have been disrupted and that they are obliged to experience such uncomfortable feelings. "I just want it all to go away" is not an infrequently expressed desire.

Anger may also be directed at professional help-givers or others in the survivor's environment. Survivors may feel that others should have recognized signs of impending crisis and intervened. Unfortunately, as was emphasized earlier in the chapter, even those who are on the receiving end of what later may be seen as inferences of suicide may not always recognize these signs, nor should they always be expected to do so, especially if they have had no training or experience in the area.

There is no stronger argument for increased community awareness through education than to point out that sensitivity for such signs can be increased through training, which is relatively easily available in most communities. Only through an aggressive approach to crisis prevention can people be spared the agony of being a suicide survivor.

Occasionally, a victim's anger may be unfocused. This represents a serious situation, in that a course of reparative action is not readily apparent. Feelings of anger may prevent the completion of grieving and leave the victim "locked" in a state where re-integration into day-to-day activities is not possible.

Guilt and Self-Reproach. Feelings of guilt and self-reproach may be related to anger. Those left behind following a suicide may feel guilt for not playing a significant role in offering the perpetrator more productive and fewer irreversible options. Guilt may also result when the prior relationship with the descendant was stressful, unhappy or in unpleasant circumstances. This easily gives rise to "If only I had . . ." statements, feelings, and self-incriminations.

The survivor-victim may encounter feelings of helplessness or experience anxiety over inability to function at perceived pre-crisis levels. In the school environment, this may give rise to academic difficulties for the student or ineffective classroom performance for the teacher. Less than satisfactory performance becomes coupled with anxiety over that performance, and survivors may as a result find themselves in a situation of circular self-fulfilling prophecy about personal adequacy. The grieving student may begin a downward spiral in performance that, if not recognized, may result in another potentially suicidal person (see Table 6-4).

TABLE 6-4

CIRCULAR SELF-FULFILLING PROPHECY RESPONSES

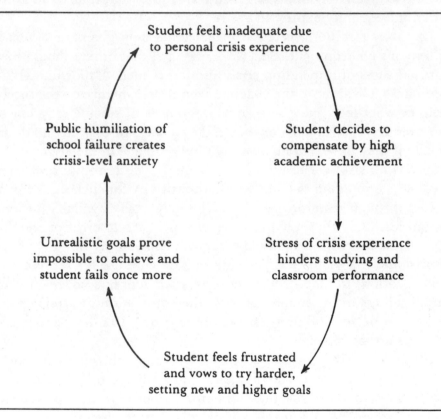

Loneliness. Survivors will frequently experience loneliness, especially in instances where the survivor and the perpetrator had typically been together for large blocks of time. A woman client whose husband was a suicide stated that she now spent a good deal of time pacing the floor or just sitting. She now felt that she had nothing to do which would fill the time previously spent with her husband as well as it had been in the past. Much of her currently unoccupied time was being spent thinking about things she and her husband had done together and how much she wished he were still alive. This lonely sense of longing for a deceased loved one is a common suicide-survivor reaction.

Emancipation and Relief. If the relationship that was lost (i.e. the one with the suicide perpetrator) was aversive, survivors may experience feelings of emancipation. This is particularly true if the perpetrator-survivor's relationship had been complicated by the perpetrator's being overprotective, jealous, or abusive. In suicide, as in death by other causes, children and adolescents in particular may angrily proclaim, "I'm glad he is dead."

Care must be taken that significant persons in the child's environment do not induce feelings of guilt through the rejecting of thoughts and emotions (of any valence, positive or negative) as being inappropriate. An initial reaction on the part of educators and other adults may be to say, "You don't really mean that." The child's feelings may not be clearly rational, but they will be honestly held and expressed. Denial by an adult may suppress them, cause them to be less overt, but it will neither extinguish them nor the emotional anguish that accompanies them. Through warm and individual understanding, coupled with professional help when necessary, the child or adolescent suicide survivor can be helped to have more settled and less destructive feelings toward the perpetrator than when he or she was alive and thus defuse a potentially incapacitating grief from developing.

Suicide is unarguably a tragic occurrence. But, with warm personal support from friends, and application of professional help as necessary, a self-inflicted death can initiate a healing process previously impossible.

However, survivor feelings of being released from an intolerable situation occur infrequently when it has been a young person who has taken his or her life. Parents may sometimes experience such feelings when family interactions and the developmental processes of the child have been particularly stressful. These feelings of relief are more often observed in situations where the survivor is a student and the suicide victim is a person in a perceived position of power, e.g. a parent, teacher, or administrator involved in a stressful or aversive relationship with at least some of the immediate survivors.

A feeling of relief may occur following a suicidal death when the perpetrator is seen as having experienced either emotional or physical suffering. Associates of the authors worked professionally with an entire school population as survivors of the suicidal death of a staff member afflicted with a very painful and incurable disease. Many of the emotions above were expressed by students and staff, but those close to the one who took her life consistently noted that in spite of their sense of personal loss and some anger at the mass effects experienced by the entire school population, they still felt that a positive purpose had been accomplished in the alleviating of their late friend's personal suffering. Years of watching their friend and colleague degenerate before their eyes had given them a profound sense of understanding of the individual's prime intent: release from pain. They experienced but were able to overlook or forgive the residual pain passed on to those who remained alive.

In dealing professionally with survivors whose lost loved one had experienced great emotional or physical pain, it is often suggested that one healing perception to consider is that, through death, the one who has chosen to end their life has indeed removed the suffering, moved on to "a better existence" so to speak. The assumption cannot be empirically demonstrated and may present a variety of philosophical difficulties for some individuals but can be truly comforting to some grieving survivors.

Yearnings to Relive the Past. For a number of survivors, assurance that the pain is over is a substantial palliative. Parents in particular are able to begin the long process of repair and recovery when they no longer feel that they have to "take care" or witness unrelievable pain or unhappiness in a dead child.

Survivor-victims will often experience a yearning for re-association with the one who has been lost. Fantasies about a reunion are often idealistic in their picturing of the relationship. One client of ours who had lost her husband through suicide stated over and over, "I want him back so bad it hurts. I would give anything I have just to talk to him one more time and then it would be all right. He always made it all right. I know it can't happen, but my wish, even my hope of seeing him again, is like a burning in my stomach that doesn't ever leave." When such feelings of longing begin to subside, the completion of mourning is often within sight (Worden, 1982).

Accurately Perceiving the Needs of the Survivor

Two sets of behavioral symptoms of post-suicide adjustment are particularly important in predicting the ease or speed of the individual's adjustment to the loss and passage through the grief process. These are: (1) indicators of clinical depression and (2) signs of withdrawal from the social-support network on which the survivor depended prior to the suicide. The presence of either of these suggests difficulties for the survivor.

Clinical depression is often accompanied by sleeplessness, crying, generalized dysphoric feelings, loss of self-esteem, or recurring feelings of lack of self-worth, loss of energy, and no hope for the future. In essence, the individual becomes less productive, more apathetic and more focused on being the responding victim than in being a self-initiating individual. Occurrence of clinical depression is usually viewed as an indication that a pathological grief reaction may be developing. Such a reaction occurs when the survivor-victim's life is totally disrupted. Even the simplest day-to-day activities may be impossible. One of our survivors had to be hospitalized, as she was completely unable to take care of herself. Care of her house and her two children became tasks that were just too difficult for her. Following a course of treatment the woman was able to return to her life, but for the moment she was genuinely incapacitated and in need of help. She has since been successfully maintaining her home and caring for her children. Intensive, but relatively short-termed therapy was all that was necessary to place her on a positive recovery road.

Our experience indicates that the other most significant variable in the recovery process is the degree to which the one who has suffered a loss through suicide interacts with others for support. Such interaction provides an optimistic prognosis for a more rapid and successful resumption of pre-suicide activity levels. Conversely, lack of an adequate support system or failure to use existing mechanisms of support is related to an increase in suffering and makes the progress toward successful adjustment slower and more difficult.

One of the authors dealt professionally with a woman who had lost her boyfriend more than a year and a half prior to seeking professional help. She had moved to another state following the death. She had hoped that a change of scene would help her recovery. Whatever potential positive effects accrued were negated by her almost total isolation. Initial contact and assessment of the client indicated that she was still actively experiencing shock and denial from the death. Through referral to a survivor's support group and gentle pushing to seek out relationships and friendships with persons in whom she could confide, the young woman was able to re-create a personal-support network. She was then able to initiate the recovery process. There seemed to be little doubt though that her recovery would have occurred earlier with less pain had she not forsaken the already established network earlier available to her.

In this case the young woman was isolated due to an absence, or perceived absence, of a support network easily taken advantage of by others due to her geographical separation. But, isolation can be gradual and self-imposed in less obvious ways. School personnel must take note of students who withdraw from friends and family following the death of someone close. When the loss is accompanied by the perceived social taboos which frequent society's perception of suicide, social isolation becomes more probable. Withdrawal from family and friends may reveal that a young person is in crisis. It may, in the worst of cases, precipitate suicidal ideation in the survivor. When self-imposed isolation occurs, the troubled student is saying, "The world is too painful for me to endure."

Thousands of suicide survivor victims are left behind each year. Each and every suicide leaves an average of six persons affected. Each of these individuals may be considered more at-risk for suicide than the general population. Assisting survivor re-adjustment most certainly should be considered as a type of primary suicide prevention.

The Impact of Suicide on Secondary Group Survivors

Secondary or extended group effects refer to the impact that suicide may have on individuals not personally interacting with the victim, sometimes extending to include the entire staff and student body of the school.

Contrasts in Intellectual and Emotional Involvement

The reaction of persons in the extended group may be less easily observed than those on primary group members, partially because it is less anticipated. But it can be very real, very strong, and experienced in many ways. The suicidal death of a student or staff member will irrevocably change the very atmosphere in a school. Even persons remotely connected with the situation can be touched. Indeed, the entire student body and staff should be considered as being potential suicide survivor victims. Each person so affected has been victimized by the act of self-destruction.

Secondary symptoms of suicide may be less dramatic than those experienced by primary group members but may induce more profound changes in the school environment over an extended period of time due to the range of their effects. The most obvious reference point in quantifying extended group effects is with students and staff who are closely associated with identified survivors. These people vicariously experience all of the reactions to the loss experienced by those more intimately involved. The primary difference is in the degree of emotional involvement that existed with the perpetrator. Guilt, anger, worry, questions of their own mortality all may arise despite the relative distance between survivor and victim.

Students and staff members in a position of trust with suicide survivors are in the ideal position to provide the first level of support in a school-wide network by providing a caring atmosphere in which healing can take place. Through pre-crisis education and peer counselor training, sensitivity and skills can be put in place to be activated when needed.

The Possibility of Modeling and Clustering Effects Upon Survivors

One of the most tragic effects of a suicide in the school setting can be the modeling of suicide as a coping mechanism.

Though the media have carried stories of alleged suicidal epidemics or "clusters," there appears as yet to be no empirical support for the phenomena (Lester, 1972). Klagsbrun (1976) has well expressed the feelings of most professionals working in the suicide area. He says, "I do not believe that young people will be incited to suicidal behavior by hearing about it, but I do firmly believe that they will continue to be prevented from helping themselves and others by being falsely protected from the subject."

Parents, community leaders, and even experts in the field of suicide have been left wondering how such apparent tragedies could occur. A partial answer to this may be found in the authors' work with junior high and high school students. Following the self-caused death of a student in a local school, an attractive and articulate young woman, who was herself a recovering suicide attempter, summed up her feelings this way: "Crystal had been having trouble with her parents. They weren't getting along and she talked about running away. She wasn't doing very well in her classes and had seemed really depressed for awhile. After she killed herself, I knew that if things got too bad for me there was always a way out. I didn't have to keep on hurting. It was like she told me it was okay to die. I didn't want to die, especially like her, hurting everybody and everything, you know, but I thought about it like I had for a long time. I was afraid everyone would think I'd done it 'cause Crystal had done it. That wasn't true. I think I thought about it long before I heard about Crystal. Her dying just made everyone think I'd copied her."

The authors do not feel that one suicide will cause others to take their own lives except in the most unusual of circumstances. Rather, it is felt that suicide of one student does add **suicide** to the repertoire of coping mechanisms available for consideration, no matter how slight. Experiencing the suicide of a significant other may increase the risk of suicide within a stated population of young people by making death, and suicide in particular, a more familiar coping mechanism. If such familiarity is not coupled with the contradictory and prophylactic information about the facts of suicide as an adaptive mechanism and the viability of more attractive options, the risk is magnified. A significant part of survivor treatment should deal in what amounts to primary prevention activities, not out of fear of epidemics, but because it makes good sense to tell our young people the truth about the ugliness, ineffectiveness, and far-reaching tragic effects of suicide!

The loss of someone through suicide is a tragic waste of human life. That loss is even more profound and far-reaching in its effects if a school population is involved. Our children are our most precious resource and one that we jealously protect. When a suicide occurs in the school setting, students, faculty, and staff are thrust into a situation that the best prepared among us would try to avoid at almost any cost. Suicide forever changes the lives of those it touches. For those close to the person who made the final decision, the shock, the grief, and the guilt may last for years. The **pain** that a suicide survivor experiences lasts a lifetime. Only through a caring and comprehensive support network can the painful effects be accommodated without manifest impact over many years. The school environment offers a unique opportunity to provide just such a support network. It can also be an important weapon against impulsive emulation of the suicidal act. Suicide is an unpleasant word but one which can and needs to be spoken and understood. Only through facing the problem can it be solved.

CHAPTER SEVEN

GUIDELINES AND RESOURCES FOR ORGANIZATION AND TRAINING

"Only by his actions can a man make himself whole."
Margaret Bourke White (1986)

PRIMARILY because of the lethality implications, suicide is generally viewed as always being an emergency situation; sometimes it is. But, as Peck (1985) points out, sudden-onset, abrupt, crisis-precipitated suicide is not the typical case among adolescents. In far more instances, though the actual act may be decided upon impulsively, there are advance behavior changes that if looked for, can be seen and noted. The adequately prepared school system should certainly have a sudden-crisis response plan in place. Though it may never be used, it will be ready when needed and in the interim will provide security and confidence for school personnel.

However, the major emphasis of this book has been on a broader plan of advance planning which deals with crisis prevention and rehabilitation as much as intervention. This approach requires considerable attention to advance planning, personnel and student-body training, and similar functions which involve the dispensing of accurate information and the acquisition of important skills.

PRIMARY FUNCTIONS OF INFORMATION AND TRAINING SESSIONS

It has been our experience that school personnel and students profit from informational and training sessions in at least two ways. Certainly,

249

such sessions help accomplish the primary purpose of preparing a school system to prevent suicide and assist those attempting to recover from suicidal behavior. But in addition to this, we have also observed that overall morale tends to improve. An **esprit de corps** usually develops. This sense of productive comradery seems to permeate many school activities otherwise unrelated to the issues at hand.

Steps in Building Morale

It has also been our observation that this uplifting of morale is no accident. It seems to come about because those organizing and planning these training sessions take care to help the involved participants become personally invested in what they are doing. There is something very special about saving a human life. Conveying this as the fundamental goal of such sessions is important.

Effective personnel enrichment and training programs involve a four-part progression in participant attitudes and feelings. These often become cyclical as staff become more involved and increasingly proficient (Sergiovanni, 1975). Failure to successfully progress through this cycle will severely truncate any training program. Planning activities designed to facilitate the accomplishment of each specific step in turn is a prerequisite to success. Once firmly established, the cycle tends to become largely self-sustaining with a minimum of extra attention. The four steps are:

1. Participants endorse the concept that what they are doing is important and meaningful, thereby making the expending of effort worthwhile.
2. Participants recognize that they are achieving growth or making progress and that the amount of effort expended is reasonable in terms of the amount of progress accomplished.
3. The participants begin to develop an intrinsic satisfaction, a personal interest and sense of accomplishment from their training activities.
4. Participants acquire a personal and individualized identification with and personal commitment to the training goals.

It is necessary to carefully blend general motivational and commitment themes with detailed content and information aspects.

Specific Goals for Training and Informational Activities

Suicide prevention training can be addressed in a number of different ways and be oriented toward several different goals. We have found it helpful to elaborate these goals to prospective participants as part of the advance publicity. We do this because we think it is important for participants to know the goals for which they are striving and because we know that people work harder and learn more effectively when they have specific target goals. We do it for another very important reason.

We know from what participants have told us that they become involved in social help-giving activities for a variety of reasons. We have found no difference in personal efficacy of suicide crisis workers based upon their personal adoption of one or another of the different motivations. Instead, by presenting a variety of reasons for becoming involved in training work we probably recruit more people. We would suggest that at least the following functions or goals be shared with prospective participants. If you can think of additional reasons, so much the better. Here are the six we use with a brief rationale for each.

Preparation for Crisis Prevention and Intervention

This is the fundamental basic reason for all suicide work. We believe it is important to emphasize the following points:

1. The high incidence of suicide
2. The need for individual response capabilities
3. The effectiveness of non-clinically-trained volunteer workers.

To negate the frequent concern over the need for large blocks of time-consuming activity, we stress the natural goodness-of-fit of crisis work with the educational system and the fact that even the most intense crisis work tends to be of rather short duration (Caplan, 1964).

In planning workshop activities it is especially productive to involve staff participants (and students too for that matter) in advance planning. We point out that a major component of primary prevention is advance planning and that a major function of these activities (with this goal being emphasized) is to allow more people to participate in this planning.

For ongoing activities, once the organization is in place and functioning, it is helpful to note that participants are encouraged to contribute to the continuous updating of the program, to offer individualized approaches and ideas, and to help in the identification of the need for any additional or different support services or materials.

Enlistment of Outside Informal Support Groups

Every community has a variety of groups that offer potential for serving as outside resources offering rich informal support to a broadly based suicide prevention plan. One of the most obvious of these is, of course, the parents of school children. Various parent-teacher or parent-school groups are already in place, actively concerned with many school issues. Enlisting their active contribution and support is very important.

In outlining this goal we include the following points:

1. Since the students' lives encompass far more than their school hours, attention to this special problem should be broader than the school.
2. Functional families offer the richest and most effective anti-crisis support available (just as dysfunctional families often have strongly negative effects).
3. Parents are in a very favorable position to prevent suicide crises, recognize signs of increasing risk, and facilitate a wide variety of tertiary prevention plans.
4. The school alone can only make a start toward thorough prevention. The family's support and involvement needs to be included.
5. The family, as an important social institution, is in a very strong position to enlist the help of other community groups and resources.

In addition to the family, we recommend soliciting the involvement of local church groups, service clubs, city and county or borough government and community leaders of all types. Support and assistance come from surprising directions. In one community where we have worked, a local motorcycle club, better known for its parties than its philanthropy, has regularly organized and carried out an annual fund drive in support of some crises services devoted to assisting young children and their families.

Responsibility to Others

We feel that person-to-person contact is the best anti-suicide treatment available. It is very apparent that deficits in personal contact and communication are frequently observed in those who have demonstrated high-risk status. Everyone who works with suicidal people has heard the same plaintive statements:

- "Am I the only one in the world with this problem?"
- "If only there was someone to talk to!"
- "I cannot handle this alone."
- "There is no place to turn to for help. I have to handle it alone."

Because of this common theme, we emphasize the importance of there being other people around who are available to counteract this lonely and hopeless feeling.

We also agree with those who say that one of the most effective ways to prevent young people from seeing suicide as a viable problem-solving option is to quit falsely protecting them from the subject (Klagsbrun, 1976). Young people not only have a right to be informed about this problem, they need to be informed in order to help save their lives and the lives of their peers.

We were once asked in a workshop question-and-answer session if using this approach didn't tend to give people guilt complexes. Our reply represents a viewpoint we firmly hold: "Indeed it may if the listener refuses to be involved, to answer or be ready to answer when a friend in need calls for help." We clearly believe and promulgate without apology the philosophy that we are our brother's and sister's keepers.

Implementing Functional Networking

As we have already extensively stressed, functional networking is important in any suicide prevention program. School-based or school-sponsored workshops and training sessions facilitate the development and implementation of a working network in several ways.

1. They provide school personnel with working information on what is available "out there" and how and when to make contact.
2. They help prepare the skills for making a prompt, efficient, and credible contact with outside help resources. The latter may be the most important of all. Those in a position to respond and provide extensive crisis help must be able to feel that the referrals they

receive are rationally prompted and based upon an adequate understanding of the problem in order for them to unreservedly commit agency or personal resources.

3. They establish the framework for subsequent flow of prevention and treatment information both to and from the school, a very valuable asset for helping youngsters in suicidal crisis.

4. They help clarify the status of community sponsored and supported helping agencies. The information gained helps motivate participants and people with whom they may have influence, to continue to support, or initiate supporting, or improve the support of those facilities and services needed for effective networking to take place.

As with the spider web, when we describe a functioning network we tend to focus on the center of activities, the center of the web. It is important to remember that in order for the center to be strong, the outreaching strands must each be firmly anchored at both the center and far end. School suicide prevention programs should provide substantial anchoring and support for a community suicide-action network.

Morale Building

There are two variables that contribute very strongly to the level of morale in any working group. One of these is the perceived meaningfulness of the work being done; the other is the degree to which the worker feels that job demands are reasonably commensurate with the worker's skills and capabilities. It is little wonder that suicide prevention workshops tend to raise the morale of schools.

The act of unselfishly helping to rescue a person's life adds meaning to anyone's life. Knowing that you have taken an active and participating step towards being in a more able and ready position to do so is very rewarding. On the other hand, knowing that one may be called upon to render assistance in a way for which one is unprepared can be frightening and depressing. If the lack of preparedness comes from deliberate choice to be uninvolved, guilt and self-depreciation is added to the equation.

Knowing the extent of the problem and the high probability of having someday to face the need to respond to someone's call for help in some way related to a suicidal experience presents a real challenge. Frightening as the overall prospect is, the acquisition of appropriate information and relevant skills brings security, increasing self-confidence, positive self-evaluation and resulting higher morale. Seeing this positive development shared by one's working peers adds a collective pride which is valuable. We point out to participants that being prepared to handle suicide-related problems is a challenge exactly like knowing where the fire alarm is or how to call the police. Each is knowledge we hope we never need to use, but it is certainly reassuring to know how if necessary.

Community Leadership Role

We happen to believe that schools and school staff are and should be recognized as community leaders. We have both worked in small villages and rural communities as well as in urban areas. We have observed with interest that the presence of a "good" school in the community is noted, appreciated, and bragged upon by everyone in town. We see no reason why the same paradigm should not hold for suicide prevention. Not only is the need for students to have these programs very high in today's social milieu, but there is also a need for the entire community to work toward better mental health and to share the pride of accomplishment.

The school, typically seen as a repository for knowledge and skills, should play a leadership role in suicide prevention, a model for all to emulate. We suggest that schools try to model in three ways: (1) by the development of functionally effective personal relationships between staff and students, (2) by working hard to develop community networking, and (3) by providing the community with regular opportunities for self-help and development experiences relevant to suicide.

DIFFERENT TYPES OF SESSIONS
AND APPROACHES

A number of different formats are used throughout the country. The professional literature (e.g. Blomquist, 1974; Peck, 1985) notes the use of lectures, seminar discussions, presentations structured for specific groups such as school nurses or PTA groups, case presentations, student discussion groups led by a trained leader, professional consultations regarding specific problems or cases, staff-oriented training sessions and others which are essentially variations of these.

It has been our experience that a useful way to approach the method-selection planning is to conceptualize major purposes and the goals which the school would wish to accomplish with the selected one(s) of these and make the decision accordingly. In consultation with schools we denote two major purposes, the first of which breaks down into two often quite different subtypes:

1. To inform and educate, i.e. to present accurate and useful information
   a. As part of the school curriculum as either a regular inclusion or a special inclusion for a limited period of time
   b. For groups of individuals which may be comprised of students (or teachers or staff or parents or various combinations of these) but not in a format or schedule so as to be perceived as part of the regular, everyday, ongoing curriculum of the school
2. To build or improve skills and techniques in any segment of or the entire school student-staff-parent population

Whatever the purpose and whichever of the many available formats is eventually selected, we would recommend that school personnel keep the following principles in mind.

1. Suicide is an emotionally loaded and frightening topic for many. Be sure to start at the level of information and sophistication of the group and move slowly. Making participants uncomfortable will dampen or extinguish motivation.
2. Accuracy of information is an absolute necessity. Be sure your figures and facts are correct and relevant to the geographical area and types of people whom you are trying to help.
3. Information acquisition should precede skill training.
4. Provide plenty of opportunity for discussion and the asking of questions.
5. Follow these rules in organizing and implementing:
   a. Sessions are usually most effective when participants have had the opportunity to be involved in the planning of them.
   b. Provide easily accessible and readily obtainable follow-up support and services.
   c. Be willing and prepared to update and amend the content and pace of your sessions as progress and participant feedback indicates.
   d. Allow for individualism and variance in approach.

Above all, do it! Planning is important, but vital intervention may be missed because nothing is ever really tried.

Guidelines for Informational Sessions

Three types of presentation formats are usually used for this purpose: lectures, seminar-discussions, and media presentations. It is impossible to categorically state that one works better than another. One needs to match the format to the situation.

Lectures

The temptation is to depend mostly upon the lecture format, especially if your community happens to have some good speakers available. The lecture format does have its place in terms of an efficient way to get information to large numbers of people quickly. It also has some serious deficits. One of the most serious is the lack of person-to-person contact and the ease of participating without really becoming personally involved. To make lecture sessions work best, make arrangements for the format to include question-and-answer sessions. The format is improved even further by being able to quickly follow-up on the lecture with small group discussion.

Large groups are difficult to handle for even the expert and experienced speaker. We seldom use the lecture method alone unless no other contact with the group is feasible. When we do use it we try to keep the lecture brief and attempt to make arrangements for other activities so we can use the lecture primarily to phase-in often more effective smaller seminar, discussion or workshop groups. We have participated in large workshops where over 100 participants have been involved. Sometimes, these have gone reasonably well due largely to the high motivation and efficient planning of the host organization or group. But these are "workshops" in name only, since little individual work is expected or possible.

If a lecture approach must be used, it should offer some opportunity for follow up with individual participants. Use handout worksheets or informational brochures, or some method to help assure that this is not a one-time-only contact with those present but rather an active enlistment and recruitment activity. It probably goes without saying (but we're saying it anyway) that only the very best public speakers should attempt the lecture method. If the listeners must suffer through boring content ineffectively presented, the recruitment goal may very well be doomed before it starts. We never recommend using the straight lecture as a format if we are dealing with the planning of curriculum inclusion activities. Having a "lecturer" talk "with" (not "at") the class followed by discussion can be very useful.

Seminars and Discussion Groups

This format works very well and avoids many of the problems inherent in the lecture approach. Two very important aspects must be considered in order to maximize success. First, the discussion leader or leaders (and frequently more than one is needed) must be well-trained, well-informed, and knowledgeable about a wide number of suicide-related topics. Questions can run far afield. It is not necessary for the discussion leader to know "everything about everything." The leader must, however, be on firm ground regarding major issues and topics, aware of important considerations to be covered and important misconceptions to be avoided. The leader must also know where and how to find additional information when necessary and be able to direct the inquiring participant to additional resources.

Second, even though seminar discussion groups appear to be informal and casual, they should not be undertaken without careful advance planning and what amounts to lesson plans. Individual sessions should have well-defined goals and objectives and may in some instances even follow a script, though the script may not be obvious to participants. If more than one discussion leader is involved, care should be taken that all leaders are aware of the goals, pace, and the importance of meeting pre-selected objectives to avoid confusion at other points in the ongoing activity.

If discussion leaders are not experienced teachers, it may be helpful to spend some advance time on giving them assistance in managing group discussion dynamics, unless the leader-participant roles become reversed due to strong or very active group involvement.

Discussion groups are very helpful in building individual commitment to the group activity while still allowing for individual differences. They are also very effective formats in which to begin to practice the interpersonal dynamics necessary to successful primary prevention. In many instances, the early discussion groups will turn out to be the beginning of the primary prevention program rather than a "gearing-up" exercise. If this is the direction that discussion groups develop, it is a pretty good sign that the overall program is on target. The only caution to really be concerned about is to be sure that facts and information are being dealt with as well as feelings. A good leader will be alert for and successfully manage such a problem without much difficulty.

Media Presentations

Media presentations can be very effective. There are a number of fine films, videotapes, and filmstrips available. Some examples of these will be noted later in this chapter. Media presentations can quickly capture participants' attention and accurately present much information in a short period of time.

We would certainly recommend the use of media in any program. At the same time, we would include all of the caveats we mentioned in regards to the lecture format. Slickness of format and ease of presentation are no substitute for personal involvement and individual commitment. Our recommendation would be to find some media pieces which very well fit program needs and then use them.

Great care should be taken to preview the materials to be sure that they are really well done, accurate, and that they match the participant population and program goals. We would strongly caution against depending upon media presentations to stand alone without discussion and follow up. We would also warn against overuse of them, since it is impossible to build and maintain really effective prevention and intervention skills without person-to-person interaction and practice of the skills involved. Watching a movie provides little of either of these.

As with any curriculum support material, media presentations work best when pre-presentation preparation has laid adequate groundwork for the material, when media themes and emphases effectively match program goals, and when follow-up discussion and face-to-face reiteration and explanation of important points takes place. Just as we believe that a "pop-psychology" paperback book doesn't adequately replace a trained therapist, so do we feel that a movie projector and a reel of film is no viable substitute for a good teacher. Carefully blend the two and you may very well have a winning combination.

Guidelines for Skill Acquisition and Training

Planning and running effective training sessions and workshops is a special skill in itself. It is critical that both principle components, i.e. content and leadership, work well. We feel very strongly that "workshops" or "working training sessions" should be exactly that: they should be sessions where individuals get "hands-on" experience and are actively involved in the process of doing. Too many so-called workshops develop into multiple-lecture sessions with the leader doing all the talking, and the participants end up going home with a folder full of notes but no real personal involvement. Because the entire process of suicide prevention emphasizes a close personal touch with individuals learning to express

and share their feelings and ideas, we feel that this "hands-on" and experiential type of training is even more important to suicide prevention
training than in other areas. As a consequence, we feel most comfortable
endorsing only those workshops and material sets that utilize this direct
approach. Some examples of good resources are available to help in the
basic concepts involved, and the material in these is easily applied to
training workshops dealing with suicide prevention. We recommend
these three:

- Bennis, W., Benne, K., and Chin, R. (Eds.). *The Planning of Change*
  (New York: Holt, Rinehart and Winston).
- Hersey, P., and Blanchard, K. *Management of Organizational Behavior*
  (Englewood Cliffs, NJ: Prentice-Hall).
- Rubin, L.J. *The Inservice Education of Teachers* (Boston, MA: Allyn
  and Bacon).

In preparing for training sessions, a number of factors, each important to workshop success, should be considered. These include the content, personalities of participants and leaders, the professional
competencies of participants and leaders, organization and structure
(the "flow") of the sessions, and the physical arrangements.

When working with adults it is also well to consider that many of
them approach a formal learning experience with more trepidation than
does the school child who faces learning challenges everyday. Individual
differences of participants in this respect will contribute to the success or
failure of the sessions. These differences may be important with school-
age participants too but are apt to be less crucial. Their effect will be
compounded, however, if young people must share training sessions
with adults.

Although total homogeneity is not necessary, it is generally better to
have cohesive and therefore more relaxed groups and this usually comes
about through the dual influence of group size and similarity of the participants. At least the following personal characteristics should be considered in the grouping of any training session:

1. Personal fears and inhibitions
2. Self-concepts and feelings of competence and self-confidence
3. Experiential background (especially in regards to suicide and other
   crisis experience)
4. Emotional readiness
5. Available time and the presence or absence of personal factors that
   may compete for attention and interest

6. Individual readiness to learn in terms of knowledge and motivational background

We do not wish to belabor the point, but it is our deliberate intention to strongly emphasize the importance of careful and thoughtful pre-session planning.

Types of Workshops

Workshops or training sessions are typically categorized according to content or characteristics of the participants. Since objectives and structure depend upon these two factors, some different types are worth noting.

Various Contents. Perhaps the easiest way to conceptualize content differentiation is to consider it as being congruent with the three stages of prevention. Thus, content may be primarily concerned with those skills and techniques most closely related to prevention or intervention or rehabilitation.

The first stage usually includes preventive mental health techniques. Based upon the participants having the necessary prerequisite knowledge, these sessions will deal with interpersonal relationships, communication, personal problem solving, decision making and similar topics.

Crisis intervention skills are typically directed at active leadership and support roles, emergency response activities, and effecting networking contacts. These may or may not be aimed at specialized staff (Fujimara et al., 1985).

Rehabilitation and recuperative skills may include the effecting of a holding environment, reiteration of prevention skills, empathetic communication and, in some instances, special aspects of handling extreme feelings and special information-sharing skills (Rosenfeld & Prupas, 1984).

Participant Characteristics. Some of the personal "readiness" characteristics were noted above. In general, participants are also grouped according to their relationship to the structure of the school, e.g. students, teachers, administration, non-teaching staff, specialized staff, parents, and community. Some mixing according to other readiness characteristics is often done, but, as noted previously, homogeneity of knowledge, feeling, and motivation among participants makes the workshop easier to run. One particular differentiation is very important. The presence of suicide attempters, survivors or those who, as significant others, have been strongly impacted by the suicidal experience is an important consideration.

Examples of Workshop Outlines and Activities

We have included three different examples, each of which has been designed for a slightly different purpose, and each of which works well when presented to the proper participants in the correct context. Only a portion of each set of material, some of which is copyrighted and should not be reproduced, is shown here. Complete packages are obtainable from the author or publisher.

EXAMPLE ONE

SUICIDE PREVENTION TRAINING MANUAL
(American Association of Suicidology)

Purpose:

"To help trainers present facts about suicide in a manner that leads to understanding of and empathy with the suicidal person." The materials cover three main areas: identifying suicide risk, taking intervention steps, and some post-suicidal experience work.

Format:

A package of materials which includes a series of 14 workshops, introductory explanations, sample publicity materials, a booklet on suicide and how to prevent it, and specific directions for the trainer. For each workshop session a "Problem" for discussion or a role-playing suggestion is presented, a checklist for the leader is included, and a worksheet is provided for the participant. The worksheet contains the "Problem" or role-playing directions and room for the participant's written response.

The leader is expected to lead the group in discussion and the noting of appropriate behaviors stimulated by the problem presentation.

Here is an excerpted problem and the leader's checklist. It is for a session early in the 14 session series focusing on acute crisis intervention:

Problem:

A friend tells you about a college student who is away from home for the first time and becomes anxious over his failure to get straight A's, even though he is doing much better than average. He breaks up with his girl friend and begins drinking and using drugs. He talks about being a burden to his friends and a disappointment to his family. You know that he recently bought a pistol, saying it was a gift for his father. What do these signs suggest and what would you do about them?

Leader's Checklist:

The problem is one of acute suicidal risk. The exaggerated sense of failure, the changes of behavior, the breaking of relationships and the conversation point clearly in that direction, and the attempt to buy a pistol shows that there is no time to waste.

What to do?

1. Notify school authorities immediately. Make sure that they understand the seriousness of the problem and are prepared to act immediately. If you are not satisfied that they are taking the situation seriously enough, call a suicide prevention center or mental health center.
2. If your friend is associated with the student's friends, see to it that they are made aware of the problem. They should be sure that he is not left alone.
3. Notify the student's family.
4. Find out who the student trusts and take advantage of that person's opportunity to talk directly with the student.

EXAMPLE TWO

LISTEN AND YOU CAN HEAR A PETAL FALL
(Johnson, 1985)

Purpose:

"To help teenagers increase their sensitivity to suicide risk among their peers." Topics covered include:

1. Dealing with the emotional topic of suicide
2. The facts and mythology of suicide
3. The ubiquity of suicide

4. The helpfulness of close everyday support
5. Learning help resources in one's own community
6. Building communication rapport with friends and acquaintances
7. Becoming familiar with signs of suicidal risk
8. Learning to judge the level of suicidal risk
9. Appropriate verbal responses to calls for help
10. How to find help in a crisis
11. Learning to neither over- nor under-react to a crisis
12. Exploring one's own personal motivations for being a help-giver
13. Dealing with one's own emotional responses in a suicidal experience
14. Some guidelines for networking
15. An introduction to grief work
16. Post-suicide attempt follow-up and response modes.

Format:

A comprehensive series of modular workshops designed to fit into a school curriculum or community action program, with each module taking approximately one hour. Materials consist of a leader's direction sheet which includes the major objectives, things to strive for in the session, things to avoid, a list of needed materials, and specific verbal statements to use along with directions for handling the material. The participants' worksheets provide some questions and answers, places for the participant to record information, and to note suggestions for application.

Here is a module that occurs fairly early in the series.

LEADER'S SHEET

OBJECTIVE:

To assist the participants in identifying (or creating if necessary) a support network for the purposes of:
1. Obtaining dependable information about suicide
2. Receiving guidance about specific problem situations
3. Establishing an immediately available resource for crisis intervention

STRIVE FOR:

Increasing the participant's knowledge about their own community and its varied resources. Work toward the assembling of exact names, locations, and telephone numbers of support resources so there is no ambiguity in the network. Explore any atypical support resources which might not be popularly known or recognized, e.g. specially trained paramedic teams at a local hospital.

AVOID:

Any presumption that no help exists. Every community, no matter how small, has some support though it may be no more than a store-keeper, e.g. a druggist who has knowledge about dangerous sub-stances. Do not focus on the poverty of resources but strive for learning how to identify, locate, or create resources.

MATERIALS:

Blackboard and chalk. Worksheet 1:5. Blank paper and pencils. Local and nearby community phonebooks, lists of known resources, hand-outs of agencies and groups which provide relevant services.

(Verbatim script is in lower and upper case, directions in capitals)

STEP 1.

VERBAL DIRECTIONS: "Suicidal problems are not something that we typically want to experience alone. They say that misery loves company. It certainly is true that it's easier to face frightening situa-tions when we know that help is either available or standing by. The type of help we might need in a suicide-related situation can vary. Sometimes the need is for help which must be obtained quickly — a genuine emergency. Let's try to identify some of the different circum-stances in which we might seek help. Let's start at the non-emergency end of the scale. What are some instances of non-emergency help we might seek?" ENCOURAGE PARTICIPANTS TO USE THEIR WORKSHEETS TO TAKE NOTES. SEEK TO IDENTIFY IN-STANCES SUCH AS THE NEED FOR ACCURATE INFORMA-TION, HANDOUTS, OBTAINING SPEAKERS, FILMS OR BOOKS.

STEP 2.

MOVE ON TO THE "OBTAINING GUIDANCE" AND FINALLY TO THE "EMERGENCY"-TYPE SITUATIONS. TRY TO

ESTABLISH THE CONCEPT THAT A VARIETY OF NEEDS FOR SUPPORT AND HELP EXIST.

STEP 3.

VERBAL DIRECTIONS: "We have identified several types of help which we might seek in our concern over suicide and suicide-related problems. Here's what we seem to be saying." SUMMARIZE INTO THREE OR FOUR MAJOR CATEGORIES AND LIST ON BOARD.

STEP 4.

VERBAL DIRECTIONS: "Now let's share what we know about how and where to find these different types of help. Let's take the first, the non-emergency level of help. What are some resources you know of in this town?" LIST ANY SPECIFIC RESOURCES THAT APPEAR TO HAVE MERIT. SEED THE DISCUSSION WITH INFORMATION FROM PREPARED LISTS OF RESOURCES. WHENEVER A WORTHWHILE RESOURCE IS MENTIONED, DEAL WITH THE SPECIFICS, E.G., NOTE THE LOCATION, PHONE NUMBER, PERSON OR PERSONS TO CONTACT.

WHERE NECESSARY, SHOW HOW TO USE THE TELEPHONE DIRECTORY TO LOCATE RESOURCES. ACTUALLY LOOK UP SOME AND NOTE THE INFORMATION ON THE BOARD. BE ESPECIALLY CAREFUL TO ADD ANY UNUSUAL RESOURCES OF WHICH AN INDIVIDUAL MAY BE AWARE AND TO AVOID WHAT IS AMBIGUOUS OR UNCERTAIN INFORMATION, E.G., "I THINK THERE'S A TEACHER AT ONE OF THE ELEMENTARY SCHOOLS WHO KNOWS SOMETHING ABOUT SUICIDE." SEEK SPECIFICITY AND ACCURACY. ENCOURAGE SEEKING OUT ADDITIONAL RESOURCES.

STEPS 5 AND 6.

REPEAT THE ACTIVITIES OF STEP 4 FOR THE OTHER CATEGORIES, BEING SURE TO BE INCREASINGLY ATTENTIVE TO THE NEED FOR ACCURACY AND SPECIFIC INFORMATION AS THE CRISIS LEVEL OF HELP NEEDED INCREASES. STRESS THE COPYING ONTO THE WORKSHEET THE USEFUL DATA SHARED DURING DISCUSSION.

STEP 7.

IF NECESSARY, ESTABLISH A PLAN FOR COLLECTING DATA WHICH DOES NOT APPEAR TO BE READILY AVAILABLE AT THIS SESSION. ASSIGN SPECIFIC INDIVIDUALS RESPONSIBILITY FOR SEEKING SPECIFIC ANSWERS AND BRINGING THEM BACK TO THE GROUP.

STEP 8.

SUMMARIZE THE CATEGORIES OF HELP AND CHECK ON EVERYONE HAVING THE CORRECT DATA. YOU MAY WISH TO OFFER TO REPRODUCE SOME SORT OF MASTER LIST DRAWN FROM THE GROUP'S ACTIVITIES.

PARTICIPANT'S WORKSHEET

This is your worksheet to use and keep. From time to time you will receive directions on using it to help with the activities. However, no one will be checking it or asking to see it in order to correct or evaluate your answers. What you write here may be very helpful to you sometime in the future. Save it for that purpose.

---

1. Types of suicide-related circumstances where we might seek help:
        (Blank space is left for responses on actual worksheet)
2. Identified categories starting with the lowest emergency type up to the real crisis situation.
3. Specific resources. Identify which category or categories fit each resource. Some will fit or match more than one.

EXAMPLE THREE

PREVENTING TEENAGE SUICIDE
THE LIVING ALTERNATIVE HANDBOOK
(Joan, 1986)

Purpose:

To provide a multiple-day program on suicide prevention for junior or senior high school students. The emphasis is on recognizing suicidal risk and knowing when and how to intervene, providing skills for living, reaching out for help themselves.

Format:

A book-long detailed outline of the two programs complete with the inclusion of optional days as seems appropriate. Topical coverage is quite thorough and, in addition to content information, suggestions are made regarding teaching methodology and visual aides. A nice feature is the inclusion of some sensitive poetry written by adolescents.

This example includes some of the notes to the facilitator or teacher and the topics covered in a single day at both the junior high and senior high level.

For Junior High Students

Goals:

To help students legitimize their feelings.

To explore with students where a young person might reach out if he or she needed help with problems.

To explore with students the concept of coping skills as methods of helping themselves get through painful times.

Means:

By story telling (A continued story is included)

By supporting the value of reaching out and making a blackboard list of possible helping persons.

By talking about pets as coping mechanisms and by forming a list of other things to do when one is feeling trapped, depressed or lonely.

Using the combination of a story about "Karen" and blackboard stick drawings, the facilitator asks the following questions as discussion leads:

1. How can suicidal feelings develop?
2. If Karen becomes suicidal as a result of this "mountain of problems," what can she do, what can you do, who can she reach out to?
3. But what if Karen doesn't reach out?
4. If you are a friend, what do you do?
5. How does an adolescent deal with depression and/or suicidal feelings when he or she is alone?
6. Is a dog useful in suicide prevention?

7. Do your pets ever help you to feel better? How? What do you do with them?
8. What are some other ways to cope?
9. What are other things one can do when one is down?
10. What do you do when you are depressed?

For Senior High Students

(This is the initial meeting.)

Goals:

To establish trust between facilitator and students.

To impart knowledge about the causes of depression and suicidal feelings.

To begin to understand what to look for as **signs of depression** and **suicidal clues.**

Means:

By creating an atmosphere of informality.

By asking questions, listening to student responses, and by adding informational content where students need a fuller explanation.

By viewing the film *Jack Was A Good Driver.*

Prior to viewing the film, the facilitator leads discussion centered around these questions:

1. What is the cause for this tragic rise in adolescent suicide?
2. What are other causes (apart from those suggested in the text) for adolescent suicide?
3. What are the feelings of a suicidal adolescent?
4. How can an adolescent become suicidal?
5. Is suicide inevitable if an adolescent is feeling suicidal?
6. What are the signs that someone is suicidal?

The film is viewed at this point, signs of depression and suicidal clues are reiterated and written on the blackboard, and then more questions and discussion follow:

7. What are the signs of depression in the film?
8. What are additional signs of depression not included in the film?
9. What are the signs of suicidal behavior in the film?
10. What are other factors to consider when trying to assess the lethality of a friend's suicidal feelings?

Programs for Inclusion in the Curriculum

Few school systems adopt a "canned" program from some outside source for use in their own curriculum without some modifications. This is probably very wise, since for the material to be effective it must match the local people and situation. More and more school systems are including material related to suicide and associated topics in the regular curriculum, and we find the requests for consultation and assistance in this direction growing.

Most of the materials are integrated into health or social science curricula. Some are broader than a single subject-matter emphasis and are integrated in a school-wide program using assemblies, special programs and handouts, and modular pieces inserted into various segments of the curriculum at all levels. Some deal with some very specific topics such as the premises regarding "death education" recommended by Schvanaveldt (1982). Because individual needs are so important, we have not tried to suggest any particular program for inclusion. Several school districts are noted for their work along this line, and we refer to several of them in other parts of this book.

The *Cherry Creek Project*, the genesis for some of the material further developed and published by Barrett (1985), has spread through a wider area encompassing several Colorado school districts (now known as S.P.A.R.E. — Suicide Prevention Allied Regional Effort) and has some limited outline material available. Some ideas may be obtained by contacting S.P.A.R.E., Holly Ridge Center, 3301 South Monaco Boulevard, Denver, Colorado 80222.

The San Mateo, California school district in cooperation with the local suicide crisis center has been a leader in involving the whole school in suicide prevention. Some of the AAS pamphlets were developed out of work in this district.

Charlotte Ross, who has authored a number of relevant publications in the journals and longer formats, is a contemporary leader highly respected in the field.

The Dayton, Ohio suicide crisis center has been very active and helped prepare materials for school use.

The Fairfax County (Virginia) Public Schools have developed a comprehensive set of materials for use in their system but has not as yet seen fit to make them widely available for the public market. Information can be obtained from them, however, by writing directly to the school board in Fairfax, Virginia.

We would encourage school systems to examine available material and then adapt what seems usuable to their own situation. The secret to success seems to be to keep working on improving the materials, encouraging participant and consumer feedback, and maintaining a high level of individual involvement in both the preparation and application of the materials.

The ultimate test, of course, is to do as San Mateo did: measure the outcomes in terms of tangible variables like adolescent use of the local crisis center, suicide rates, teacher and student feedback, community-wide adoption of the program and similar indications that the program is working.

BUILDING A RESOURCE LIBRARY

Most school systems will ultimately wish to either write or assemble their own materials for use in the various aspects of a suicide prevention program. However, there is no reason for individual systems or schools to have to depend entirely upon their own creative resources. A wide variety of materials — written as well as in the audio and visual media — are available. The information in this chapter should be helpful in the process of building individual resource holdings as well as giving assistance as to how and where to find specific types and pieces of resource material.

There are no special rules for assembling resources in suicide prevention work. The cataloging and accessing procedures already available in most school systems and in use with other materials (special education resource-room material, for example) will work well here, too. Probably, the most helpful suggestion we can make is that the materials should be easily accessible, clearly designated or annotated as to utilization objectives and type of consumer, and (a very important point) be widely publicized as being readily available to identified consumer groups.

We would stress the importance of the presence of some organized access and availability system for two reasons. The most obvious one is purely pragmatic. It is easier and faster to find and get material that is organized in some way. But there is another important reason. Some volunteer workers with whom we have been associated use the slogan "Three C's to Help!" The three "C's" are **caring, commitment,** and **consistency.** We have uniformly found each of these to be a vital and critical component of successful programs. Individual motivation can provide a major part of these three components, but a visible institutional and group effort is necessary, too. There is an implicit message in the efforts that a school system makes to organize and publicize the accessibility of suicide prevention and intervention materials. Such effort speaks of cohesive group involvement in the three C's, adding tremendous strength and ongoing commitment to individual efforts.

Categorizing According to Utilization Objectives

In our experience there seem to be four major utilization objectives that are useful in categorizing or cataloging materials in this area. These are noted and used here because we have found them to be workable and easy to use with broad groups of consumers. Other taxonomies may be just as useful in certain situations, and there is no reason for any school system to feel bound to the organization structure used here.

For Use as a Basic Personal Information Resource

These materials include those items that meet three general criteria:

1. Informational content is broad and general, not requiring a particular background of preparatory activity or information.
2. Content is of a type and level to be readily understood and used with a minimum of guidance or instruction (including such practical aspects as being able to run a projector or video playback machine).
3. Topics are such that they can be individually accessed by those seeking specific information, e.g. suicide rates, myths of suicide, resource centers in the county, etc.

For Curriculum Content and Support

These materials should be arranged or cataloged in a fashion that matches the curriculum presentation(s) of the prospective user. The classification or accessing system should include reference to curriculum level, specifically related classes, identified segments of separate lesson plans where appropriate (e.g. background film for ninth grade health and fitness class sessions on mental health), and cross-references to other related aspects of the curriculum or other resource materials.

For In-Service Work

These materials are typically of two types. Some of them will be modular capsule programs ready to check out and use with a minimum of integrative effort. Other items will be less self-contained, prepared for careful insertion and integration in programs of broader or more detailed scope. It is very helpful to have both types, since schools will be called upon for two types of in-service presentations. Some will be requested to meet a specific need in a specific situation (often with less than optimal time for advance planning). An example might be a request for an in-service workshop on handling group grief as a result of a sudden loss of a student or faculty member. In other instances, in-service activities related to suicide will be scheduled as part of broader programs. For example, a district may choose to address the whole topic of "Teaching, Teachers, and Stress" of which crisis-related stress may be an important but only segmental topic.

For Network Use

Schools becoming involved in prevention and intervention networks for the first time are apt to view the outside members of the network solely as sources of help and assistance. They quickly discover, however, that these outside agencies will also depend upon the schools for a substantive contribution, as well. Typically, these expectations fall along the lines of activities and services for which the schools will already have a community reputation. These are particularly likely to include expectations of ideas and materials relevant to the acquisition of information, e.g. the learning process, factual background information, primary resource material, and information relevant to special age groups, e.g. children and youth. It greatly strengthens feelings of security and a type of helpful symbiosis if the school is ready to respond quickly and efficiently with information and items of these types.

Categorizing According to the Type of Consumer

When material already cataloged because of its demonstrated value doesn't seem to fit the needs of a prospective user, the problem is most often due to one or two main factors. Either the user hasn't sufficiently clarified utilization objectives (and a system such as that outlined above will help solve that problem) or the material itself is correctly categorized by objective but does not match the preparation, orientation, and/or topical sophistication level of the prospective user. There is probably no simple, tactful way to evaluate the level of sophistication of a user and certainly no readily available checklist to use even if it were easy to make the inquiry.

This categorization principle is not assuming the condescending attitude that "there are some things one of your sophistication just shouldn't know!" It is assuming instead that anyone should have access to anything they might find helpful, but that the most useful match will be between the materials designed for a particular group (and their assumed interests and typical topic-sophistication level) and the primary group identification of the user. The application of the principle is one of helpfulness, not any kind of exclusiveness, and should neither be presented nor applied in the latter light.

In our experience, few significant errors are made if one operates on some broad assumptions about the general level of sophistication typically found in different user groups rather than individual users. Cataloging or characterizing materials as particularly useful to certain designated groups of users goes a long way towards solving the match between level of material and the sophistication of the user. Individuals who appear to be of one group but self-perceive themselves as also having knowledge in another will tend to self-select in a type of cafeteria approach to materials of different levels. This is neither harmful nor misleading.

We have found it useful to note when materials are particularly suited to the following five broad groups. Overlap and dual group membership are obviously commonly encountered and present no particular problem or concern.

1. **General instructional staff.** This group is comprised of exactly what is says, those involved in teaching, whether by contractual definition or assigned activity involvement. Materials pinpointed for this group carry the assumption of usefulness and ready application in the instructional process. They may or may not be relevant to formal curriculum content.

2. **Specialized staff.** Definitions here will vary some from system to system. In our experience, we have encountered identified subcategories of specialized staff which have included the following groups: student personnel workers (psychologists, guidance personnel, nurses, speech therapists, etc.), office and secretarial staff,

administrative staff, custodial and building support staff, volunteer workers and aides, cafeteria workers, bus drivers, and citizen advisory group members. Other groupings certainly are feasible.

3. **Students.** Group designation is fairly obvious here. In some instances we have found sub-groupings such as student leadership group members, sub-sets of special versus regular students, groupings according to grade levels, of course, and in one instance the inclusion of adults involved in "community-school non-credit adult extension" classes.

4. **Parents.** The only sub-groupings we have encountered in this segment have differentiated between parents of students currently on the school roles and those with children not yet in or already out of the system.

5. **Members of the community.** This group is often combined with the "parents" grouping, though the differentiation may be helpful at times. Materials designated as matching this group are often those types of items that can be used in a variety of community settings such as with church groups, service club luncheons, community agency inservice, etc. The material is usually quite basic, with emphasis on information dispensing and commitment enlistment. More detailed or advanced materials might be better listed under "specialized staff," with some special note of how this could be meant to include certain related or affiliated segments of the community.

Major Sources for Information and Material

There is good supply of useful information and fine materials available that will help any school system with suicide prevention and intervention planning and activities. Assistance can be obtained from national organizations dedicated to suicide and related topics, from local organizations and local offices of national organizations, as well as from the literature and material distributed by publishing houses and media distribution centers.

There are also a number of smaller independent distributors who have material available. The quality of these materials will vary considerably, though some very good things are available. There are two important criteria to use, particularly when dealing with an author or publisher or distributor who is not nationally recognized. The credentials of the author should be clearly established and the user should be very sure that the material really meets the individual needs of the purchasing school.

Much of the independently prepared and distributed material has initially been designed for a local situation. This does not mean that it cannot be generalized to a broader population of users, but it may be less useful than desired without modification. Unfortunately, as in any other field, mental health has its share of charlatans and individuals whose primary motivation is to make money. These are relatively few in the area of suicide prevention, but some care should be exercised. Any bona fide author or distributor will be more than willing to provide information regarding the professional credentials of its authors. If in doubt, ask! If there are doubts, you may find it useful to check with one of the national organizations listed below or with local mental health professionals whose integrity is unquestioned.

Individual needs will vary, though later in this chapter we have made some suggestions for a set of basic resource holdings. Probably, the most useful information we can share is how and where to find these major sources.

Agencies and Organizations

The major organization that will probably be of the most specific help in this area is the *American Association of Suicidology* (AAS). In addition to being the organization with which many professionals in the nation affiliate, it offers several important services. These include:

1. Sponsoring of a large national convention each year which draws not only clinical professionals but many educators and others interested in suicide prevention and study. Sending an observer to one of these conventions would be an excellent preliminary step in organizing a school progam. Many useful ideas and concepts are made available each year and a printed set of proceedings is published, as well.

2. Distribution to members of an organizational newsletter, *Newslink*, which includes interesting information about current events in the area of suicide study and also offers reviews of materials, names, and addresses of new and interesting programs and information about local, state, and national programs. Membership may be obtained by someone representing your school.

3. Certification of local suicide crisis centers, guaranteeing therein that the services offered, staff involved, and materials used meet professional standards. Of particular interest to those seeking local help or information about a specific geographical area is the annually updated directory of suicide prevention centers. This directory is available from *AAS* for a nominal fee.

This organization may be contacted by writing to:

American Association of Suicidology
2459 South Ash
Denver, Colorado 80222

A *Directory of Survivor Groups,* often a way to contact resource people working in the area of suicide, is available from:

Suicide Prevention Center Inc.
184 Salem Avenue
Dayton, Ohio 45406

The Suicide Information and Education Centre is a Canadian organization that serves both Canada and the United States as a clearinghouse for a tremendous amount of information about suicide. By writing or phoning this service one may obtain bibliographies, a list of workshops scheduled for the coming months, and even job listings. The service is either free or with only copying costs charged. Contact may be made by writing to SIEC, Suite 201, 723-14 St. N.W., Calgary, Alberta, Canada T2N 2A4.

Schools should not overlook the help they may receive from community mental health centers. These centers very often have very fine materials available. In many cases the material will include informative handouts with accurate dependable information, mental health films, program outlines and other similar useful help. Many centers also will provide speakers and consultants to school systems. And, of course, if networking is to be successfully implemented, the school will want to establish firm communication and operational arrangements with these local centers.

Locations, addresses and telephone numbers and other useful contact information regarding community mental health clinics may be obtained from two sources:

National Mental Health Association
1800 N. Kent Street
Arlington, Virginia 22209

and

National Institute of Mental Health
Public Inquiries
5600 Fishers Lane
Rockville, Maryland 20857

You may obtain brief information by telephoning the first organization. A listing of all community mental health centers in the country is available from the latter one.

Professional therapists may be very useful to schools, though their availability may vary greatly. When affiliating with a therapist or counselor, the school should be sure that the individual is properly credentialed, certified or licensed. The exact requirements are not the same in every state and province. Referrals and information on how to check on whether or not an individual meets these important criteria may be obtained from one of these three organizations, depending upon the profession of the therapist:

American Psychiatric Association
1700 18th Street, N.W.
Washington, D.C. 20009

American Psychological Association
1200 17th Street, N.W.
Washington, D.C. 20036

The National Association of Social Workers
1425 H Street, N.W.
Washington, D.C. 20005

You should have no reservations about checking on a professional's credentials. Ethical responsibility and integrity is prized by bona fide professionals, and they are as concerned about charlatans or well-intentioned but improperly trained individuals as is the consumer.

Periodicals and Journals

A number of professional journals frequently carry articles relating to suicide. These include journals written for and distributed to social workers, psychologists, psychiatrists and other physicians, school counselors, special education workers, and similar professions. Many of these are available in the public library, and the librarian can demonstrate how to use various kinds of professional abstracts (e.g. *Psychological Abstracts*) to facilitate quickly finding the article or type of article sought.

There are two publications of particular interest to those working in suicide. One of these, *Newslink,* mentioned previously, is regularly distributed to members of the *American Association of Suicidology.* The other, the *Journal of Suicide and Life-threatening Behavior,* is also sent to *AAS* members along with their membership but is available by subscription as well and can also be found in many public and university or college libraries. Individual or institutional subscriptions may be obtained by writing to Guilford Press, 200 Park Avenue South, New York, New York 10003.

Major Publishers of Suicide-Relevant Materials

Almost every one of the major textbook publishers includes some suicide or suicide-related titles in its listings. The quality of the publication cannot be judged from the number of titles that a publisher lists, however, since some publishing firms may offer only a single listing, but that one offering is very good. Several houses do list a number of works about suicide, and being on their mailing list would be useful. These include:

> Charles C Thomas, Publisher
> 2600 South First Street
> Springfield, Illinois 62794
>
> Guilford Press
> 200 Park Avenue South
> New York, New York 10003
>
> Human Sciences Press
> 72 Fifth Avenue
> New York, New York 10114
>
> Springer Publishing Company
> 200 Park Avenue South
> New York, New York 10002

Recommended Holdings for a Basic Suicide Prevention Resource Library

Any selected listing of books and other materials must, of course, be arbitrary and highly personalized. We have no intention of suggesting that these materials listed are exactly what every school system needs to have. We do feel confident that those items that we recommend have some worth and application and may be of use if they match other parameters of the individual school or school system. Obviously, there are many other items that might have been legitimately included additionally or in place of these we list. Others will continue to be published after this book has gone to press.

The best advice we can give is for school users to spend some time reviewing what is available. Many publishers offer free 10-day to 30-day review opportunities, and most of the media materials may be obtained for preview prior to purchase or rental. Many of the publications and releases are reviewed elsewhere in professional journals and magazines. Once contacts have been established with other systems and agencies involved in suicide prevention work, it will be discovered that they will not only have some of the materials already at hand for you to preview but will be able to make recommendations particularly relevant to your own distinctive situation and population.

As a starter, we would recommend the following list. We have deliberately not included multiple selections under the same heading for all areas. In some instances, this has seemed necessary, but in others we have tried to keep in mind that this list is just what it says: a "start" toward acquiring a basic suicide prevention resource library.

Basic Personal Reading and General Information

Some of these materials are useful for other purposes (the AAS pamphlets are a good example). We list them here because they can be used for general reading without other instruction or activities.

For General Staff

Hoff, L.A. *People In Crisis: Understanding and Helping*. Menlo Park, CA: Addison-Wesley, 1984.

This book is a good one to pair with Janosik (see following), since both deal with the same topic but do not cover the same material. Hoff includes separate sections on suicide and suicide survivors and covers some very important topics (such as understanding people's varying behavior under crisis-level stress) in some detail.

Janosik, E.H. *Crisis Counseling: A Contemporary Approach*. Monterey, CA: Wadsworth Health Sciences, 1984.

This is a very readable coverage of a large number of crisis concerns. While suicide does not receive extensive coverage per se, much of the general material is very applicable.

Shneidman, E. *Definition of Suicide*. New York: Wiley-Interscience, 1985.

This author has long been one of the nation's leaders in the study of suicide and he has written extensively on the topic. This book is his latest and offers many new and useful insights into suicide and the suicidal person.

Slaikeu, K.A. *Crisis Intervention: A Handbook for Practice and Research.* Newton, MA: Allyn and Bacon, 1984.

This is a very good work crammed full of useful information well presented. Slaikeu should be required reading for anyone interested in really pursuing the concept of psychological first aid.

For Specialized Staff

Cain, A. (Ed.)., *Survivors of Suicide.* Springfield, IL: Charles C Thomas, Publisher, 1972.

Grief therapy and adjustment therapies and techniques are discussed in a format suitable for student personnel workers.

Hatton C., and Valente, S. *Suicide: Assessment and Intervention.* New York: Appleton-Century-Crofts.

A fairly brief paperback which provides good introductory coverage of a number of important areas including some grief work and ethical considerations. Some clinical training is helpful, but a lot is not required to understand the book.

Heillig, R.J. *Adolescent Suicidal Behavior: A Family Systems Model.* UMI Research Press.

Knowledge of the family systems model is very helpful in networking with social-service agencies since many of them use this model in planning treatment. This book will be especially useful to school counselors or any staff member who will be working with the parents of students.

Moustakas, C.E. *Loneliness.* Englewood Cliffs, NJ: Prentice-Hall.

This short paperback does a very nice job of helping the reader really understand what loneliness is all about and what it actually feels like to be experiencing feelings which are so often a correlate of suicide. It is probably most useful for school staff and some parents. It probably would not be useful to any but the most mature of students.

Slaikeu, K.A. *Crisis Intervention: A Handbook for Practice and Research.* Boston, MA: Allyn and Bacon, 1984.

School psychologists, nurses and counselors will find many parts of this book directly applicable to their own profession. We encourage all of our advanced graduate counseling students to include this book in their professional library.

For Students

Madison, A. *Suicide and Young People.* Boston, MA: Houghton-Mifflin-Clarion, 1978.

This short work offers a non-condescending examination of the realities of suicide among today's young people. It is reasonably heavy reading from an emotional standpoint but not beyond the involved high school student's capability.

For Parents and the Community

Giffin, M., and Felsenthal, C. *A Cry for Help*. Garden City, NY: Doubleday, 1983.

This is a very readable and useful book. It would also be suitable for some adolescents and certainly for teachers, as well.

Klagsbrun, F. *Too Young to Die*. New York: Pocket Books, 1976.

A relatively brief but generally helpful broad coverage of youth and suicide.

McCoy, K. *Coping With Teen-age Depression: A Parent's Guide*. American Library.

A good practical sourcebook for some workable ideas. It also includes some information about sources and types of professional treatment plans.

My Son, My Son . . . A Guide to Healing After A Suicide In The Family. Available from Iris Bolton, Link Counseling Center, 218 Hilderbrand Avenue, Atlanta, Georgia 30328.

Ms. Bolton is an established public advocate for suicide prevention, and this work of hers is helpful for survivors or those who wish to understand more about working with them.

In addition, we would recommend having a supply of the pamphlets available through the American Association of Suicidology. Their current stock may vary, but we have found these to be very helpful. Packets containing samples of the entire set are available and quantity discount orders are offered.

- *Suicide In Young People*
- *Suicide In Youth and What You Can Do About It: A Guide for Students* (This pamphlet should be available for both parents and students!)
- *Suicide in Youth and What You Can Do About It: A Guide for School Personnel*
- *Suicide — It Doesn't Have to Happen*
- *Before It's Too Late*

Curriculum Content And Support

For Instructors

Janosik, E.H. *Crisis Counseling: A Contemporary Approach*. Monterey, CA: Wadsworth Health Sciences, 1984. (See also under previous section, "Basic Personal Reading and General Information.")

Hoff, L.A. *People In Crisis: Understanding and Helping.* Menlo Park, CA: Addison-Wesley. (See also under previous section, "Basic Personal Reading and General Information."

Pfeffer, C.R. *The Suicidal Child.* New York: Guilford.

This is a very recent publication that deals extensively with the younger child. Many of its insights can be easily generalized to older youth, as well.

For Student Reading

Clifford, E. *The Killer Swan.* Boston, MA: Houghton-Mifflin.

Through the process of trying to protect a young cygnet from being killed by its swan father, a young boy works his way through problems with his own father's suicide (for grades 6 to 9).

Friedman, M. *Buried Alive: The Biography of Janis Joplin.* New York: Morrow.

A good portrayal of loneliness, insecurity, and drug use as related to suicide (for grades 9 to 12).

Gordon, S. *When Living Hurts.* New York: Union of American Hebrew Congregations, 1985.

In our opinion this is one of the finest crisis resolution works written for the young person that we have ever seen. Warm, friendly, compassionate, and understanding, the author (well-known for several other works related to children and adolescence) writes for teenagers in terms they will understand and appreciate. The short book is designed for youth in crisis. We have used it as a crisis prevention tool, as well.

Guest, J. *Ordinary People.* New York: Viking Press.

A 17-year-old experiences guilt over his brother's death and attempts suicide. Story focuses on post-attempt establishing of new peer and parental relationships (for grades 9 to 12).

In-Service Training

For General Staff

A Teacher's Manual for the Prevention of Suicide Among Adolescents (The Samaritans, 33 Chestnut Street, Providence, Rhode Island 02093).

This is a helpful piece of material prepared by an iternational group well-known for their work in suicide prevention.

Barrett, T.C. *Youth In Crisis: Seeking Solutions to Self-Destructive Behavior.* Longmont, CO: Sopris West, 1985.

This manual, designed to be used with teachers, students and other school personnel, is one of the consequent results of the well-known Cherry Creek Public Schools (Englewood, Colorado) Demonstration Project funded under a Title IV-C federal grant in 1980-1982. Some reference has been made to this project and the author's work in other places in this book. We highly recommend this to be a part of any school's suicide resource library.

Slaikeu, K.A. *Crisis Intervention: A Handbook for Practice and Research*. Newton, MA: Houghton-Mifflin-Clarion, 1984.

Parts of this may be too heavily clinically focused for general staff, but its many other sections are very useful for this broader group.

For Specialized Staff

The Student Assistance Model (Prevention Services, Wheeler Clinic, 91 Northwest Drive, Plainville, CT 06062)

This inexpensive handbook has been prepared for use by school personnel faced with what appears to be a growing epidemic of suicidal ideation or behavior in their school. It is useful for all school personnel but may work best when used with the direction of administration or school personnel staff.

Getz, W.L., Allen, D.B., Myers, R.K., and Lindner, K.C. *Brief Counseling With Suicidal Persons*. Lexington, MA: Lexington Books/D.C. Health, 1983.

We have found this book useful to shool counselors who, though they may never find themselves doing formal psychotherapy with a student, do often have the need to apply professional counseling skills and techniques to the problems faced by school staff and students experiencing crisis.

Meeks, J.E. *The Fragile Alliance*. Baltimore, MD: Williams & Wilkins, 1971.

Very well written, this empathetic work explores the difficulties of the adult therapist/ adolescent relationship. While it is clearly written for the professional counselor, its many insights into the adolescent's world make it a very worthwhile book for any interested staff member with even a little clinical training.

Worden, J.W. *Grief Counseling and Grief Psychotherapy: A Handbook for the Mental Health Practitioner*. New York: Springer, 1982.

The title should not frighten those without extensive formal clinical training. This short book has many useful suggestions that might be applied to survivor work in the schools.

For Aides and Volunteers

Madison, A. *Suicide and Young People*. Boston, MA: Houghton-Mifflin-Clarion, 1978. (See also under previous section, "Recommended Readings for a Basic Suicide Prevention Resource Library.")

Network Support Use

Focusing On Networking Functions

Rueveni, U. *Networking Families in Crisis: Intervention Strategies With Families and Social Networks.* New York: Human Sciences Press.

This is one of the classics regarding networking. It is good basic reading for anyone who must plan or implement networking functions or organization.

Slaikeu, K.A. *Crisis Intervention: A Handbook for Practice and Research.* Boston, MA: Houghton-Mifflin-Clarion, 1984.

Several of the chapters deal with how special-focus groups (police, attornies, hospital emergency room personnel) deal with a crisis. These sections provide useful information and also lay a foundation for understanding the work and approaches of other professionals who must be involved with the school in any successful prevention network.

Focus On Content Information

Hoff, L.A. *People In Crisis: Understanding and Helping.* Menlo Park, CA: Addison-Wesley. (See also under previous section, "Basic Personal Reading and General Information.")

Focus On Skills and Techniques

Slaikeu, K.A. *Crisis Intervention: A Handbook for Practice and Research.* Boston, MA: Houghton-Mifflin-Clarion, 1984. (See also under previous section, "In-Service Training.")

Media Materials

There are a number of different media items that we feel have merit. Since the cost of media materials tends to run much higher than books and pamphlets and most of them are available for preview, we have chosen not to recommend any particular item. We would recommend instead that a number of items be previewed and then selections made on the basis of good application to a particular program and budget considerations.

Many universities have film-rental distribution centers. These centers, and many local school systems as well, will have available a copy of the *Educational Film Locator.* This publication will help locate a nearby distributor for most films. Filmstrips are often available through the same distributors as well as from individual publishing houses. Videotapes come from many sources. A number are from individual distributors.

A good source for a large number of videotapes is the Public Broadcasting System. Catalogues and tape publication notices can be obtained by writing to PBS Video, 1320 Braddock Place, Alexandria, VA 22314.

The following publishers or distributors have films, videotapes, audiotapes, or filmstrips available in the area of suicide. Catalogs or listings are available from most.

Alan Landsberg Productions, 1554 Sepulveda Boulevard, Los Angeles, CA 90025.

American Association for Counseling and Development, 5999 Stevenson Avenue, Alexandria, VA 22034.

American Association of Suicidology, 2459 South Ash, Denver, CO 80222.

Audio Visual Narrative Arts, P.O. Box 9, Pleasantville, NY 10507.

Avna Media, Box 1040, Mount Kisco, NY 10549.

Behavioral Sciences Media, The UCLA Neuropsychiatric Institute, 760 Westwood Plaza, Los Angeles, CA 90024.

Coronet/MTI Teleprogram, 108 Wilmot Road, Deerfield, IL 60015.

Kidsrights, 120-A, West Fifth Avenue, P.O. Box 851, Mount Dora, FL 32757.

Linda Gottsman-Filmmaker's Library, 133 E. 58th Street, Suite 703A, New York, NY 10022.

McGraw-Hill Films, P.O. Box 641, Del Mar, CA 92014.

Media Guild, 11722 Sorrento Valley Road, San Diego, CA 92121.

MI Media, University of Michigan, 416 Fourth Street, Ann Arbor, MI 48109.

Paulist Productions, P.O. Box 1057, Pacific Palisades, CA 90272.

Simon and Schuster Communications, 108 Wilmot Road, Deerfield, IL 60015.

Sunburst Communications, Room LM 8, 39 Washington Avenue, Pleasantville, NY 10570.

UAHC Television and Film Institute, 838 Fifth Avenue, New York, NY 10021.

Vidcam Inc., 6322 Kings Point Road, Grand Blanc, MI 48439.

Walt Disney Media, 500 South Buena Vista Street, Burbank, CA 91521.

Wombat Productions, Inc., P.O. Box 70, Ossining, NY 10562.

Youth Suicide National Center, 1825 I Street, N.W., Suite 400, Washington, D.C. 20006.

REFERENCES

_____ (1985). How we die. *Science 85,* October, 38.

_____ (1985). Associated Press release, June 21.

Albert, G., Forman, N., & Masik, L. (1973). Attacking the college suicide problem. *Journal of Contemporary Psychotherapy, 6* (1), 70-78.

Allen, N.H. (1976). The health educator as a suicidologist. *Suicide & Life Threatening Behavior, 6* (4), 195-201.

Andress, V.R., & Corey, D.M. (1973). Survivor-victims: Who discovers or witnesses suicide? *Psychological Reports, 42,* 759-764.

Baldwin, B.A. (1979). Crisis intervention: An overview of theory and practice. *The Counseling Psychologist, 8,* 43-52.

Barrett, T.C. (1985). *Youth in crisis.* Longmont, CO: Sopris West.

Berkovitz, I.H. (1985). The role of schools in child, adolescent, and youth suicide prevention. In M.L. Peck, N.L. Farberow, and R.E. Litman (Eds.), *Youth suicide.* New York: Springer.

Bernard, M., & Joyce, M. (1984). *Rational-emotive therapy.* New York: Wiley.

Blomquist, K.R. (1974). Nurse, I need help — The school nurse's role in suicide prevention. *Journal of Psychiatric Nursing and Mental Health Services, 12* (1), 22-26.

Bolton, I. (1985). *Statement before the subcommittee on human services of the select committee on aging* (H.R. 98th Congress Committee Publication No. 98-497). Washington, D.C.: U.S. Government Printing Office.

Bourke-White, M. (1986). In V. Goldberg, In hot pursuit: The life and times of Margaret Bourke-White. *American Photographer, 16,* 38-61.

Brammer, L., & Abrego, P. (1981). Intervention strategies for coping with transition. *Journal of Counseling Psychologists, 9,* 19-36.

Brammer, L.M., & Shostrom, E.L. (1982). *Therapeutic psychology: Fundamentals of counseling and psychotherapy.* Englewood Cliffs, NJ: Prentice-Hall.

Cain, A.C., & Fast, I.M. (1972). Children's disturbed reaction to parent suicide: Distortions of guilt, communication, and identification. In A.C. Cain (Ed.), *Survivors of suicide.* Springfield, IL: Charles C Thomas.

Calhoun, L.G., Shelby, J.W., & Faylstick, M.E. (1980). Reactions to the parents of child suicide: A study in social perceptions. *Journal of Consulting and Clinical Psychology, 43,* 535-536.

Caplan, G. (1964). *Principles of preventive psychiatry.* New York: Basic Books.

Cohen-Sandler, R., Berman, A., & King, R. (1982). Life stress and symptomatology: Determinants of suicidal behavior in children. *Journal of the American Academy of Child Psychiatry, 21,* 178-186.

Cowgell, V.G. (1977). Interpersonal effects of a suicidal communication. *Journal of Consulting and Clinical Psychology, 45* (4), 592-299.

Crook, T., & Raskin, A. (1975). Association of childhood parental loss with attempted suicide and depression. *Journal of Consulting and Clinical Psychology, 43,* 277.

Danto, B.L. (1978). Crisis intervention in a classroom regarding the homicide of a teacher. *The School Counselor, (26)* 69.

Diekstra, R. (1985). Suicide and suicide attempts in the European economics community: An analysis of trends, with special emphasis upon trends among the young. *Suicide and Life-Threatening Behavior, 15,* 27-42.

Duraj, L. (1984). School and teenage suicide. *Education Canada, Spring,* 42-47.

Ellis, A. (1977). The basic clinical theory of rational-emotive therapy. In A. Ellis & R. Greiger (Eds.), *Handbook of rational-emotive therapy.* New York: Springer.

Ellis, A. (1971). *Rational-emotive therapy and its application to emotional education.* New York: Wiley.

Ellis, A., & Greiger, R. (1977) *Handbook of rational-emotive therapy.* New York: Springer.

Ellkind, D. (1974). *Children and adolescence: Interpretative essays on Jean Piaget.* New York: Oxford.

Erickson, E.H. (1968). *Identity, youth and crisis.* New York: Norton.

Fowler, D.E., & McGee, R.K. (1973). Assessing the performance of telephone crisis workers: The development of a technical effectiveness scale. In D. Lester & G.W. Brockopp (Eds.), *Crisis interaction and counseling by telephone.* Springfield, IL: Charles C Thomas.

Fritz, D. (1986). *The effects of disruptions in the primary family of origin on the development of suicide ideation.* Unpublished master's thesis. University of Alaska-Anchorage, Anchorage, AK.

Fujimura, L., Weis, D., & Cochran, J. (1985). Suicide: Dynamics and implications for counseling. *Journal of Counseling & Development, 63,* 612-615.

Getz, W.L., Allen, D.B., Myers, R.K., & Loner, V.C. (1983). *Brief counseling with suicidal persons.* Lexington, MA: D.C. Health.

Giffen, M., & Felsenthal, C. (1983). *A cry for help.* Garden City, NY: Doubleday.

Gill, A.D. (1982). Outpatient therapies for suicidal patients. In E. Bassuk, S. Schoonover, & A. Gill (Eds.), *Lifelines: Clinical perspectives on suicide* (pp. 71-82). New York: Plenum.

Gilligan, C. (1982). New maps of development: New visions of maturity. *American Journal of Orthopsychiatry, 52,* 199-212.

Gordon, S. (1985). *When living hurts.* New York: Union of American Hebrew Congregations.

Hafen, B.Q., & Peterson, B. (1983). Parenting adolescent suicide. *Nursing, March,* 47-48.

Hafen, B.Q., & Frandsen, K.J. (1986). *Youth suicide: Depression and loneliness.* Provo, UT: Behavioral Health Associates.

Haim, A. (1974). *Adolescent suicide.* New York: International Universities Press.

Hansell, N. (1976). *Person-in-distress: On the biosocial dynamics of adaptation.* New York: Human Sciences Press.

Hawton, K., & Catalan, J. (1982). *Attempted suicide: A practical guide to its nature and management.* New York: Oxford.

Hoff, L.A. (1984). *People in crisis: Understanding and helping.* Menlo Park: CA: Addison-Wesley.

Holmes, T.H., & Rahe, R.H. (1967). The social readjustment rating scale. *Journal of Psychosomatic Research, 11,* 213-218.

Husain, S., & Vandiver, T. (1984). *Suicide in children and adolescents.* New York: SP Medical and Scientific Books.

Jacobs, J. (1971). *Adolescent suicide.* New York: Wiley-Interscience.

Jacobsen, G.F., Strickler, M., & Morley, W.E. (1968). Generic and individual approaches to crisis intervention. *American Journal of Public Health, 58,* 339-343.

Janosik, E.H. (1984). *Crisis counseling: A contemporary approach.* Monterey, CA: Wadsworth.

Joan, P. (1986). *Preventing teenage suicide: The living alternative.* New York: Human Sciences Press.

Johnson, S.W. (1985). *You can hear a petal fall.* Anchorage, AK: Johnson.

Keith, C.R., & Ellis, D. (1978). Reactions of pupils and teachers to death in a classroom. *The School Counselor, 25,* 228-234.

Klagsbrun, F. (1976). *Too young to die: Youth and suicide.* Boston: Houghton-Mifflin.

Kohlberg, L. (1969). *Stages in the development of moral thought and action.* New York: Holt, Rinehart and Winston.

Kohlberg, L., & Gilligan, C. (1971). The adolescent as a philosopher: The discovery of the self in a preconventional world. *Daedalus, 100,* 1051-86.

Kubler-Ross, E. (1969). *On death and dying.* New York, Macmillan.

Kubler-Ross, E. (1975). *Death: The final stage of growing.* Englewood Cliffs, NJ: Prentice-Hall.

Lawton, A. (1978). Two new approaches to helping young people—coping at festivals. In V. Aalberg (Ed.), *Proceedings of the 9th International Congress for Suicide Prevention, Helsinki; 1977.* Helsinki: Finnish Association for Mental Health.

Lazarus, R.S. (1980). The stress and coping paradigm. In L. Bond & R. Rosen (Eds.). *Competence and coping during adulthood.* New Hampshire: University Press of New England.

Leenaars, A.A., Balance, W.D., Wenckstern, S., & Rudzinski, D. (1986). An empirical investigation of Schneidman's formulations regarding suicide. *Suicide and Life Threatening Behavior, 15,* 184-195.

Lennox, C. (May, 1986). Personal communication.

Lester, D. (1972). *Why people kill themselves.* Springfield, IL: Charles C Thomas.

Lester, D., & Brockopp, G. (1973). *Crisis intervention and counseling by telephone.* Springfield, IL: Charles C Thomas.

Levinson, D., Darrow, C., Klein, E., Levinson, M., & McKee, B. (1978). *The seasons of a man's life.* New York: Knopf.

Madison, A. (1978). *Suicide and young people.* New York: Houghton-Mifflin-Clarion.

Maris, R. (1984). Why 30,000 Americans will commit suicide this year. *U.S. News and World Report,* pp. 48-50.

Maris, R. (1985). The adolescent suicide problem. *Suicide and Life Threatening Behavior, 15,* 91-109.

Maslow, A. (1970). *Motivation and personality.* New York: Harper & Row.

Matter, D., & Matter, R. (1984). Suicide among elementary school children: A serious concern for counselors. *Elementary School Guidance and Counseling,* April, 260-267.

Matthews, K.E., & Brunson, B.I. (1975). Allocation of attention and Type A coronary-prone behavior. *Journal of Personality and Social Psychology, 37,* 571-577.

Mayer, N. (1978). *The male mid-life crisis: Fresh starts after forty.* New York: Doubleday.

McBrien, R.J. (1983). Are you thinking of killing yourself?: Confronting students' suicidal thoughts. *The School Counselor, (31),* 75-82.

McGee, R.K. (1976). *Perspectives on suicide.* Speech delivered at National Conference on Preventing the Youthful Suicide, Dallas, TX.

McIntire, M., & Angle, C. (1980). *Suicide attempts in children and youth.* Hagerstown, MD: Harper & Row.

McKenry, P.C., Tishler, C.L., & Christman, K.L. (1980). Adolescent suicide and the classroom teacher. *The Journal of School Health, 50,* 130-132.

Meeks, J. (1971). *The fragile alliance.* Baltimore, MD: Williams & Wilkins.

Menninger, K. (1938). *Man against himself.* New York: Harcourt-Brace-Jovanovich.

Miller, J.G. (1978). *Living systems.* New York: McGraw-Hil.

Motto, J.A. (1985). Treatment concerns in preventing youth suicide. In M.L. Peck, N.L. Farberow, & R.E. Litman (Eds.), *Youth suicide.* New York: Springer.

Moursand, J. (1985). *The process of counseling and therapy.* Englewood Cliffs, NJ: Prentice-Hall.

Murray, H.A. (1967). Dead to the world. In E.S. Shneidman (Ed.), *Essays in self-destruction.* New York: Science House.

Murray, H.A. (1938). *Explorations in personality.* New York: Oxford University Press.

Neill, S.B. (1977). Crisis counseling. *American Education, 104,* 43-44.

Nelson, E.R., & Slaikeu, K.A. (1984). *Crisis intervention: A handbook for practice and research* (pp. 247-262). Newton, MA: Allyn & Bacon.

Newman, B., & Newman, P. (1978). The concept of identity: Research and theory. *Adolescence, 13,* 157-166.

O'Roark, M.A. (1982, January). The alarming rise in teenage suicide. *McCalls,* pp. 14-22.

Otto, U. (1972). Suicidal acts by children and adolescents: A follow-up study. *Acta Psychiatrica Schandinavica, 233,* 5-123.

Pasewark, R.A., & Albers, D.A. (1972). Crisis intervention: Theory in search of a program. *Social Work, 17,* 70-77.

Peck, M.L. (1985). In M.L. Peck, N.L. Farberow, & R.E. Litman (Eds.), *Youth suicide.* New York: Springer.

Peck M.L., & Litman, R.E. (1974). Current trends in youthful suicide. In J. Bush (Ed.), *Suicide and blacks: A monograph for continuing education in suicide prevention.* Los Angeles: Charles R. Drew Postgraduate Medical Center, Favor Research & Development Center.

Peck, M.L., & Schrut, A. (1971). Suicidal behavior among college students. *HSMHA Health Reports, 86* (2), 149-156.

Perr, I.N. (1979). Legal aspects of suicide. In L.O. Hankoff & B. Einsidler (Eds.), *Suicide: Theory and clinical aspects* (pp. 91-101). Littleton, MA: PSG Publishing.

Polak, P.R. (1971). Social systems interventions. *Archives of General Psychiatry, 25,* 110-117.

Ray, L.Y., & Johnson, N. (1983). Adolescent suicide. *Personnel and Guidance Journal, 62,* 131-134.

Robbins, D., & Conroy, R.C. (1983). A cluster of adolescent suicide attempts: Is suicide contagious? *Journal of Adolescent Health Care, 3* (4), 253-255.

Rogers, C. (1951). *Client-centered therapy.* Boston: Houghton-Mifflin.

Rosenbaum, C.P., & Beebe, J.E. (1975). *Psychiatric treatment crisis/clinic/consultation.* New York: McGraw-Hill.

Rosenfeld, L., & Prupas, M. (1984). *Left alive.* Springfield, IL: Charles C Thomas.

Rosenthal, N.B. (1981). Attitudes toward death education and grief counseling. *Counselor Education and Supervision, 21,* 203-210.

Ross, C.P. (1985). Teaching children the facts of life and death: Suicide prevention in the schools. In M.L. Peck, N.L. Farberow, & R.E. Litman (Eds.), *Youth suicide.* New York: Springer.

Rusk, T. (1971). Opportunity and techniques in crisis psychiatry. *Comprehensive Psychiatry, 12,* 249-263.

Samaritans, The. (1978). *Answers to suicide.* London: Constable.

Schvanaveldt, J.D. (1982). Developing and implementing death education in high schools. *The High School Journal, March,* 189-197.

Selye, H. (1976). *The stress of life.* New York: McGraw-Hill.

Sergiovanni, T.J. (Ed.). (1975). *Professional supervision for professional teachers.* Alexandria, VA: Association for Supervisors and Curriculum Development.

Shaffer, D. (1982). Diagnostic considerations in suicidal behavior in children and adolescents. *Journal of the American Academy of Child Psychiatry, 21,* 414-416.

Shaw, C.R., & Schelkon, R.F. (1965). Suicidal behavior in children. *Psychiatry, 28,* 157-168.

Sheehy, G. (1976). *Passages.* New York: Dutton.

Shneidman, E.S. (1985). *Definition of suicide.* New York: Wiley.

Shneidman, E.S. (1979). An overview: Personality, motivation and behavior theories. In Hankoff, L., & Einsidler, B. (Eds.): *Suicide: Theory and clinical aspects.* Littleton, MA: PSG Publishing.

Shneidman, E., Farberow, N., & Litman, R (1976). *The psychology of suicide.* New York: Jason Aronson.

Slaikeu, K.A. (1984). *Crisis intervention: A handbook for practice and research.* Newton, MA: Allyn & Bacon.

Slaikeu, K.A. (1983). In L. Cohen, W. Claiborne & B. Wolman (Eds.), *Crisis Intervention (2nd ed.)* New York: Human Sciences Press.

Slaikeu, K.A. (1979). Temporal variables in telephone crisis intervention. Their relationship to selected process and outcome variables. *Journal of Consulting and Clinical Psychology, 47,* 193-195.

Slaikeu, K.A. (1977). The clinical-community approach to community psychology. In B. Wolman (Ed.), *International encyclopedia of psychiatry, psychology, psychoanalysis and neurology.* New York: Van Nostrand Reinhold.

Slaikeu, K.A., Lester, D. & Tulkin, S. (1973). Show versus no show: A comparison of telephone referral calls to a suicide prevention and crisis service. *Journal of Consulting and Clinical Psychology, 40,* 481-486.

Slaikeu, K.A. & Willis, M.A. (1978). Caller feedback on counselor performance in telephone crisis intervention: A follow-up study. *Crisis Intervention, 4,* 42-49.

Smith, D.F. (1976). Adolescent suicide: A problem for teachers? *Phi Delta Kappan, 57,* (8), 539-542.

Snyder, J.A. (1971). The use of gatekeepers in crisis management. *Bulletin of Suicidology, 7,* 39-44.

Steele, W. (1983). *Preventing teenage suicide.* Ann Arbor, MI: Ann Arbor Press.

Tishler, C.L., & McKenny, P.C. (1982). Parental negative self and adolescent suicide attempts. *Journal of the American Academy of Child Psychiatry, 21,* 404-408.

Toolan, J.M. (1978). Therapy of depressed and suicidal children. *American Journal of Psychotherapy, 32,* 243-251.

Viney, L.L. (1976). The concept of crisis: A tool for clinical psychologists. *Bulletin of the British Psychological Society, 29,* 387-395.

Viorst, J. (1986). *Necessary losses.* New York: Simon & Schuster.

Wilhem, R. (1967). *The book of changes.* Princeton, NJ: Princeton.

Wilson, L. (1981). Thoughts on Tarasoff. *The Clinical Psychologist, 34,* 37.

Winters, R.A., & Modine, A. (1975). High school students as mental health workers. *The School Counselor, 104,* 43-44.

Worden, J.W. (1982). *Grief counseling and grief therapy: A handbook for the mental health practitioner.* New York: Springer.

AUTHOR INDEX

295

SUBJECT INDEX

299